About the Author

Ian Wishart is an award-winning journalist and author, with a 30 year career in radio, television and magazines, a #1 talk radio show and more than twenty bestselling books to his credit. Together with his wife Heidi, they also edit and publish the news magazine website www.investigatedaily.com.

Dedication

To the memory of Olivia Hope and Ben Smart, and for their parents Gerald and Jan Hope, and Mary and the late John Smart, and their extended families. May this end the uncertainty.

ELEMENTARY

Ian Wishart

HOWLING AT THE MOON PUBLISHING LTD

First edition published 2016
Howling At The Moon Publishing Ltd
PO Box 188
Kaukapakapa
Auckland 0843
NEW ZEALAND

Email: editorial@investigatemagazine.com
Web: www.ianwishart.com

Copyright © Ian Wishart
Copyright © Howling At The Moon Publishing Ltd

The moral rights of the author have been asserted.

Elementary is copyright. Except for the purpose of fair reviewing, no part of this publication may be copied, reproduced or transmitted in any form or by any means, including via technology either already in existence or developed subsequent to publication, without the express written permission of the publisher and authors.
All rights reserved.

ISBN 978-0-9941064-6-9

Cover photo by Dreamstime
Typeset in Adobe Garamond Pro and Apex New
Cover concept: Ian and Heidi Wishart
Book design: Bozidar Jokanovic

Contents

Introduction 11
The Psychology Of A Murderer 15
Scott Watson: The Psychopath Test 25
Is This The Evolution Of A Killer? 49
Violent And Dangerous 67
An Attempted Rapist 79
Who Was That Mystery Man? 89
Who Is Guy Wallace? 93
Who Was In The Naiad? 109
Conflicting Descriptions? 131
The Camera Never Lies—Or Does It? 145
The Mystery Ketch 155
Another Ketch Bites The Dust 183
Wallace Waffles 191
Diversions 215
The Two-Trip Theory 249
The Real Sequence Of Events 257
Which Water Taxi? 277
Keith Hunter's Taxi Theory Sinks 289
The Deception Widens 295
Cracking The Case 305
The Final Piece Of The Jigsaw 347

LEGAL WARNING

What you are about to read has been drawn from the police investigation files into the murders of Olivia Hope and Ben Smart. The opinions expressed in this book are those of the people expressing them and they are not necessarily the opinion of the author. Critical expressions of opinion by the author about individuals named in this book are made on the basis of the facts set out in this book or otherwise known at the time of writing.

Introduction

In 1999, I co-wrote and published the very first book on the Scott Watson case. It was called *Ben & Olivia: What Really Happened?* The title was rhetorical, because as readers discovered we didn't know what had really happened—even after a court trial and guilty verdict.

Jayson Rhodes, my co-author on the case, was a TV3 journalist who'd been assigned by the network to cover the High Court trial of Scott Watson on double murder charges. So Rhodes was on the case, day in, day out.

It was my job to review the daily reports he was filing for us, edit them, work in some context from media coverage at the time of the disappearance, and guide the narrative plot of the book.

Like many New Zealanders, I came away from that trial with a distinct sense of unease. Based on the timings given in evidence and cross examination, it seemed like there was volumes of room for reasonable doubt. Scott Watson could not have been in two places at the same time, and the witnesses were wildly divergent on differences between the scruffy unshaven 'mystery man' and the clean shaven, short haired Watson.

Even key witnesses like Guy Wallace were spooked, admitting under cross examination that if the 'clean-shaven photo' was really Scott Watson on the night then he can't have been the mystery man.

For those of us who were hardened crime reporters, the trotting out of secret jailhouse witnesses was a sure sign prosecutors were clutching at flash to make up for the lack of substance in their case. Tension-inducing testimony about harrowing scratch marks made by fingernails on the inside of the hatch cover on Scott Watson's yacht *Blade* gave way to ridicule when it emerged the scratches extended beyond the accessible boundary of the lid when it was closed, meaning the scratches could only have been made on an open lid.

The Crown's sole piece of forensic evidence was a sample of two of Olivia's hairs found on a tiger blanket of Watson's. The problem was, those hairs had not been found on the original forensic examination and only turned up the same day that a ripped bag of Olivia's hair samples arrived at the ESR desk where the blanket was being examined.

It didn't look good. The conviction didn't look safe.

We originally titled the book *Ben & Olivia* because that's how people remembered the case. Over the years, the victims have become mere footnotes to a bigger headline: "Scott Watson is innocent". Today, Scott Watson is the brand, the name people talk about in the same breath as Arthur Allan Thomas as an example of miscarried justice.

Yet if you go back and read that first book, you'll know we never gave Scott Watson a clean slate—there was no get out of jail free card. We floated the possibility that he was involved, somehow, even if the missing pair had disappeared on a ketch.

Over the following 17 years since, I've leaned heavily to the belief that Watson could not have killed the pair, not if they were alive on the back of a ketch sailing out of Cook Strait on 2 January 1998 while he was happily painting his boat at Erie Bay.

One thing differentiates *Elementary* from its predecessor. The first book was primarily coverage of the actual court trial. The quotes were taken from evidence given.

We asked for but received no cooperation from the police—no access to the Operation TAM files. That privilege was reserved for Prime Minister Jenny Shipley's press secretary John Goulter, who decided to do his own book with the full cooperation of Rob Pope.

That book, however, *Silent Evidence*, was also largely a rehash of the trial from the police perspective.

What I can now say is that every book written on the Scott Watson case up to now, including *Ben & Olivia*, is wrong. Every news article written on this case has been wrong. For reasons that will become disturbingly clear, events did not transpire the way we all thought they did.

Elementary breaks new ground on the Scott Watson case, and it does so because it is the first book ever to fully peer review the police files, previously unavailable to us when we published *Ben & Olivia*.

I had asked Scott's father, Chris Watson, for access to the police files the defence team had. There was umming and ahhhing, it was too big, it was all too hard, and I never pushed the issue further.

Waiheke yachtie Mike Kalaugher did, obtaining an electronic copy of the police database from the Watsons which he used for his 2001 book *The Marlborough Mystery*, arguing Watson's innocence. Kalaugher did the best he could, but he was not an investigative journalist.

Keith Hunter was, though. He too obtained access to the police files and produced a TV documentary, *Murder on the Blade*, then a book, *Trial by Trickery*.

These were unashamed examples of pure advocacy journalism—Scott Watson is innocent, he's been defamed and convicted of crimes he did not commit.

Both Hunter and Kalaugher had access to police files that I didn't. This didn't worry me, I had no intention by then of revisiting old ground. But over the years I've had pressure from some quarters to reinvestigate. I couldn't see the point—what could I possibly uncover that Hunter and Kalaugher had missed?

Then, eventually, in late 2015, the Defence legal files from this case were sent to me. You will be stunned when you read what's in them.

This is the story of the Scott Watson case that has *never* been published before. You won't believe what you are about to read, but it is—as documents buried deep within the police files show—almost certainly the real story of what happened to Ben Smart and Olivia Hope. The information has come from long-overlooked witness statements from eighteen years ago. Sightings have been cross-checked, corroborated and, in many cases, published in expanded detail so you can see the full context.

No matter which side of the debate you are on, you will find the content of this book confronting—to say the least. But this book is not about tribal allegiance, it's about using the intelligence gathered by police to shed new light on the key issues.

The police witness statements are much more useful than court testimony. When a crime first happens, dozens of police officers fan out and simply collect evidence. The officers on the ground don't know initially what will be relevant and what will not—that's a job for prosecuting lawyers down the track—so all they do is vacuum up as much information as they can. Witness statements are a goldmine, a treasure trove taken when witnesses' memories are still fresh, which is why John Goulter, Mike Kalaugher and Keith Hunter have relied on them previously. Statements only half-explored, however, only tell half the story.

Up until now, the police file has only been half-explored. All that is about to change. This is the story you have never been told, with a twist you never expected.

CHAPTER ONE

The Psychology Of A Murderer

No one really knows what happened to Marlborough students Ben Smart and Olivia Hope in the pre-dawn hours of January 1st, 1998, although many trees have been harvested, processed and reproduced as books and court files fuelling the speculation.

It's as if, somewhere between 3am and 5am, Ben and Olivia stepped into another dimension and never returned. For all practical purposes, that may as well have been the case. In the 18 years that have passed since that day, no trace of 17 year old Olivia or 21 year old Ben has ever been found.

Yet, like the Crewe murders a generation earlier, it has become an enduring murder mystery that continues to captivate the attention of a nation.

The Crown case has hinged on 7 main factors:

1. That Scott Watson was the mystery man seen by many, pestering women at Furneaux Lodge during New Year's Eve 1997

2. That there was no "mystery ketch"
3. That Watson was the "mystery man" on board Guy Wallace's water taxi that dropped himself and Ben and Olivia off to a boat
4. That Watson cleaned his boat to erase forensic evidence
5. That Watson dumped the bodies at the entrance to Tory Channel
6. That Watson confessed to prison inmates
7. That hairs from Olivia were found on his blanket

Over the course of this book, we are going to address some fundamental questions that go to the core of the case:

Did Scott Watson have the character of someone prepared to kill in cold blood?

In other words, while virtually anyone in the right circumstances is capable of killing (in self defence, or in a jealous rage for example), those prepared to murder a stranger for the purposes of some kind of thrill or gain to themselves are a different breed. People who fall into the first groupings actually commit the most killings—you are more likely to be killed by someone you know. Those who fall into the latter category—for thrill or gain—are the people our parents warn us about, the people cast as villains in fairytales and literature. Sometimes we call them psychopaths—those narcissistic individuals seemingly bereft of empathy who are more capable of cold-blooded murder.

"The term psychopath is often used interchangeably with sociopath," says an analysis on the website CriminalProfiling.com,[1] "and psychopathy is often diagnosed as antisocial personality disorder (Hare, 1993). However, antisocial personality disorder merely describes behaviours, this diagnosis does not measure emotion and

---

[1] http://www.criminalprofiling.com/psychopathy-an-evolutionary-perspective/

conscience. Psychopaths are individuals who lack remorse and guilt, they are selfish individuals who only look out for themselves, they are cunning and resourceful, often leaving behind a trail of individuals whom they have victimized, sometimes physically, sometimes emotionally, and sometimes financially (Cleckley, 1982; Hare, 1993)"

Scientists believe psychopathy is an inherited trait passed down through families.

Mark Olshaker, co-author of the bestselling book *Mindhunter* puts it this way, saying individuals can be[2] "referred to as a sociopath, or sometimes a psychopath. DSM-IV, the Diagnostic and Statistical Manual of Mental Disorders, Fourth Edition, replaced the term for this condition with 'anti-social personality disorder,' though we think that sounds a bit mild for what it represents.

"Whatever you call it, it is characterized by 'a pervasive pattern of disregard for, and violation of, the rights of others that begins in childhood or early adolescence and continues into adulthood.'

"So what does all of this actually mean? Well, the easiest way to summarize what is admittedly a fairly complex subject, is to enumerate some of the characteristics we would expect to see.

"The first is narcissism. Again, this trait will lie along a continuum, but in extreme instances like this one, it manifests as a total involvement with self to the exclusion of consideration for others. This goes hand-in-hand with a total disregard for the truth. For these types, truth is a commodity rather than an absolute; that is, it is a tool to achieve an end. And if that end is better served with a lie, that is a completely acceptable "moral" choice.

"I put "moral" in quotes in an earlier paragraph because that leads to the second characteristic, which is that there is no morality for this individual other than what is best for her. Other people have no rights.

---

2 http://mindhuntersinc.com/what-makes-jodi-arias-tick/

"A third characteristic is actually a modus operandi, and that is manipulation. These people are very good at manipulating those around them to achieve their own ends.

"And a fourth—a perfect fit with what has preceded—is a projection onto others for all of their own faults and flaws."

Hervey Cleckley, author of *Mask Of Sanity*, adds another characteristic:[3]

"Fantastic and objectionable behavior, after drinking and sometimes even when not drinking. Vulgarity, rudeness, quick mood shifts, pranks for facile entertainment."

Robert Hare, a psychology professor and author of *Without Conscience*, rates it this way:

1. GLIB AND SUPERFICIAL CHARM: the tendency to be smooth, engaging, charming, slick, and verbally facile. Psychopathic charm is not in the least shy, self-conscious, or afraid to say anything. A psychopath never gets tongue-tied. He can also be a great listener, to simulate empathy while zeroing in on his targets' dreams and vulnerabilities, to be able to manipulate them better.

2. GRANDIOSE SELF-WORTH: a grossly inflated view of one's abilities and self-worth, self-assured, opinionated, cocky, a braggart. Psychopaths are arrogant people who believe they are superior human beings.

3. NEED FOR STIMULATION OR PRONENESS TO BOREDOM: an excessive need for novel, thrilling, and exciting stimulation; taking chances and doing things that are risky. Psychopaths often have a low self-discipline in carrying tasks through to completion because they get bored easily. They fail to work at the same job for any length of time, for example, or to finish tasks that they consider dull or routine.

---

3 https://psychopathyawareness.wordpress.com/2011/10/03/the-list-of-psychopathy-symptoms/

4. PATHOLOGICAL LYING: can be moderate or high; in moderate form, they will be shrewd, crafty, cunning, sly, and clever; in extreme form, they will be deceptive, deceitful, underhanded, unscrupulous, manipulative and dishonest.

5. CONNING AND MANIPULATIVENESS: the use of deceit and deception to cheat, con, or defraud others for personal gain; distinguished from Item #4 in the degree to which exploitation and callous ruthlessness is present, as reflected in a lack of concern for the feelings and suffering of one's victims.

6. LACK OF REMORSE OR GUILT: a lack of feelings or concern for the losses, pain, and suffering of victims; a tendency to be unconcerned, dispassionate, coldhearted and unempathic. This item is usually demonstrated by a disdain for one's victims.

7. SHALLOW AFFECT: emotional poverty or a limited range or depth of feelings; interpersonal coldness in spite of signs of open gregariousness and superficial warmth.

8. CALLOUSNESS AND LACK OF EMPATHY: a lack of feelings toward people in general; cold, contemptuous, inconsiderate, and tactless.

9. PARASITIC LIFESTYLE: an intentional, manipulative, selfish, and exploitative financial dependence on others as reflected in a lack of motivation, low self-discipline and the inability to carry through one's responsibilities.

10. POOR BEHAVIORAL CONTROLS: expressions of irritability, annoyance, impatience, threats, aggression and verbal abuse; inadequate control of anger and temper; acting hastily.

11. PROMISCUOUS SEXUAL BEHAVIOR: a variety of brief, superficial relations, numerous affairs, and an indiscriminate selection of sexual partners; the maintenance of numerous, multiple relationships at the same time; a history of attempts to sexually coerce others into sexual activity (rape) or taking great pride at discussing sexual exploits and conquests.

12. EARLY BEHAVIOR PROBLEMS: a variety of behaviors prior to age 13, including lying, theft, cheating, vandalism, bullying, sexual activity, fire-setting, glue-sniffing, alcohol use and running away from home.

13. LACK OF REALISTIC, LONG-TERM GOALS: an inability or persistent failure to develop and execute long-term plans and goals; a nomadic existence, aimless, lacking direction in life.

14. IMPULSIVITY: the occurrence of behaviors that are unpremeditated and lack reflection or planning; inability to resist temptation, frustrations and momentary urges; a lack of deliberation without considering the consequences; foolhardy, rash, unpredictable, erratic and reckless.

15. IRRESPONSIBILITY: repeated failure to fulfill or honor obligations and commitments; such as not paying bills, defaulting on loans, performing sloppy work, being absent or late to work, failing to honor contractual agreements.

16. FAILURE TO ACCEPT RESPONSIBILITY FOR OWN ACTIONS: a failure to accept responsibility for one's actions reflected in low conscientiousness, an absence of dutifulness, antagonistic manipulation, denial of responsibility, and an effort to manipulate others through this denial.

17. MANY SHORT-TERM RELATIONSHIPS: a lack of commitment to a long-term relationship reflected in inconsistent, undependable, and unreliable commitments in life, including in marital and familial bonds.

18. JUVENILE DELINQUENCY: behavior problems between the ages of 13-18; mostly behaviors that are crimes or clearly involve aspects of antagonism, exploitation, aggression, manipulation, or a callous, ruthless tough-mindedness.

19. REVOCATION OF CONDITION RELEASE: a revocation of probation or other conditional release due to technical violations, such as carelessness, low deliberation or failing to appear.

20. CRIMINAL VERSATILITY: a diversity of types of criminal offenses, regardless if the person has been arrested or convicted for them; taking great pride at getting away with crimes or wrongdoings

That last point is sobering: if Scott Watson did kill the couple he will be getting a real ego boost out of every article suggesting the public believe he is innocent.

These, then, are the signs of psychopathic behaviour. Not all, in fact not even many, psychopaths are murderers. Psychopathic traits are sufficiently common that all of us have come into contact with a full or borderline psychopath at some time in our lives. Many successful business leaders, praised for their "killer instinct", are psychopaths. But conversely, nearly all cold-blooded killers turn out to be psychopaths. It is that willingness to step outside the boundaries of moral behaviour that leads them into rape or murder. It is Gordon Gekko with a gun.

Psychopaths comprise around four percent of the population, although criminal psychopaths are a much smaller subset of that. There were undoubtedly several psychopaths at Furneaux Lodge the night Ben and Olivia were taken. The question is, which one did it? And does Scott Watson fit the profile?

Could Scott Watson Be The Mystery Man?
This is the $64 million question, and you will find it extensively answered.

Did Scott Watson have the opportunity to commit this crime? Could he have done it, based on the evidence now available?
We all know the police investigation of the case was a dog's breakfast, and the evidence presented in court at Watson's 1999 trial left enough discrepancies that numerous commentators including this author have argued the conviction was not sound. But what if the case had been argued differently? What if the prosecution made a strategic error by running with straw-man "evidence" like the scratched hatch cover, in a bid for emotional imagery, when they had better but less gut-wrenching evidence in their toolkit?

What if a genuine case can be made that Scott Watson did indeed commit this crime? And what if you've never heard that story because of the distractions around the stuff-ups? That's something, surely, that needs investigation.

Court hearings are strange beasts. They come months or even years after the events in question, and people's memories can fade. The testimony actually given in court is often more vague, or conversely more contaminated with invented detail, than the statements originally given to police at the very beginning of a criminal investigation when events were still fresh in the mind.

Just as there is a "golden hour" to save the life of a road crash victim, so too is there a "golden hour" to solve a major crime. Gathering evidence in the immediate aftermath of a murder is critical, before witnesses have a chance to discuss it with each other and compromise their own crucial recollections. If Witness A starts comparing notes with Witness B, they can end up with a consensus view of what happened. The danger of that is that Witness A may have seen something vital that Witness B didn't, and if Witness A self-edits his or her unique memory out of the picture, police could be left without that vital clue.

Even worse, a witness can have a false memory of the event programmed into their mind by discussing the case with others.

Dr Helen Paterson of the University of Sydney calls this "false memory syndrome":[4]

"Memories can't be trusted and become contaminated when people discuss their memories of an event with others," she said in 2010. "Sharing memories can contaminate people's recollections and create false memories.

"A false memory is the recollection of an event, or details of an event, that did not actually occur."

You will find in this particular case—the disappearance of Ben and Olivia—there were so many witnesses discussing what they had seen with each other that memories quickly became corrupted. The most obvious example is Guy Wallace. He actively discussed his recollections with other witnesses right from the start and created a nightmare mix. It is possible that Wallace's memories of the water taxi trip and the mystery man and the ketch are hopelessly compromised.

Dr Paterson describes it as "memory distortion" and says "that is, witnesses who discuss an event with a co-witness are very likely to incorporate misinformation presented by the co-witness into their own memory for the event. Once their memory has been contaminated in this way, the witness is often unable to distinguish between the accurate and inaccurate memories."

The idea that Scott Watson is definitely innocent relies in a large part on the memories of Guy Wallace and others he talked to. What if they have contaminated each other's recollections? What if their testimony cannot be trusted for that reason? This, too, needs investigation.

---

4 "Sydney study finds false memories are common", University of Sydney news release, 9 August 2010

So the question of whether Scott Watson could have had the opportunity to commit this crime is necessarily entangled in the debate about memories of the mystery man and the ketch. We will look at that.

Which leads to the next point this book will examine: *Was there a mystery ketch?*

This book identifies the mystery ketch.

Let's get started.

CHAPTER TWO

Scott Watson: The Psychopath Test

To say the Scott Watson case has captured the public imagination is an understatement. It has happened gradually. It has taken 18 years. But it has happened. In the December 2015 issue of *North & South,* journalist Mike White printed the result of a long awaited interview with Watson which, as New Zealanders discovered on the eve of Christmas, resulted in a million dollar payday for White and a film crew from taxpayer funded NZ On Air.[5]

White is merely the latest in a line of writers who have chronicled this tragic case. Yours truly co-wrote the first book on the murders with Jayson Rhodes, *Ben & Olivia.* John Goulter followed in 2000 with *Silent Evidence.* Mike Kalaugher in 2001 wrote *The Marlborough*

---

5 http://www.stuff.co.nz/entertainment/film/75238723/Scott-Watson-interview-leads-to-million-dollar-television-documentary

Mystery and Keith Hunter produced the *Murder on the Blade* TV documentary, watched by more than half a million viewers, and wrote the book *Trial by Trickery*.

In his book, Keith Hunter paints a portrait of a man being unfairly picked on by police. It's a similar line to the one we took in the original book on the case, *Ben & Olivia*. But that book was written on the basis of the court hearing, not the police evidence folders that we were forbidden to have access to, and it is the latter that appear to cast a disturbing new complexion on what we know of Scott Watson and his family.

The image of Scott Watson sold to the public by his defenders has utterly trivialised his background.

It was, says Keith Hunter,[6] "almost entirely non-violent adolescent delinquency. Watson had a criminal record but it was not of adult criminal behaviour. It was historical and patently obsolete. The picture it painted was of a man who in his youth had used marijuana and other people's cars and bicycles from time to time. Most serious was that he had been an occasional burglar. Allowing for a minor error in the archived record, only one offence had occurred in the previous eight years.

"This related to Watson's objection to the theft of his dinghy, when he had pulled out a three-inch, pocketknife-sized marlinspike to persuade two people he discovered taking the dinghy away on a truck to return it to him. In January 1998 this was 26 year old Watson's only recorded offence since the age of eighteen and a half," writes Hunter.

Hmmm. We'll return to Hunter's version of Watson's past shortly, but here's how it was painted in *Ben & Olivia*:[7]

"Firstly, a process of tracking down boats known to be in the

---

6 *Trial by Trickery*, Hunter, p29
7 *Ben & Olivia*, Rhodes and Wishart, p42, 2013 edition (all references are to this edition)

area had led them to *Blade* as part of routine inquiries. But instead, they find a yacht with its name painted over, and a lifebuoy on the yacht carrying a different name again. Then they check the criminal background of the owner—again, a routine inquiry—and discover he has previously run afoul of the law, although he has no major convictions.

"They did discover something, however ... a minor infringement that nonetheless heightened police suspicions about Scott Watson. We cannot reveal the context at this point as Watson has been charged with theft of a dinghy, a matter that is still before the court.

"In police parlance this is known as the "sniff test", and it was the best lead the police felt they had. It was certainly the only lead they could physically hold onto."

In *Ben & Olivia*, we at least held open the possibility that Scott Watson was somehow involved in the disappearance, not least because he kept talking about his "ketch":[8]

"This is not the first time that Watson has allegedly linked himself to a ketch during discussions with other boaties. Is it possible that there really was a ketch anchored there, as well as *Blade*, and that not only did Watson know the occupants but he had also been invited to crew on a voyage to Tonga? Could this be the missing link in the prosecution scenario? Given the significance of a ketch in this investigation, it seems extremely unusual that Watson should be allegedly big-noting about a double-masted ketch, when he had sailed in on a small sloop."

Hunter writes in his book that there has been a "profound defamation and tunnel-visioned pursuit of Watson" which, he asserts, "has been entirely unearned".[9]

Hunter goes even further, saying Watson "was cheaply labelled

---

8 *Ben & Olivia*, p107
9 *Trial by Trickery*, Hunter, p9

a liar...The documentation does not support the label. He emerges from an inspection of it lie-free."[10]

The author then thanks Watson's father for his help researching *Trial by Trickery*:

"Finally, I must acknowledge Chris Watson, father of the wrongly-convicted Scott, for his tireless and patient assistance in allowing me to check my research against his encyclopaedic knowledge of the documentation of the case."[11]

Yet there are revelations in the "documentation" that cast Watson and his supportive family in an entirely new light. Revelations that Keith Hunter never shared when he did his *Murder On The Blade* TV documentary or his book.

First, let's look at how Keith Hunter reported one of these revelations:[12]

> For four months in 1998 Inspector Pope had microphones secretly planted in their homes. During that time the microphones picked up two brief conversations which he parlayed into a conspiracy to murder. The conversations involved were brief exchanges of family banter after two months of public accusations that their son and brother was a murderer. They reflect a family under the pressure of attack by the entire New Zealand press, the Police Force and Detective Inspector Pope's strategic lie, trying to make light of it all with black humour. Here follows the transcript of one of those exchanges in its entirety. It was recorded on 4 March 1998. The stage instructions are by the police transcriber.

---

10 ibid
11 Ibid, p16
12 *Trial by Trickery*, Hunter, p61

B00601 / NIGHT / 040398 / CR7175 / BLUE

BEV: (sarcastically) I keep, I keep seeing him on TV, I can't sleep, he gives me nightmares. Keep seeing his face.
SCOTT: Just go and walk into his little office and shoot him in the head.
SANDY: Yeah...no have to do it with a knife.
SCOTT: (Whispering) With a razor.
SANDY: Kitchen knife.
SCOTT: (Inaudible whispering)
BEV: And what did that guy say he does for a hobby?
SANDY: Oh yeah, a guy that comes into the Toot 'n' Whistle,...
SCOTT: Mmmm.
SANDY: And he come, he comes, he reckoned that Rob Pope's hobby is throwing knives. That's why he wants to know about all the knives. (long pause) Good hobby isn't it.

Pope promoted this chit-chat into a serious plot to murder him, for a High Court judge who would never see the evidence of it.

OK. That's what investigative journalist Keith Hunter told the public of New Zealand was the substance of the "conspiracy to murder" allegation, or "defamation" of the Watsons as he then called it in his book. However, the keen-eyed reader will have noticed that Hunter referred to "two" conversations, but published only one of them. The second conversation is reprinted here exclusively for the very first time. Here's what Hunter failed to tell you the police also caught on tape during the discussion between parents Chris and Bev Watson and their children Scott and his sister Sandy:

SCOTT: Be nice to have that, get rid of Pope.

CHRIS: Mmm.
SCOTT: Nice to just get rid of Pope.
BEV: Well I, ask [name withheld] to let, to get [name withheld] out and do the right thing.
(long pause)
(Inaudible conversation between Bev and Sandy in background)
SCOTT: Surely there (inaudible) f**ker around that'll do it.
CHRIS: It costs five grand.
BEV: Yeah.
SCOTT: Is that all it costs?
CHRIS: To have it happen.
BEV: Now who had that, five grand?
SCOTT: It's f**k all.
BEV: Yeah.
CHRIS: Ah somebody's, Ian's mate.
BEV: Oh yes cause he was offered.
CHRIS: Mmm.
SANDY: Oh that's right yeah.
SCOTT: It's probably double for a detective.
BEV: Mmm.
SCOTT: But you'd f**ken....
SANDY: What a loser.
BEV: Oh no, you could go to the Mongrel Mob with (inaudible).
SCOTT: No they'd f**k it up.
SANDY: Then they'd get the blame.
BEV: Yeah (laughs). They'd just keep killing them until they get rid of them all. I don't know, that guy at Walls? he decided he was going to kill a cop.

Watson has been portrayed as a "rascal" whose worst days were in his teenage years, but the excerpt above appears to show the psychology of someone with a calculating view of killing, who weighed up the risk of detection and likelihood of success, rather than the larger moral argument of right vs wrong.

Readers can make their own call on whether that previously unpublished excerpt is banter, or whether it's evidence of a family prepared to be staunch to the point of crossing the line, and a family that appear to be on speaking terms with the criminal underworld. It was Scott Watson's parents after all—Chris and Bev—who appeared to know the cost of a hit, and who to approach.

On the other hand, maybe you want to read more of the evidence that does not appear in Keith Hunter's book yourself before making a decision. Very well, let's continue.

At issue here is whether Scott Watson is innocent. If New Zealand is going to make that call and even, possibly, down the track, offer compensation for wrongful imprisonment, then the country has to be comfortable that he really is innocent. If Watson cannot withstand the scrutiny in this book, he may not succeed in his aim to clear his name.

The bugging of the Watsons was codenamed *Operation Celt*. Hunter is correct that Pope obtained the interception warrants under the flimsiest of pretexts. Arguably they should never have been allowed. However, Chris Watson chose to release those transcripts to selected people and a copy fell into our hands. Keith Hunter chose to publish selected portions of *Operation Celt* in *Trial by Trickery*. Here, though, are some of the other bits he left out:

QUENTIN:[13] Okay now and the other thing that Scott had the ability to say, according to what this person I was speaking to yesterday…
SANDY: Mmmm.
QUENTIN: …is that if he saw a young lady walk past, orrr ahh, just a tourist or something like that…and he say [sic] to the guys that he was with "rape the bitch".

---

13 Quentin Doig, former Detective Inspector turned private investigator, hired by the Watsons

SANDY: Ohhh no, he's never said that about me (chuckles).
It's a strange thing for Sandra Watson to laugh about, especially as she's his sister.
QUENTIN: Have you ever heard that?
SANDY: No.
QUENTIN: No.
SANDY: That's, I think that's um…mouthing off isn't it?
QUENTIN: Oh it's big, big man talk.
SANDY: What, yeah what, the discussions that males have together, can be pretty um extreme.
QUENTIN: Mmmm, can be. It just worries me if um…
SANDY: Yeah there's…
QUENTIN: …if it's been said to the Police that's all…person who I was speaking to yesterday hasn't told the Police that.

Normally when children are murdered, consideration is shown and allowance made for the grieving parents. It's still seen as unseemly to speak ill of the dead, but look at Scott's parents' comments:[14]

BEV: (Laughs) He's got Olivia's glasses on…he wanted her glasses (laughs)…It's only her father that sez that she never went anywhere voluntarily…
SANDY: Yeah.
BEV: …but she obviously did go, voluntarily…
CHRIS: He is not…he is obviously, um…
BEV: (inaudible)
CHRIS: …no as far as his darling daughter, his little angel, and an innocent by-stander and all that.
BEV: Oh no he had high hopes for her.
CHRIS: Yeah.

---

14 41045/B00102/LATE BLUE COMPOSITE/CR7175/230298

BEV: Yeah was going to make her do this, that and everything else.

A couple of days later:[15]

SANDY: ...if he was genuinely mistaken about...yeah...so...and (sarcastically) anyway it sounds like that, that Olivia was actually having a temper tantrum during all this, because she was upset, because she was quite upset that her bloody, that her bed had been taken.
BEV: Yeah she had an argument.
SANDY: Yeah.
BEV: Yeah...they had an argument.
SANDY: Oh she was having a temper tantrum, she was all sour and...
BEV: She was very emotional was Olivia, which means (laughs) her and Lisa[16] would get on well...they could lay on the concrete together holding onto your legs.(Laughing)
SANDY: Yeah...spoilt brat having a temper tantrum.
BEV: Yeah it wen', the more ya think about it the more, I mean even if you're drunk, do you really just go and hop on somebody else's boat, some one that was...
SANDY: ...someone that was weird...
BEV: Yeah someone funny lookin' like that.
SANDY: Yeah that's right...well if I didn't know Scott I wouldn't go and jump on his boat.
BEV: Well he wouldn't offer ya probably, oh no he'd might offer you, just try and pick you up (laughs).
SANDY: ...no....um...
BEV: But he wouldn't offer you and a guy.
SANDY: No, no.

---

15 B00203 / Early / 250298 / CR7175 / Blue
16 Sandy's toddler

It is possible the Watsons may not be happy at details from these transcripts being published, but they appeared to delight in the bad publicity about Olivia Hope being leaked to the media. You cannot claim the moral high ground in such circumstances, and given what is at stake (including calls for a public inquiry, exoneration and compensation) there is a legitimate public interest in everything surrounding the innocence or guilt of Scott Watson.

The other interesting thing about Bev Watson's comments, apart from the attack on another mother's 17 year old murdered daughter, was what Bev thought her son would say to Olivia if he'd been in the water taxi with the young couple:

"No he'd might offer you, just try and pick you up (laughs)…But he wouldn't offer you and a guy."

The comment is haunting, because here's how eyewitness Guy Wallace described the conversation in the water taxi:

"You can come but he can't," the mystery man in the Naiad told Olivia while nodding in Ben's direction.[17]

The *Operation Celt* bugging tapes reveal more callous commentary about Ben and Olivia:[18]

> SCOTT: Yeah how's f**ken long is this gonna go on for though. This f**ken pisses me off!! I got a good mind to walk in there and f**ken shoot them.
> SANDY: Well Beryl mum and I were talking about…..about, oh cause they said now, oh they wanted to know all about our kitchen knives. About you know, knives that you cut up your vegetables and that you eat with and, and they were going (whispering) oh it was probably done with a kitchen knife, it'll (inaudible) and Beryl was goin' "Yeah stainless steel knives are strong, they don't bend" (laughs).

---

17 Guy Wallace in police interview, 11 January 1998, doc 12635, line 1438
18 B00501 / Night / 040398 / CR7175 / Blue, recorded discussion at 2am

SCOTT: (Laughing) Is that right.
SANDY: …had it all worked out…And I wear my skeleton earrings now.
SCOTT: Do ya?
SANDY: Yeah, the left is Ben and the right's Olivia. Um oh yeah and they had psychics, Carl and Quentin had the psychics phone them up…
SCOTT: Did they?
SANDY: ……and they're very very concerned that they say that Scott Watson is a hundred percent innocent. It was two guys and the boat's hidden over in Nelson somewhere. In Tasman Bay somewhere…and they're in the Pelorus Sounds…and so I don't know what, but they checked them out and apparently they're very good ones. There's one in Blenheim and a mate in Auckland.

But the attacks on the murder victims just kept coming—Scott Watson's mother Bev appeared to find it hilarious when a confidential police profile on the missing students was leaked to yacht clubs, while Scott Watson wanted to know if his mother had obtained a copy:[19]

BEV: You know when I was talking to Chris Clark he said they're probably listening, they'll be listening on every phone, and I said yeah I know. He said they'll to this conversation. I sez year I know. What's good, what good's it gonna do them, they only hear what, how, what idiots they are. And that doesn't make any difference to them because everyone's tellin' them things like that…But sometimes ya just don't care.
SCOTT: (inaudible) It's all f**king going on.
BEV: Yeah, and unless they find them……F**kin' Olivia
SCOTT: This'll go on for f**ken ever.

---

19 B00601 / Night / 040398 / CR7175 / Blue, recorded discussion at 2.40am

BEV: Even Beryl says "That f**kin' little bitch!!" (laughs) I said why do we all say "That f**kin little bitch" and we never co', never swear about him.
SANDY: Oh cause they go on about her, oh her father's gone on about her all those...
BEV: Yeah.
SANDY: ...and all those things he's done and his darling daughter, that's why.
BEV: Yeah, yeah, but he, the other guy hasn't said anything... wonderful darling little daughter. How come you just got one page on ya, Olivia had about fourteen pages on her.
SCOTT: Did she!! Did you ever get them?
BEV: No they went round all the yacht clubs up north

You might think that a mother might understand another mother's anguish at the disappearance and murder of her 17 year old daughter. But not if you are Bev or Sandy Watson who began talking about Jan Hope's "nervous breakdown":

BEV: He wanted ev'...all the resources, as much spent, money spent as possible, Mr Hope did. Well I hope he realises that if they pop up again, she's up for the bill.
SANDY: Yeah.
BEV: Cause he's been a f**ken nuisance. (Laughs)
SANDY: Yeah...yeah.
BEV: His kids are up for the bill. But he's been very quiet, he's been trying to straighten some of these coppers. He's been very quiet since...
SANDY: ...the Smart's went on holiday.
BEV: Mmmmm, oh yeah, no.
SANDY: Since his wife had a nervous breakdown.
BEV: Yeah.

SANDY: Funny that!!!
BEV: The last we heard of her, is she went on and on and on and then they, when they had to paste those kids names over TV.
SANDY: Oh yeah.

It seems even Watson's private investigators were beginning to wonder what kind of character their client was.

QUENTIN:....it just isn't (inaudible)...I mean he's obviously a bit of a rascal.[20]
SANDY: Yeah, oh yeah he's no angel, he's a little shit. I always tell him that.
QUENTIN: And um and, and he's quite clearly stealing things and...but...that doesn't make him a double murderer.
SANDY: No.
QUENTIN: And you know your brother well and you would know if he had the ability of doing it...now unfortunately there's one, one of the guys I spoke to yesterday was scared shitless of him.
SANDY: Yeah, Andrew, mum said.
QUENTIN: Mmmm.
SANDY: I can't imagine that.
QUENTIN: But I think the longer he thinks about it...the more he's....
SANDY: Oh right it's all turning another direction in his mind....
QUENTIN: Yeah, yeah his mind and that's and he's an unusual vague little person, but.....the Police will be able to turn him into being quite a...um quite a useful witness for the prosecution.

Andrew Averill was a friend of Watson's, but as the family put it, Andrew knew better than to do anything that would "piss him off":[21]

---

20 B00202/Early/250298/CR7175/Blue
21 B00201/Early/240298/CR7175/Blue

Cue 0170: General discussion about Police interviews and how they are intimidating. Andrew wouldn't sign statement. Andrew told Police Scott un-nerved him a few times.

Cue 0225

BEV: Hey did Scott just go out to his boat the night after the Police had talked to him......at night?
SANDY: I dunno...Oh! after the media, Scott went out there, yeah, he went round to see him.
BEV: Yeah well it frightened Andrew.
SANDY: Why did it frighten him?
BEV: Andrew thinks Scott was threatening.
SANDY: Scott was probably angry.
BEV: Mmmm, yeah but they, he un-nerves people, you know how he (inaudible) and (inaudible) them.
SANDY: Oh yeah.
BEV: Well Andrew's quite frightened of him they think.
SANDY: They think Andrew is?
BEV: They sez yeah...He told the Police he is too.
SANDY: But, but he knows Scott.
BEV: Yeah.
SANDY: And he knows that he's not, like...Andrew would never do anything to piss him off.
BEV: No.
SANDY: No.
BEV: (inaudible) pipe wrench (inaudible) told him
SANDY: He must of taken the pipe wrench out of my car cause I just let him take my car (laughing)
BEV: I think that's so funny (laughs).....
SANDY: (inaudible)
BEV: ...oh it really frightened Andrew.....

SANDY: But he does un-nerve people.
BEV: Yeah, he un-nerved those Policemen, that's why they decided that it was him.....
SANDY: Spose yeah, he doesn't un-nerve me.
BEV: No he doesn't un-nerve me either.
SANDY: So, then, cause they said to me last night, ah Quentin said to me "now Scott, you know, have you ever seen Scott lose it" and I said shit yes!!....we used to try and kill each other when we were kids!!! (laughs) and that, um and that, and when the Police interviewed me and they said now you and Scott are be, always been quite close, I said shit no!! we used to try and kill each other when we were kids (laughs) and they.....but we did!!

Cue 0665: *General conversation about Bev's meeting with Quentin Doig.*

Cue 0707

BEV: He's going, he mouths off, I said oh yeah. He told someone he stabbed someone in prison or something and that made them intimidated. I said, oh god! I said he would of been charged with it if he had've stabbed someone in prison...(inaudible)...I said no he's got a smart mouth, he's always had a smart mouth, he hasn't got a smart mouth very much now, just when he was younger.
SANDY: Jumped up little twerp (laughs).
BEV: Yeah. Tries to be better than anyone else. (talking over top of each other).

Cue 0799: General talk about how Scott has a way of un-nerving people. It would have to be a pretty strong person to censure him. A few school teachers and Policemen have. Scott would never understand why Andrew would be frightened of

him. Scott needs to be told that he un-nerves people and that they get frightened. He doesn't know how the look that comes over his face affects people. He can definitely stand up for himself verbally. He can get a bit too personal. He says what he thinks and you don't want to hear it sometimes.

The family discussion about Watson's bravado and methods of unnerving people is revealing from a psychological point of view: it fits the definition of psychopathy. Either Watson was telling the truth about stabbing a prison inmate, or he was lying about it in a bid to intimidate someone else.

The family saw it as merely a "smart mouth", but taken in conjunction with other factors it could also be significant.

Let's look at what Andrew Averill told police he had experienced with Scott, across a number of statements:

STATEMENT 2:[22] "The nights he was interviewed by the Police he came to my boat shed after the interview. He spent about an hour with me and we walked over to the boat here. We walked back through the gap. He was ranting on in the shed, Mafia type talk. He believed the Police were going to nail him. I was telling about the forensic type things the Police can do. I did a bit of chemistry.

"When we parted here he shook my hand as though we were parting. He came over to see if you had his boat. He thought his dinghy had gone but he found it here still. He expected it had gone. He brought a piece of rope out of my shed. He was stressed out and mentioned he might commit suicide but later said he wouldn't do it. I had asked him what the line was for. He was using it as a garrote. He may have been trying to intimidate me with my young son.

"Last night around 10.30 pm he rowed up to my boat in the

---

22 Second statement of Andrew Averill, doc 10310, dated 14 January 1998

aluminium dinghy. I called out if it was Scott. He told me to shush. He hopped on. I told him I didn't want him and basically told him to bugger off. He told me to keep my mouth shut and not to talk to the Police. He wanted to know what you had been asking me but mostly to tell me to keep my mouth shut. He had a wrench, a pipe wrench, in the dinghy with him.[23] He was with me for only five minutes. I was abrupt. I explained why I'd been on TV. He'd seen me.

"I have seen Scott with a knife. He is always picking up my knives and chisels and things. He often pokes knives and the like at me in the shed and will stab them into the wall, things like that. He brought a knife back with him on the boat *Galerna* when he was on it. It was a small fold-up knife with a knob on the blade past the handle and you flick the blade out by touching the knob with your thumb. He said the whole crew off the *Galerna* bought knives. The handle would fit in the palm of your hand and it had similar sized blade. He said he'd left it with his sister after a Policewoman at Picton had seen him flicking it around in a pub in Picton. I last saw the knife in my shed I think, the day he got back in the *Galerna* I think it was. I haven't seen the knife this year. His sister may still have it if she had it ever."

STATEMENT:[24] "I remember while I was talking to Scott in my shed that I felt threatened by Scott's manner. He had my hammer in his hand and was acting quite aggressive and he was very on edge. I felt like he was trying to intimidate me. I told him to put the hammer down and he did. He then picked up a piece of heavy fishing line. As we were walking back to Shakespeare Bay I saw the fishing line

---

23 A wrench which, based on the evidence, Watson must have physically removed from his sister's car and taken with him on the dinghy to see Averill. He wasn't visiting his friend's yacht to fix the plumbing, nor did the dinghy have pipes.
24 Statement of Andrew Averill, doc 12493

hanging out of his pocket. I asked him what he was going to do with it. He said "I'm going to top myself".

"My son, Tim was walking with us and I started to feel uneasy about him being there listening to that, so I told him to go on ahead.

"Scott said "Don't worry I'm not going to do anything."

"We sat in the bay talking for a while. Scott had the fishing line wrapped around each hand and was pulling it like you would if you were going to wrap it around somebody's neck, but he never made any kind of threats with it."

Remember, this is not behaviour dredged up from Watson's teenage years. This was the here and now. The question objective readers have to consider is whether such behaviour displays a manipulative character capable of murder or whether it was simply someone showing signs of stress. If the latter, you then have to ask yourself 'why?'. Why, if he had no connection to the events at Furneaux, was Watson suggesting he was suicidal? Things would get a lot tougher for Watson in the months to come and as history shows suicide was never attempted. Which again raises the question: why did he say it then?

Quentin Doig, an intelligent and capable former police detective inspector whose security firm had been hired by the Watson defence, spoke to Andrew Averill on 24 February 1998. This is Doig's account of that conversation:[25]

"Andrew has got to know him quite well and has spent quite a bit of time with Scott. He describes Scott as not a loner as the media have painted him out to be. He is the first guy who is always looking for company or someone to talk to. He said Scott does, however, have the habit of saying stupid things. He considers Scott as hard and cunning and he is typical of a person who has been inside prison.

"Andrew would not trust Scott and that if anything ever went missing, he would at first suspect Scott as having taken it, but

---

25 Jobsheet: Interview Andrew Averill, 24 Feb 1998

would then later find out some other explanation for something going missing. Andrew said he didn't want to run Scott down and that he had been interviewed by the Police and had said things to the Police that didn't put Scott in a good light.

"On the last time Andrew saw him, which was just over a week ago, he told Scott he was nothing but an arsehole. Scott had called in to see him to see what he had told the Police. Andrew said that he had been interviewed by the Police on four or five occasions and that he had made one signed statement. He said that he was in a difficult situation and that he didn't want to say things that might get back to Scott. He said that Scott has an attitude and that he was cautious of him. He said Scott behaves as though he likes you to know that he is a hard man.

"He said he had seen Scott on a number of occasions since Ben and Olivia went missing. He saw him first in January, 2-3 days after New Year when Scott brought his boat into Shakespeare Bay. He said Scott likes to walk around creating an image of being a suspect little bugger. He supposed that he, Scott, identified himself as being in charge or tough.

"Andrew said he did not want to see him done for something he didn't do and that he is prepared to keep an open mind on things. He said the day on which the police seized Scott's boat; Scott visited him at a shed he has at Picton Marina—C29. Scott sat there and was very uptight. He was holding a hammer and was weighing it up and down in his hands. He also had a fishing line in his hands on occasions, which he held like a garrote.

"Later that evening Andrew, Scott and Andrew's eight-year-old son walked across the hills to Shakespeare Bay. Andrew felt uneasy about Scott having the fishing line in his pocket and at one stage said to Scott, "what's the fishing line for, Scott?". Scott replied, "I might do myself in". Andrew said to Scott, "you can get your kicks any way you like, but leave me and my eight year old son alone".

"The next day some television reporters went out to Andrew's boat. He refused to talk to them, and told them to go away. Later that day some Police visited and took Scott's dinghy. Andrew went over to speak to them and he was seen by the television crew talking to the Police. He later heard he was on television that night talking to the Police. He said that Scott rode out to see him at about 10:30—11:00 p.m. at night. He came very quietly. Andrew saw him coming and told Scott to bugger off. Scott told Andrew to keep his mouth shut. Andrew noticed a pipe wrench on the floor of the dinghy. At that stage Andrew hadn't told the Police anything, but as a result of Scott's attitude that night, he felt more inclined to talk to the Police. Andrew said that the pipe wrench remained on the floor of the dinghy throughout their conversation that night.

"Andrew recalled on one occasion Scott telling him about how he had stabbed a guy in the guts in jail. Andrew said that Scott told him about it in such a way that he believed what he was saying. Scott told Andrew that the guy had a look of surprise on his face. Although Andrew didn't know if Scott was telling the truth, he took it as a boast of some sort, an ego-type thing. He still believed him and told the Police about that.

"Scott also told Andrew on one occasion how once in jail he walked up to a Christian guy who was playing darts. The Christian guy was in prison for murdering his girlfriend. Scott claimed to Andrew that he stabbed this Christian a number of times in the arm, with a dart. Andrew didn't tell the Police about this.

"He said that on a lot of occasions when Scott had visited him while he had been working on the boat around in his shed at the Marina, he has been present when Scott has said silly things to females, or about females, as they walked past. He would regularly say, "rape the bitch". Andrew said that Scott talks a lot about rape—it's the tough guy type of talk, according to Andrew. You can either read nothing into it, or now when Andrew compares it to what has happened to Ben and Olivia, he now wonders whether there was some truth to what Scott was saying. Andrew said he didn't tell the Police about either the darts stabbing or the "rape the bitch" comments.

"Andrew said that Scott was a funny type of guy—he can either be a likeable person or absolutely abrasive.

"After New Year, Andrew noticed that Scott had different oars in his boat. He then had an old dunger set of oars, whereas the ones he had before weren't "half bad oars". Andrew didn't discuss the oars. Also after New Year, Andrew got the impression that Scott was removing things from the yacht. He recorded on one occasion finding two cans of food on the beach. He thought they belonged to Scott. He remembers asking Scott whether there was anything on Scott's boat that he could get in to trouble for. Scott replied, "no, that it is all cleaned up". Andrew took that as relating to trivial things. He said that Scott was into a lot of trivial things, such as petty theft and cannabis use. He described Scott as a brash young sod."

That was Quentin Doig's report to the Watson defence team, but here's something Andrew Averill *did* tell police:

"I remember on one occasion we over sitting in my second boat at the Picton Marina and a tourist walked past. Scott said "Rape the bitch". Another time a young girl walked past and he said "Show us your tits". He yelled it out so she could hear. He actually said "Show us your tits, you slut".

"He was always saying things like that. He told me since that the way to make money was to make movies of raping women and killing them. He called them snuff movies. He was stoned when he said this. He was always talking about things like this, and he would quite often get really worked up about it."

Murder on the Blade documentary-maker Keith Hunter apparently had access to these witness statements, but you won't find them quoted in his book *Trial by Trickery*.

Perhaps it's what Al Gore would call "an inconvenient truth": Scott Watson was more than just a posterboy "rascal"—he was displaying character traits in the profile of a sexual killer. Perhaps Hunter and others didn't want to let the facts get in the way of a good martyrdom story. Some of these stories you will read are covered a little bit in *Ben & Olivia*, but they were only the snippets read out in court by people whose memories had faded over the 18 months it took to come to trial. That testimony often lacked the edge and detail of what witnesses had initially told police at the time of the disappearance. When we wrote *Ben & Olivia*, Jayson Rhodes and I had no access to the police files, and the Watson family later failed to provide the files either, so at least we can plead ignorance as to what was buried inside when we wrote at the conclusion of our book:[26]

"And yet, one is left with that niggling fear: maybe, in our need to put a name to the unspeakable evil that stalked Endeavour Inlet that dark New Year's morning, we have put an innocent, even if somewhat antisocial, man in jail for a crime that he truly did not commit."

Maybe, maybe not. "Antisocial" or "psychopath"? That's the real question. At least for this part of the book. A Google search for "Scott Watson" and "rape the bitch" turns up no hits, so it's a pretty good bet that his attitude towards women is not widely known. It appears never to have been discussed online, yet it is highly relevant to the charges he faced. He was not afraid to vocalise criminal fantasies about raping random women.

How did Keith Hunter describe Watson's criminal tendencies again?[27]

"Watson had a criminal record but it was not of adult criminal behaviour. It was historical and patently obsolete. The picture it

---

26 *Ben & Olivia*, p252
27 *Trial by Trickery*, p30

painted was of a man who in his youth had used marijuana and other people's cars and bicycles from time to time. Most serious was that he had been an occasional burglar."

The police, wrote Hunter, painted "a picture of Scott Watson as an active criminal who has a long history of violence. The picture is false[28]...on the basis of his criminal record it was apparent that Watson had matured and left his growing pains in the past."[29]

The police, he added, attempted to fabricate "this adolescent misbehaviour into the criminal record of a violent psychopath."

Reading *Trial by Trickery* you'd come away thinking of Watson as a "defamed" veritable Thief of Hearts. Andrew Averill, however, wasn't the only one of Watson's associates to tell much more sinister stories than Hunter was publishing. Snuff movies and "Show us your tits" were about to emerge in another totally independent witness statement, along with alleged attempted rape at knifepoint, a vicious beating of a man who crossed Watson and a loaded stolen rifle.

---

28 Ibid, p57
29 Ibid p30

CHAPTER THREE

Is This The Evolution Of A Killer?

In October 1997, Scott Watson had crewed on part of the delivery journey from Tonga to Picton of millionaire Alasdair Cassels' massive 87' ketch, the *Galerna*. Watson had met the vessel in Whangarei, and agreed to join it in Auckland for the trip down the coast.

During the voyage, "occasional burglar" Watson graduated to knife-play after *Galerna* stopped off in Napier on 14 October: "While there," fellow crewman and drinking buddy James Frueh told police,[30] "Scott bought a knife from a knife shop. It was a stainless steel knife with an aluminium handle. The handle was silver or blue. It had a folding blade. The whole knife was about 20 cm long.

"During the rest of the trip then Scott would always play with the knife. He would just sit there opening and closing the blade. It would

---

30 Statement of James Frueh, doc 10212, dated 14 January 1998

make a clicking noise. He would do it so much that people would take the knife off him. He would try and open the blade as fast as he could."

Cassels, according to Frueh, ended up confiscating the knife but returned it to Watson when he left *Galerna* on its arrival in Wellington.

It was only a brief parting of company. By late November Watson had been hired to do maintenance work on *Galerna*, which was rafted alongside Cassels' other smaller ketch, *Faith*, at Erie Bay in the Tory Channel northeast of Picton. Richard 'Ricardo' Rusbatch was *Faith*'s skipper and acting as Cassels' overseer. Frueh told police Rusbatch fell out with Watson.

"Scott thought that Ricardo was talking about him behind his back. That was the main reason. He thought that Ricardo was telling Alistair about him. Their relationship really started to deteriorate. This was then I started to try and get them to talk about it.

"On the last day that Scott was aboard we had a barbecue in Waikawa Bay.

"There was me, Scott, Sandy and her two kids. We had a few drinks. We came back to the boat. I ended up going to bed at about 11.00 pm. I had a few drinks. Scott had been drinking too. He doesn't drink a lot but when he drinks he drinks a lot. I like him when he's not drinking. I don't like him when he's drinking. He can really change.

"The following day we went for a tour around the Sounds in his sister's car. We got back about 5.00 pm.

"When we got back Ricardo came to me and told Scott to ring Alistair. He didn't say what for. He said that the cops were coming to see him. He rang Alistair and Alistair fired him over the telephone. I remember him saying, "You can't fire me, I have done nothing wrong".

"This was when I found out that the reason he was fired was because he cut up Ricardo's jeans with a knife.

"The Police arrived and told Scott that they had a complaint about him jumping on someone's boat. Later I asked him why he had jumped on this person's boat and he just said, "Because he was a c**t".

"Scott spent the night on the boat. The following day he left. He told me that he was going to take the ferry and go up north. When he left he had an argument with Ricardo. They were yelling at each other. It ended up with Ricardo saying that he was going to end up in a prison. He left. I was quite glad to see him go because the situation on the boat had got so bad."

Rusbatch tells a similar story:[31]

"My job once Alistair had left was basically to just keep an eye on things. Over the next month Scott worked around the boat. I found that when Alistair was around Scott worked well but when Alistair wasn't there, Scott was pretty slack. I noticed that when Scott was drinking his attitude changed drastically and he became anti."

That's two men each describing a Jekyll and Hyde personality switch in Scott Watson when fuelled by alcohol. Rusbatch continues:

"Towards the end of the month I was finding Scott pretty hard work. He wasn't responding to my suggestions in relation to work that he could have been doing around the boat. A guy by the name of Tommy who was a boat builder working on board also wasn't happy with Scott. As a result I rang Alistair and told him I would like to see the back of Scott. Alistair agreed and as a result I told Scott that work had run out for him. I told him to ring Alistair if he had a problem with that.

"Scott did ring Alistair and Alistair backed up what I had said. When Scott got off the telephone he said to me that I had set him up to get the sack. He said that he was going to "get me for this and that I wouldn't even see it coming". I was pretty concerned about his attitude.

3110292 / ST / RICHARD RUSBATCH / MW7124 / 140198

"That night I was sleeping on *Faith* which was rafted up alongside *Galerna*. Scott, his sister and James had been out to the pub. I had three pairs of jeans hanging on the line of *Galerna*. I was woken by them turning the music up on *Galerna* then I heard the slap of wet clothing hitting the deck of *Faith*.

"The next day I found three pairs of my jeans on the deck of *Faith* with knife holes in the crotch of each of them. I confronted Scott about the jeans but he denied doing the damage to them."

Which brings us to a visit around this time by Scott Watson to the home of a former work colleague from Carey's Boat Yard, Warwick Eastgate, and his wife Vicki.

"We started talking about Scott's trip on the boat. That's the big boat [*Galerna*] that was moored at the wharf.

"Scott started going on about the antics of what was going on on the boat. He said that one of the guys had a lot of kinky toys and dirty movies. I know that animals were mentioned in relation to the movies and it got worse from there. I don't remember exactly what was said but I felt he started talking about snuff movies. That is movies where someone actually gets killed. I remember thinking I don't need to hear about this.[32]

"Scott talked about it for probably half an hour I suppose. I remember Scott saying that the guy with all this stuff was [withheld]. The gist of what I picked up from Scott was that there was a lot of weird things going on on the boat. It was definitely more than just a group of guys watching a few blue movies. I said I didn't want to hear any more and stood up and walked away."

Remember, this is direct testimony of a conversation Watson had with the Eastgates.

Again, none of this appears to be in Keith Hunter's book. Here's

---

[32] In a later statement Vicki clarified it: "I can't recall what Scott said but it was apparent to me that some person was murdered during the sexual act on the movie." 12373 / ST / VIDA EASTGATE / AHD181 / 160698

something else I couldn't find. Watson and Warwick headed off to the Federal pub for a drink:

"While they were away," said Vicki, "I noticed that Scott had left his knife behind. I had a play with it. It had a silver blade and handle and you could sort of flick the blade out. The blade was about four inches long.

"When they arrived back they were very merry. They weren't that drunk that they were falling over or anything and I could understand their speech quite clearly. They both sort of told me in stages of what had happened at the Federal. Apparently they were the only ones in the bar apart from a female and the bar staff.

"After they had been there for a while the female started pestering them. Warwick said that he thought she was a prostitute. They apparently started being rude to her, saying things like, "Show us your tits" and carrying on. Scott was going on about how she was a real dog. At about that stage Scott started saying something to the effect of how they should have bumped her off.

"I can't remember how it came up but Scott started going on about murder and how easy it would be. He started going on about if I wanted anyone murdered he would do it for me. He had this real evil look in his eye and he was very intense. It takes a bit to make me nervous but the way he was talking was making me scared. He seemed to have psyched himself into it.

"Every time I changed the subject he would bring it back to murder and murdering someone. I got the impression that if I had said to him, "Go and murder the girl in the pub", he would have done it. I don't remember him saying anything about how he would actually commit a murder.

"This carried on until I went to bed at 10.30 or 11.00 pm. Not long after Warwick came to bed as well.

"The next day I spoke to Warwick about Scott and what had happened at the Federal with the girl. Warwick said that Scott had started going on at the pub about murdering the girl. He said that he tried to change the subject but Scott kept coming back to it. Warwick was more specific than this but I don't remember exactly what he told me. I told Warwick that I didn't want Scott back here again.

"I remember reading in the paper the description of the person at Furneaux Lodge that the Police were looking for. As soon as I read it I thought of Scott. I know Warwick thought of Scott too when he read it."

This incident happened in November 1997, more than a month before Olivia and Ben disappeared at Furneaux Lodge.

Let's remind ourselves for a moment of University of British Columbia's Professor Robert Hare's definition of the "antisocial psychopath":[33]

"This type of psychopath is considered the archetypical delinquent, openly pursuing a diverse range of antisocial behaviors and often in trouble with the law. The antisocial psychopath is the main type found in prisons, whose availability for psychological testing results in a disproportionate representation of this type in psychopathy descriptions. The American 'Diagnostic and Statistical Manual' (DSM) description of psychopathy is based on this group of offenders, to whom the manual gives the name 'antisocial personality disorder'. Descriptive criteria for this category are as follows:

1. failure to conform to social norms with respect to lawful behaviors as indicated by repeatedly performing acts that are grounds for arrest
2. deceitfulness, as indicated by repeated lying, use of aliases, or conning others for personal profit or pleasure
3. impulsivity or failure to plan ahead

---

[33] http://abusesanctuary.blogspot.be/2006/10/seventeen-faces-of-psychopath.html

4. irritability and aggressiveness, as indicated by repeated physical fights or assaults
5. reckless disregard for safety of self or others
6. consistent irresponsibility, as indicated by repeated failure to sustain consistent work behavior or honor financial obligations
7. lack of remorse, as indicated by being indifferent to or rationalizing having hurt, mistreated, or stolen from another

Keith Hunter wrote that Scott Watson emerged from the documents "lie-free".[34] Yet the documents show Watson repeatedly lied about the identity of his boat, giving it a range of alias names—none of them actually appearing on the boat—so that he could slip out of marina berths without paying.

"Scott said that his boat did not have a name," holidaymaker Jennifer Skelton told police of an encounter her family had with him. "He said that this was handy as he could go wherever he wanted, moor anywhere and then leave.[35]

"He said how he had sailed down the North Island and did not pay for any moorings. He told us where he had been but I cannot remember where that was.

"Scott said that if he did name his boat he would call it 'Mad Dog'. He did not say why. I thought he looked like a mad dog and it would suit him."

The evidence of the Skeltons and Cassidys is fascinating for a whole range of reasons, not least because it paints a picture of Scott Watson as an explosive device in search of a fuse. Jennifer and her husband Simon were holidaying at Momorangi Bay near Picton on 27 December 1997 with another couple, Debbie and Gary Cassidy and their baby. This was four days before New Year's Eve.

---

34 *Trial by Trickery*, p9
35 11130 / ST / JENNIFER SKELTON / MK8254 / 190198

Jennifer told detectives she and the two men arrived back from waterskiing at 5pm to find Scott and Sandy Watson in their tent, drinking. Apparently Sandy had recognised Debbie Cassidy—who'd stayed behind to look after her baby—as an old schoolfriend. Sandy and Scott downed most of a bottle of rum.

"Scott got drunk as the night went on. They would have stayed till about 9.30 pm. During the evening Sandy had left for about an hour and Scott was with us by himself. We were quite pleased to see him go. He had been ok until he started drinking. He then became a pain. It was nothing in particular, just his general demeanour.

"He got quite close to me at one stage until my husband told him to leave me alone and moved closer between us. It wasn't a violent incident, more just pushing away a drunk. We had been trying to get him to go for sometime before he did.

"When he did leave he came back with Sandy almost straight away. This was because Sandy had been away for about an hour and was obviously on her way back when we got Scott to leave.

"Sandy asked what Scott had done. We said "nothing" and they chatted for a couple of minutes before they left.

"Scott was very drunk and staggered away. He stopped for a pee on someone's caravan. They said that they were going to go back to Picton that night as Sandy wanted to meet her boyfriend 'Jimmy'. He is Swiss."[36]

A drunk Watson revealed he'd been in prison, and boasted of his drug connections:

"Somehow it came up in conversation and Scott said that Zappa grows the best grass around. He gave the impression he got drugs from Zappa and I got the impression Zappa was an older guy. I can't remember his exact words but it was words to that effect. He said that Zappa lived in the Tory Channel. He said that Zappa was

---

[36] The 'Jimmy' referred to is James Frueh, the crewman on the Cassels' ketch.

alright if you gave him drugs but if he had alcohol he turned into a murderer.

"Sandy also knew Zappa and she also talked about him. Sandy said that she thought Zappa fancied her as he always grinned when he saw her.

"Scott said that he would take us out fishing but made no firm offer. We would not have gone out in the boat with him. He said he knew the best places and that you had to throw blood and bone over to attract the fish and sharks."

As to Watson's description, Jennifer said he "had stubble, probably a day or so growth. He had homemade tatts on his hands.... Scott had told us he was going to Furneaux Lodge for New Year."

Gary Cassidy remembered the Watson visit to his tent vividly:[37]

"Scott was quite rapt how he had just sailed around the North Island in his boat and that he hadn't paid any mooring fees. To do that he said he would go into a marina or such like and then take off early. He said that his boat was unnamed and because no one knew whose boat it was he could slip away untraced.

"Scott mentioned that he wanted to change the colour of the boat to blue because everyone else's boat was blue. As I understood it, he intended to change the colour of his boat so that he could continue to avoid paying the mooring fees.

"He said his next trip was going to be to Tonga... He did say that he was thinking about giving the boat a name at some stage—Mad Dog. I think he mentioned that later in the evening when he was drunk.

"Scott also was very drunk. He kept saying to Deb—where was her blonde hair and her leopard skin outfit that he had seen her in some ten years previous. He was becoming obnoxious and we became tired of him going on about it. We eventually persuaded

---

37 11637 / ST / GARY CASSIDY / DRD506 / 180298

him to leave. He never lost his temper or got abusive. He had some cannabis mixed up in his tobacco, I think that's why he was dribbling shit later on.

"He said to me that if I ever wanted some cannabis, to go and see his mate Zappa in the Tory Channel. He said that Zappa is fine on the dope, but if he gets on the alcohol he kills people. Sandy also mentioned the same thing, that Zappa goes mad and kills people when he drinks alcohol. They said this about three times during the night.

"He said this when he was in his "waffling" stage, so I didn't read much into it. I certainly had no intention of going to meet this Zappa character. I don't care for cannabis and nor does my wife.

"When I spoke with Scott he had about two days stubble on his face. His hair was curly, it was on his shoulders and looked scruffy."

Simon Skelton, Jennifer's husband, told police of Watson's Jekyll and Hyde transformation when he drank:[38]

" As the evening developed and Scott consumed the rum his personality changed. He became loud, obnoxious, boasting about getting away with a lot without paying for it.

"He began talking to Debbie about her changing her hair colour and style. Debbie previously had blond hair below shoulder length but had changed it to red hair bob. Scott mentioned he didn't like her changing her hair I suppose about six times. I got the impression Scott liked Debbie and particularly blond hair.

"Now I think about it, it was more like Scott liked blond hair as he would say things like "it's a shame you cut your hair and why did you change the colour." Scott said this aloud around three times and because I was sitting next to him I heard him say it at least another three times. I just put it down to Scott being drunk and I knew Debbie wasn't happy.

---

38 12117 / ST / SIMON SKELTON / DH6260 / 010598

"Debbie also wears glasses and Scott made some comments about her glasses. I remember him saying "four eyes" which didn't go down too well. Scott also mentioned Debbie's dress but don't know what exactly was said.

"By this time I was getting uncomfortable being with Scott. He was getting drunker and drunker and was getting scared of him. I wanted him away and out of the camp site.

"When I was scared about Scott I was scared because he looked confrontational. He was lean, had a couple of days stubble, olive skinned, tattoos on forearms and was a bit wary of him. When we first met him he seemed okay but when he was drunk his whole personality changed and I didn't like him.

"I must admit once the incident occurred at Furneaux I immediately thought of Scott because of the way he had acted at the camp site.

"When I mentioned earlier the stubble on Scott's face I imagine he appeared to be the sort of guy who after a day or a day and a half would give the impression of a few days growth. His beard would appear to grow heavily."

Debbie Cassidy testified in Depositions that Watson, despite knowing she was married with a child, began invading her space and continually asking about her leopardskin outfit and blonde hair:[39]

"He continually went on about what I was wearing at Sandy's 21st party. He moved his chair closer to me and shut himself off from the rest of the conversation and the rest of the group. He began focussing all his attention on me.

"He wasn't being abusive but he swore a lot. His behaviour was just annoying. I didn't fear for my own safety because Gary was there and because he was drunk. I was embarrassed because Sandy was my friend and of how her brother was behaving.

---

[39] 11530D / DEBORAH CASSIDY

"I started suggesting to him to leave and go look for Sandy. After several of these requests, I became more blunt and told him to leave."

Watson and his sister ended up in someone else's tent moments later, where he drunkenly invited one of the women there to sail to Tonga with him.[40]

"During the conversation, he mentioned that he wanted me to be his cook on his boat and Jimmy, my brother in law to be his crew. He said he was intending to go to Tonga and wanted us to go with him but first he had a trip to do back up the coast to Napier.

"He said he'd go to Tonga when the trade winds were right. I think in about June he said. He was pretty drunk and when he did say something he would keep repeating what he said."

"He leaned over to me and pointed at me and said, "Hey you in the blanket I want you to come on board and cook my breakfast, you be my cook" and then pointed to Jimmy and said, "You be my crew". My reaction was just to laugh because I thought he was drinking.

"He just said, "What do you think about that, what do you think about that".

The woman said they asked the name of his boat, "I think he said it was Chandlair but that he had changed it. He said he'd been up to Napier and mentioned to some guys in a bar the name of his boat. He said they had had him on about the name and told him it was the name of a faggot movie and had been upset this.

"He said he took the name off and now called it Mad-dog with a real emphasis on Mad-dog and yelled this name out quite loud often during the conversation. If any of us referred to the boat by Mad-dog he would say "No it's Mad-dog" and repeat himself. He would say "Got to kill the dog, kill the dog". He seemed agitated when he said this and sat up and gestated [gesticulated] with his hand in a fist motion."

---

40 20298 / ST / YVONNE GREER / LC8773 / 140198

The woman's husband, Gary, remembered Sandy Watson using the term Mad Dog and Scott mentioning Furneaux:[41]

"When he talked about Mad Dog the female Sandy seemed to back it up by saying, "Yeah, Mad Dog". She didn't seem that drunk.

"When he mentioned about Furneaux being the place to go he really emphasised the word *Furneaux* like when he said Mad Dog. He mentioned something about there being plenty of babes at Furneaux. Whenever someone mentioned Furneaux he would repeat, "Yeah Furneaux".

"It was like he was half asleep while he was there and would catch on to someone's conversation and speak up and go on about Mad Dog and "Kill the dog". He had quite a husky voice.

"The people in the tent next door the next day asked us about who the hell Mad Dog was, asking about the guy Scott and what he was going on about."

When he wrote *Trial by Trickery* and produced his documentary *Murder on the Blade*, Keith Hunter had not met Scott Watson. He wrote, "A study of the documentation reveals that a demonstrably innocent and very wronged New Zealander has been imprisoned for life. The facts which underlie this pronouncement are set out in the pages that follow, all sourced to relevant publications and to the judicial process."[42]

Search Keith Hunter's book all you like, but very little of the eyewitness testimony you'll read in *Elementary* appears in Hunter's book. Arguably, then, "facts" highly relevant to whether Scott Watson is "demonstrably innocent" are mysteriously missing from Hunter's tome. Hunter would say they are not relevant. You might agree or you might think otherwise, but you actually can't reach an informed conclusion unless the evidence is before you.

---

41 0302 / ST / GARY GREER / LC8773 / 140198
42 *Trial by Trickery*, p25

Even the evidence you do already know about has questionmarks over it.

"Only one offence had occurred in the previous eight years," wrote Keith Hunter.[43] "This related to Watson's objection to the theft of his dinghy, when he pad pulled out a three inch, pocketknife-sized marlinspike to persuade two people he discovered taking the dinghy away on a truck to return it to him...this was Watson's only recorded offence since the age of eighteen and a half."

Reading that paragraph you'd have to have sympathy for Watson. Finding two men (implied) loading his boat onto the back of a truck, he grabs the only tool he can find, a marlinspike for untying ropes, and tries to "persuade" the men to give it back. Hell, he shouldn't even have been prosecuted!

Fast-forward to the *North & South* interview with Watson in 2015, where journalist Mike White wrote:[44]

"His only other conviction before Ben and Olivia went missing was from May 1995, when he discovered someone stealing his dinghy in Picton. 'I just said, 'Hey, that's my boat—I want you to put it back'. And he's one of the local rednecks in his four wheel drive—gets out and you think, 'Oh, here we go, you're going to get your head kicked in in the middle of the night'.

"So Watson pulled a marlinspike from his pocket—a 10cm sharpened spike he used at the boatbuilding yard where he worked—and the guy gave back his dinghy, but Watson was charged with possessing an offensive weapon."

There's been a bit of creative writing taking place, it appears. The police files reveal the "two people", the "local rednecks", turn out to be a man and his wife:[45]

"I went down to the Waikawa Marina with my wife, Petrice, to

---

43 *Trial by Trickery*, p30
44 "Scott Watson: The Interview", by Mike White, *North & South*, Dec 2015 p42
45 20516 / JS / LAWRENCE GLEDHILL / KY7541 / 120198

uplift a dinghy. By mistake we collected the wrong dinghy and as we were departing Scott Watson arrived on his motorcycle and told us to put the dinghy back. Watson produced a knife. After we put the dinghy back we reported the matter to the Police."

If they were truly boat thieves, would they have gone to police to complain about Watson?

Marlinspikes, real ones from boat yards, are between six inches (15cm) and 24 inches (60cm) long. You don't generally carry them in your pocket any more than you would carry a pickaxe in your pocket. On the other hand (and here's the rub) you can often find a miniature marlinspike as one of the tools on a Swiss Army pocket-knife. But it's not likely to be the tool you would specifically pull out to threaten "rednecks" with. Not unless you wanted to be laughed at. No, if you were carrying your flick knife as Watson always did, you'd push the button and pop out the blade. Describing the knife as a 'marlinspike' is like describing the knife as a 'corkscrew' or a 'nail file' just because it carries one of those tools.

Lawrence Gledhill was under no illusions what he saw:

"Scott Watson threatened me with a knife. We had to go to court and Watson was fined $400.00. He even got to keep the knife."[46]

---

[46] Interestingly, Watson later stole a friend's dinghy: " In about February/March last year (1997) Scott WATSON took my dinghy, which had been tied up to the back of my boat. The dinghy was white hardchine wooden dinghy about 8' long, with splashes of yellow paint on the inside. The dinghy was worth about $100, with a black rope lashed to the outside gun hull with a white braid rope. At that time WATSON's yacht was moored out from Picton wharf and he needed to row out to his yacht. I know he didn't have a dingy at that time.

I saw WATSON using my dinghy one day, to row out to his yacht. At the time I wasn't using my dinghy and thought he'd return it.

He never asked for permission to use it, and after a couple of weeks when I next saw him using it, I actually asked him for it back.

He said to me "F**k off I'll give it back to you when I'm good and ready" or words to that effect.

Shortly after that WATSON moved his yacht to Waikawa Bay, and then he moved it to my own mooring, (#31) that I own in Shakespeare Bay. (He never had permission to use my mooring.)

It would have been a good month later that I spotted WATSON's yacht on my mooring, and it was then that I saw my dinghy on the shore at Shakespeare Bay. I then went down and uplifted my dinghy and took it

Even Watson was calling it a knife when boasting about it to a workmate:

"He also told me about a time when he got arrested for pointing a knife at someone who was trying to steal his dinghy," Greg Curling told police.[47]

To another witness, Brian Kinder, Watson claimed it was "a putty knife", to which Kinder made the observation that Watson used his flick-blade to remove rotten wood from boat hulls. It was a long stretch of the definition "putty knife", but arguably more accurate than the word "marlinspike" which does not appear in the Operation TAM database.

Journalists Keith Hunter and Mike White can explain in their own time why they chose to play the weapon down.

Up in Whangarei, Watson's former girlfriend told police he had opened up to her:[48]

"On the night we first went to dinner, Scott told me that he had been in trouble for drugs. He said he'd been in jail where he'd been in solitary confinement because he'd been a bad bastard. He said that he had grown some cannabis in Picton but the Police had found his plot and taken it—from the way he spoke that had happened a short time before I met him. He said that he used drugs and I told him that I wasn't into that. He never used drugs around me at all.

"A couple of days after we went out to dinner he told me that he had stabbed some people and from the way he was talking it sounded like it had happened whilst he was in prison. I understood that he had stabbed two people but not both at the same time. He

---

back to my yacht. That would have been about April 1997.
WATSON's yacht at that stage still didn't have a mast on it. I never made a complaint to the Police about him taking my dinghy, and don't want to make any complaint now.
11436 / ST / MICHAEL MEADS / MR8667 / 040298
47 12884 / ST / GREGORY CURLING / PMC692 / 220798
48 10235 / ST / SUPPRESSED / WM7683 / 130198

said that one of the persons was from Invercargill and that he could never go there. I understood that it was to do with gangs."

The woman also discovered Watson's Jekyll and Hyde personality change once he started drinking:

"When we went to my boss's birthday party Scott got absolutely drunk and was being a real arsehole during the party. I was told on the Monday after the party by people who went to the party that Scott had been telling my boss's 15 year old son the benefits of drugs, that he'd been feeling up two women and that he'd been drinking bath oils from the bathroom."

"Feeling up two women" would be indecent assault if the women concerned had decided to press charges - another sex offence. His girlfriend dumped him after this.

Let's read some more things you haven't been told by Keith Hunter or Mike White, testimony from people who—unlike all the book authors to date—have actually met Scott Watson and know what he is really like.

CHAPTER FOUR

Violent And Dangerous

Much has been made of the fact that Watson is a bicycle thief, not a violent psychopath. Michael Coutts would disagree.

In 1994 Coutts was a 31 year old boat builder in Picton who went halves with a then 23 year old Watson in the purchase of an old yacht to renovate and sell. The pair found it harder to shift on to a buyer than they'd expected, and Coutts began bad-mouthing Watson behind his back as they fell out over the best sales strategy.

"I wanted to hold out for a higher price and Scott just wanted to get his money out so he could start building his own boat. This was causing friction between us."[49]

The storm seemed to blow over, and weeks later the pair were sitting together discussing ways of adding value to the yacht.

"Scott came round to where I was and we sat on the beach chat-

---

49 20343 / ST / MICHAEL COUTTS / ASD279 / 180198

ting and there seemed to be no animosity between us and I thought that things were going along okay. Scott and I knew of a winch that was half buried on land between the snout and the marina. Somehow our conversation turned around to this winch and Scott and I decided to go out and have a go at digging it up.

"We motored out in my dinghy and when we got ashore we both walked up the track to where this winch was and when we got there I bent down to have a look at it and at that time Scott said to me that he had heard that I was bad mouthing him behind his back.

"Things had been fine up to that point and when he said that to me it kind of took me by surprise but I told him that I had been saying a few things about him.

"I wasn't really sure who had been talking to him and I kept asking him what the problem was.

"Scott then started hitting me with a manuka stick that he had picked up. He hit me several times around the legs and my arms as I was fending off the blows. I ended up with some pretty big welts on my legs the next day.

"While he was hitting me with the stick he kept inviting me to have a go. I was saying to him that I didn't want to have a go and I was trying to calm him down. At the time I had a steel bar in my hand that had been lying next to the winch. I think I picked it up after he started hitting me.

"I think his stick ended up breaking over my arm. The situation was then that if I threw my bar away then he would throw his stick away. So I threw the bar away and he dropped his stick and he walked off back down the track and I followed him.

"When we got back to the dinghy he hopped in and said, 'I'm taking your dinghy you can walk'.

"I told him that he wasn't taking my dinghy and I had to grab hold of the dinghy cause he had already pushed it out. We were in knee deep water and had a punch up. A few punches were thrown by both of us and then I said to Scott to just get in the dinghy and I'd drop him off at the marina.

"He hopped in and we didn't talk and I motored into the marina which was only about five minutes away and I dropped him off either at his boat or in the marina.

"At the time this happened I had been a bit stunned at what had happened. I was a bit worried that because he lived in a boat in the same marina that this wasn't finished. That night I was thinking of the best way to resolve things and I went to work the next morning and the guys at work could see the bruises on my arms and legs and they asked me what had happened and I told them.

"After work I put a note in his dinghy which basically said that we didn't like each other and that if he wanted $1,000 I [would] buy him out of the boat. Scott rang me at work the next day and he accepted the offer and I got $1,000 out of the bank and met him the next day in town (Picton) and gave it to him. I think I still have the receipt.

"It would have been about two to three months from when we bought the boat to when Scott assaulted me," stated Michael Coutts.

Watson had shown, consistent with psychopathic behaviour, the ability to hold a grudge and plot—in this case luring his target to a secluded location with the intention of meting out rough justice. The incident does not appear on Watson's criminal record because it was not reported to police. But it happened, and Keith Hunter had access to the files disclosing it. Arguably it was a bit disingenuous to say police were "defaming" Watson as violent, when the author was sitting on testimony like this.

On 14 January 1997—a year before Ben and Olivia disappeared—Watson had moored his boat on a private jetty used by livestock barges and marked by a large "Keep Clear At All Times" sign. Barge operators Peter McManaway and Michael Jones were navigating into position at 5am as they often did. They saw Watson's boat parked illegally and went around it, but in the process they clipped a mooring rope Watson had strung across the entrance, causing the barge carrying a load of sheep to nudge the corner of Watson's yacht.

"There may have been a chip of paint on his boat but no real damage," McManaway told police.[50] "As soon as that happened Watson came out of his cabin and started yelling at Mike. I couldn't hear what he was saying but I could see him and he appeared to be shouting and yelling and carrying on. At the time I was on the flybridge of my boat.

"I backed out a wee bit and Watson untied his ropes and backed out past us on our right side and he went back out to the mooring. As he was backing out he was yelling and carrying on. He brought up something about me having to watch my back or there would be a knife in it and also for the boys to watch their cars. It's not any sort of threat that I took seriously and I just told him to 'f*** off'," said McManaway.

His employee Mike Jones says it didn't end there, however.[51]

"I saw Watson about two days later. He was outside the fence at McManaways walking past and he stopped and saw me and got abusive. He was saying things like, 'I'll get you, I'll get you'. He was still saying that he would slash my tyres. I never said anything back to him. Peter was there and he just told me to leave it and not worry about it.

"A couple of days after that I saw Watson again and the same sort of thing happened again. He stopped outside the fence and became abusive and was saying the same sort of thing, like he'd get me and slash my tyres. I got sick of listening to him and I went inside."

On that occasion, the threats came to nothing. Others however were not so lucky in their run-ins with Scott Watson. In *Trial by*

---

50 10386 / ST / PETER McMANAWAY / ASD279 / 190198
51 10242 / ST / MICHAEL TAYLOR / ASD279 / 160198

Trickery, Keith Hunter says Watson had never been involved in "home invasion, beating someone up while breaking and entering their home, a very serious offence."[52] Maybe not, but arguably this next incident comes close:

"One morning at about 2.30 am, Scott paid me a visit on my boat. He was uninvited," DOC worker Albert Matheson told police.[53] "I was in bed at the time and Scott rocked the boat to wake me and then he stepped on board.

"I told him straight away to get off my boat. He ignored that and then asked me why I hadn't been out on my boat and I told him that I had been working and that it was my business anyway. I continued telling him to get off my boat. I tried to talk him off rather than get into a confrontation.

"Scott said words to the effect that he was going to kill me. I can't remember his exact words but I do remember him threatening to kill me. I don't think he was drunk so much, more a mixture of being slightly drunk and a bit high.

"He eventually left the boat after threatening me. He was probably on the boat for about ten minutes or quarter of an hour. He was pretty much saying the same sort of things, that he was going to get me."

You might think that Matheson had committed some major offence against Watson to warrant a 2.30am 'boat invasion' and threat to kill. But no. According to Matheson he had helped Watson move his boat on several occasions at the marina they shared, but the DOC worker had made the mistake of not jumping to attention the instant he was summoned on the last occasion.

Watson, he said, had turned up early evening to ask Matheson for help later that evening after Watson returned from having a meal

---

52 *Trial by Trickery*, p57
53 10326 / ST / ALBERT MATHESON / ASD279 / 180198

at the Federal pub in Picton. Not a problem said Matheson, just don't make it too late because his kerosene lamp was running low.

"I waited for Scott to return and while I was waiting my kerosene ran out and the batteries in my radio went dead. When that happened I thought I'd wait for Scott because he shouldn't be too much longer. I went to sleep very late in the evening, perhaps about 9.00 or 10.00 pm.

"Next morning I got up at about 7.30 am and noticed water in my power box which is on the jetty."

It hadn't been raining, and other boats using the power box told Matheson the electricity had gone out at 8.30pm.

Matheson noticed Watson's boat had now been moved—without his help. Watson admitted returning at 8.30 but decided not to get Matheson to assist. Matheson suspected Watson had deliberately shorted out his powerbox by throwing water into it, and he made the mistake of later voicing that suspicion in front of one of Watson's friends.

"About a month later nonsense started happening and I suspected Scott for doing it. I got rubbish dumped on my boat. He would walk past with a silly grin on his face and on a couple of occasions he would make veiled threats saying that he would get me. On one occasion when I had the flu real bad I had my boat parked on the wharf and Scott parked his stern to mine so both cabins were facing each other.

"While I was down below he chucked rubbish and eggs at my boat. The following morning I shifted my boat adjacent to Ted Church's yacht (*Lady Margaret*) and explained to him the troubles I'd been having with Scott and that I was getting fed up and at that stage where I would go to the Police and he said, "Fair enough" or words to that effect.

"That night Scott chucked another egg at the boat and was seen by Bryan Badger. I contacted the Police (Jem Belcher). Scott was made to clean up the boat and apologise and was explained the situation regarding the law."

It is little wonder police had Watson in the frame as a psychopath capable of involvement in murder. Picton yachtie Barry Johns could also see what was happening to Albert:[54]

"I was here the day that Ted Churches towed Albert in. Albert had been out sailing and Scott had come out of Shakespeare Bay and had been running in at him and veering off. Albert hailed Ted and got a tow to the wharf. Watson returned to Shakespeare Bay.

"Albert had also had stuff thrown onto his boat by Watson. He called the police and they came down and made Watson clean it up.

"I decided to go and speak to Watson. Things were getting out of hand. I thought that Albert was unable to look out for himself. I walked over to Watson's boat at the wharf after the police had left.

"He was below and came out. I told him to leave Albert alone. I said if he wanted to pick on somebody to pick on me.

"He told me, 'F**k off old man or I'll get the heavies'.

"I took that to mean that he'd get somebody to look after me. I'd seen him round with some rough looking guys whom I don't know.

"Every time after that when I'd meet him up town he'd pass comments. He told me that I was f***ing my mother. If I'd pass him on the ocean he'd yell across to me the same thing. I was never too concerned about his insults.[55]

"The day that Watson threatened to get the heavies onto me that night me and Faye had to go to Waikawa as my mum was crook. Brian Badger off the *Bette Helene* later told me that that evening while we had been away, Watson had turned up at my boat with another one or two men.

"They'd stood on the wharf yelling out for me to come out. When

---

54 30074 / ST / BARRY JOHNS / SD5025 / 270198
55 There is a certain dark irony in this. Keith Hunter notes that police later investigated a rumour of Scott Watson being involved in incest, for which there was utterly no evidence. Hunter said the suggestion was a grossly offensive defamatory smear. However, Watson flinging a similar insult at someone did not rate a mention in Hunter's book.

I didn't appear they jumped onto the boat and realised there was no-one there. This was at 2.00am in the morning or so Brian told me."

Brian Badger confirmed the story to police:[56]

"I got woken up in the early hours of the morning by some shouting coming from the opposite finger of the wharf to me. I just heard something like 'If you don't come out of here by the time I count to 10 I'm coming to get you'.

"Next minute I heard the words 'There's nobody here'.

"I poked my head up out of my boat because the voice was quite loud. The light was on the wharf. I saw two persons. I'm 95% sure one of them was Scott Watson but it was reasonably dark and I couldn't see properly."

Significantly, they had boarded someone's boat—a home. A violent crime of the sort Hunter acknowledged would be "very serious".

Also significantly, *North & South* correspondent Mike White wrote off this incident in one sentence: "He'd once thrown an egg at a guy on his boat near the ferry terminal and had a cop tell him to leave the area."[57]

That's it. One throwaway minimalistic line trivialising what really happened. One witness described Watson's ongoing stalking of Albert Matheson as "mentally tormenting" him.[58] It's as if the media have turned a blind eye to reality when it comes to the background of Scott Watson. What else haven't they told you?

Scott Watson told *North & South* he'd been "demonised", but those who knew him well say he had more than enough of his own demons without anyone else having to invent extras.

Picton man Rodger Burrows used to work with Scott's mother, Beverley Watson:[59]

---

56 20595 / ST / BRYAN BADGER / LC8773 / 230198
57 "Scott Watson: The Interview", by Mike White, *North & South*, Dec 2015, p42
58 10437 / ST / RICHARD WISHART / RMC084 / 270198 (no relation to author)
59 20206 / ST / RODGER BURROWS / SD5025 / 170198

"I am aware that Scott pulled a knife on Lawrence Gledhill at the Waikawa Marina over a dinghy. The cops took him to Court over that.

"I know he pulled a knife on his dad over an incident at their home. Beverley told me about that."

Another of Watson's few friends, Dean Ryder, told police Scott was a Jekyll and Hyde character:

"He would change when only after a few beers. He became quite scary. It almost was a f**k the world attitude and f**k you too. One of his favourite sayings when he was on the booze was 'who's the best?, I'm the best'. It was a definite noticeable change and it would start only after a small amount—a rigger or two."

Watson, he said, had a pathological hatred of Christians.

"One of my mates, Funghi, used to work at Westside Marine on boats. He was an older guy, he'd be in his 50's now…He was a religious guy and was a hell of a good friend. Scott Watson hated him simply because he was religious. His attitude was, Christians—burn them. His hate was fairly strong towards him for no reason."

Thus, it disturbed Ryder greatly when he found out Watson was in possession of a loaded .303 rifle. A psychopath with a gun: not an ideal combination.

"I know Scott stole a rifle from Jorgenson's boat yard approximately 5 years ago. Watson told me on my then yacht that he had a rifle. He said it had a carved stock, which he'd got rid of. He said he got it off a little yacht of Jorgenson's. I realised later that it had come off a launch which had been at Jorgenson's. I can't remember the launch name or who owned it.

"Watson wanted to swap the rifle with me for a small outboard that was on a boat that I was looking after for a guy. I said no. Initially I said 'bullshit you've got a rifle!', but he took me to see it.

"We went to the area between Shakespeare Bay and Picton Harbour. We walked on the track up the hill towards Shakespeare Bay. Near the top off a side track he pulled out the rifle. It was wrapped in Hessian cloth which had been stolen from Westside Marine's yard. I recognised the cloth straight away and thought you cheeky shit.

"He unwraps it and shows me the rifle. He told me the stock had been carved so he had got rid of it. It was a .303 or .308 with a black magazine underneath it. There were 9 bullets in the magazine. It was a bolt action rifle. He wrapped it back up and then he stashed it nearby.

"When he had done this he walked back and found the magazine which he had forgotten to wrap up. He picked this up and carried it down the hill. He threw the magazine, or placed it behind one of the freezing work buildings.

"I was surprised and stunned by this and later that night I went back and got the magazine. I threw it in the sea in the Picton Harbour. I thought at the time the gun is no use to him."

When Ryder found out Watson had taken to Michael Coutts with a manuka branch, he confronted him over it. The three men ended up at the pub discussing their differences over a beer, before adjourning to a nearby boat owned by a friend named Ivan.

"We had a couple of beers there. Me and Mike came out in our own boat and Watson in his own. When we were preparing to leave I told Watson not to untie our boat until we were on. I knew his attitude too well. He then went and untied the boat and let it drift.

"I'd had enough by then with the incident with Mike and now this. I gave him a hiding then. Me, Mike and Ivan jumped in the boat to leave. Watson then grabbed a flare and was holding it pointing it at us. He didn't say anything, he just pointed it like a gun.

"Luckily he did not fire the flare at us when we motored away. We dropped Ivan back at the ferry terminal and then Mike and I went back to Westside Marine."

It was then that Ryder decided to raise the issue of the hidden rifle with Coutts:

"We both then agreed that Scott shouldn't have access to a rifle," remembered Coutts. "Dean was quite worried about it and he told me that the rifle was wrapped up and buried and that it had a full magazine.

"He was worried that some kid might pick it up. I think Dean told me that Scott had cut the barrel off it, that it had been shortened. He didn't tell me where at Shakespeare Bay it had been buried.

"The next time I saw Dean was the next day at work. He came down to tell me that he had got the rifle and handed it into the police station."

"Stuff was also going missing from Westside Marine," said Dean Ryder, "and I'd caught him with a scraper which belonged to Funghi. I'd had enough so I went and got the rifle. I handed it into the Picton Police. It worried me Watson having access to the rifle.

"All I knew of Watson's associates were me, Mike and Albert. He had mates in Blenheim but I never met them. He used to take pills with his mates in Blenheim. He did not say what sort of pills he was taking. It appeared to me that he did not have any real friends in Picton."

Scott Watson's past included several years as a skinhead in Christchurch at the turn of the nineties. Although Watson and his family have all these witness statements with names and contact details, we've chosen not to identify the witness behind the next story—a woman who believes she came within a whisker of being raped at knifepoint by Scott Watson.

CHAPTER FIVE

An Attempted Rapist

While Keith Hunter erroneously wrote off Scott Watson's past as "adolescent misbehaviour" that he had grown out of, we've now seen that he didn't grow out of it—that he was violent and dangerous right up to the time Ben and Olivia went missing.

Such a pattern of ongoing behaviour fits the psychopath diagnosis. According to psychologists, psychopaths are leopards who do not change their spots. Therapy doesn't 'cure' them, because there is no cure. It's not an illness, it is a personality type that appears to be genetic. It is their core being. A psychopath imprisoned at 18 will still be a psychopath on release at 40, no matter how well behaved they have been inside.

Bearing that in mind, this story from Watson's skinhead days in Christchurch was never heard by the jury, but you can make up your own mind about how it places him on the psychopath scale.

The woman concerned, and her friend, were teenagers infatuated with a group of skinheads. Scott Watson happened to be there one afternoon.

"I found this guy Scott to be very greasy, sleazy. I felt uncomfortable and had a bad feeling about him. He was overly friendly but quite funny at times but I was very cautious about him. I thought he could just turn on me. I got the feeling that if we, Tracy and I, didn't leave then we'd be in trouble. He was different from the other guys and made me feel uncomfortable. We spoke generally, I don't recall what about.

"Scott had Doc Martens on and a green type of Army jersey and probably black jeans. I'm pretty sure they were cherry red Docs. He had very short hair, he was wiry in build, he's quite short but appeared quick in physical movements. The other features about him that stood out were his eyes.

"I recall his eyes because they looked mean eyes and were slitty. They really looked mean. His eyes really scared me. He looked a lot older back then, more than his years. He had a very smug aura about him. Very self assured, cocky and arrogant. They are traits that I recall about him.

"In winter of 1989 I had blonde brown hair. More blonde than brown. To my shoulders. I have a natural curl in my hair with a fringe. I would have been wearing boots of sorts (not Docs), jeans, or fish net stockings and a leopard skin skirt and a black top. I used to straighten my hair out because I didn't like the curl.

"I recall that I was not comfortable being there. Tracy had gone to the toilet. She took a bit of organising to leave places so I decided to make my way in to the hallway to leave when they came out of the toilet. The other guys Dave etc were not there so that with feeling uncomfortable with Scott I decided it was time to go.

"I went out into the hallway and Scott followed me down. He stood in front of the front door. It was a large older style door. He said 'don't leave, don't leave, why don't you stay for a while?' or similar.

"Scott then said, 'come into a bedroom.' I said no. I tried to keep things light and not antagonise him. I felt that if I antagonised him I could get into trouble with Scott.

"Scott carried on trying to get me to stay. He pushed me up against the wall and pulled a knife out from his boot and waved it in front of my face. He again asked me to stay. I again said no and he held the knife up to the side of my throat. He was speaking, going over, 'come into the room'.

"He was sort of laughing/sniggering about the situation. Scott really made me feel uncomfortably and uneasy. I felt terrified. I had no doubt he'd knife me. He had nothing to stop him. He was serious.

"I really don't think he was aware of the consequences, like of knifing me. Scott had no appreciation of what he was doing.

"I may have screamed/called out and this caused Jason to appear out of the lounge and say to Scott, 'what's happening?'. I think Tracy may have appeared then and seen it too.

"Scott just backed away. Tracy and I made a run for it and just left. We ran away from the address. I don't recall if he followed us out or not. I was really upset and crying. I told Tracy what had happened.

"The knife he pulled out was possibly a flick knife, if he had it in his boot. It was about 5 inches long. I had not seen it before that. I was shocked when he pulled it out of his boot."

Keith Hunter had access to that eyewitness testimony, but it does not appear in his book or documentary. What was it Mike White wrote in *North & South*?:[60]

"Watson's criminal record—extending to 48 convictions—is frequently presented as a reason he's likely to be guilty of murdering Ben and Olivia," opined White. "The fact that all but one of these convictions were from when he was aged 15 to 18 years—eight years before Ben and Olivia disappeared—is usually ignored. The fact none were for sexual offences and only one involved any degree of violence is also generally missing."

Yes. Just as that woman's story was missing from the *North &*

---

60 *North & South*, Dec 2015, p41

South article or the questions White apparently asked Watson.

As readers will now appreciate, Watson's criminal behaviour had *not* stopped but in fact had worsened right up to Ben and Olivia's disappearance. It's just that now no one was daring to lay a formal complaint because it just resulted in more harassment.

Watson, however, wants New Zealand to believe he'd been on the straight and narrow for the eight years leading up to his arrest, that he was fingered because of an out of date criminal record and that he had lived the life of a virtual saint up to the point of his arrest:[61]

"I never did anything major. I think I've got one assault charge, from when I was 16 years old. Common assault. It was me and another 16 year old having a fight outside a pub.

"I was an over-exuberant bloody boisterous teenager who got into trouble as a juvenile…I wasn't mugging anyone. I stole a couple of cars, got caught with some weed, some pot, got wasted, got drunk, couple of burglaries. And everything that did happen was basically because I'd been wasted—drunk, stoned. And then I got over it and got on with life. You grow up, you get a job."

Except, Watson didn't get over it and 'grow up'. He was a drug grower and drug user throughout the nineties. Sandy Watson told her brother's defence team what she'd seen:[62]

"Over the two weeks we were sailing there [in 1997], he would have smoked about a dozen joints. I smoked with him. I don't think he is a heavy smoker. He smokes 'Port Royal' roll your owns also."

The pattern of drinking, drug use and Jekyll and Hyde behaviour did not end at 18. It ended only when a cell door clanged shut on Watson in 1998.

A man who spent eight weeks in close quarters with Watson working on the Cassels boat in 1997 says he was a dopehead:[63]

---

61 Ibid p41
62 Statement by Sandy-Jo Watson to Quentin Doig, 23 Feb 1998
63 12884 / ST / GREGORY CURLING / PMC692 / 220798

"I don't really know a lot about his drinking habits in terms of what he liked to drink and how much etc. He drank a little bit of whiskey on the boat from time to time but not much really.

"He was a good worker and he seemed to know his way around the boat.

"I saw Scott using dope probably twice a day during the eight weeks I spent with him. I have no idea where he was getting it from but he didn't seem to ever be in short supply. That was the only drug I saw him use.

"[He] told me he had used (LSD) acid previously, magic mushrooms, and cactus juice. He said he would black out occasionally on drugs and that he would wake up occasionally with bruises all over him and not know how they got there after tripping on acid.

"As far as I know Scott did not use the ship girls at all. He didn't really talk about sex or his sex life at all other than to say he normally ended up with the fat chicks."

Erie Bay owner Alasdair Cassels told police his employee was unpredictable:[64]

"I think it was when we were out on the water after having left Napier that I took this knife off Scott. Scott was playing with the knife a lot and was flicking it out. He was also poking people with it and I thought it was dangerous so I took it off him. He wasn't being threatening with it, just playing with it.

"The other incident that Scott was involved with was with Seppo. Apparently Scott hit Seppo with a sword on his arm and cut him with it. It would have been a year ago in Lyttelton but it can't have been that bad because I didn't hear about it at the time. Seppo told me about it yesterday.

"Scott had told me that he was going to stick Seppo with a knife or something similar to this. I took this as a joke because Seppo

---

64 10213 / ST / ALASDAIR CASSELS / RHD188 / 140198

used to get drunk and came back to the boat and woke people up. This was before the incident where Scott hit Seppo with the sword.

"I had also taken Scott down to Dunedin when '*Galerna*' was in the slip there for about two weeks. He went down there to work on her.

"On the way down we stopped at Akaroa for the night and Scott got really drunk on Rum. He was paralytic on the Rum. I didn't see him get aggressive at all but he appeared to be uncontrollable on it. I heard my nephew Andrew say yesterday that he had pulled a knife out that night and played with it.

"When Scott is sober I would say he is friendly, capable and a hard worker. He is good at working on boats. I would not call him trustworthy. Things went missing from my boat like paint and I accused Scott of taking it but he denied it. Scott was quite convincing and believable when he denied taking the paint but I still think he may have taken it.

"Scott appeared to be a normal guy when sober."

Andrew Averill, one of Watson's closest friends, made similar observations according to a police job sheet:[65]

"Averill was asked about Watson's general character. He stated that Watson was a very direct person and he liked him for that. He said that he was predatory and even if you were a friend you couldn't trust him. 'If you put something down and looked away it would be gone'. He stated that Watson had 'had a run in' with another permanent boat resident from Shakespeare Bay, a returned serviceman and indicated that he was capable of violence and in fact probably capable of murder. He said that the police would have problems sorting out what was truth and what was lies when talking to Watson because everything he said was a lie.

"Averill stated that Watson was a compulsive thief and stole

---

[65] 20830 / JS / ANDREW AVERILL / WS5242 / 270298

dinghies and outboard motors and anything else he could lay his hands on. He stated that he was not backward in going up to people and asking them if they wanted to swap these stolen things for something legitimate that he needed."

In a formal statement, Averill told police he'd challenged Scott about the murders and got no denial:[66]

"Scott did not deny killing Ben Smart or Olivia Hope at anytime when he spoke to me that day. He told me that he couldn't remember what happened on New Year's Eve because he was so out of it."

A police job sheet notes:[67]

"Averill stated that Watson was using cannabis excessively to the point where he thought he had lost it. Watson had told him the 'choppers had got his patch'. It is unclear whether this was in the present year's operation or the previous year's operation."

The bigger question, to be answered not by journalists but by those who knew Watson best, was: could Scott Watson have murdered the missing couple?

Dean Ryder's view:[68]

"I knew Watson for between 2 and 3 years—probably only 2 years in Picton," Dean Ryder told police. "I would describe him as a strange guy. He was always untrustworthy and unpredictable.

"I knew Watson smoked dope but not a lot, with me. If he could get it he would smoke it. Watson did not really like alcohol when I first met him but as I said he would change considerably in attitude. I knew he did a few pills because that is what he told me. I don't know about other drugs he could have done.

"It was Watson's attitude that worried me.

"I believe he would be capable of killing someone. Having seen

---

66 12493 / ST / ANDREW AVERILL / TFD573 / 170698
67 20830 / JS / ANDREW AVERILL / WS5242 / 270298
68 10680 / ST / DEAN RYDER / JSC422 / 090298

him under the influence of alcohol he is very unpredictable. A couple of riggers of beer and he became very scary and quite intimidating in a way.

"Knowing that Watson was at Furneaux the night the young couple went missing, I would think he was a very good suspect, particularly if he had been drinking.

"If he is the man I'd guess he would have headed straight out to Cook Strait and dump the bodies where no one was around him. He's done a bit of off shore sailing before, to the North Island and it would not be a problem. There would be too many problems with people around in the Sounds and he would not be seen easily further out.

"I'd guess also that he will have scrubbed the boat from head to toe. I say this because I know Watson and he is extremely cunning. I think he would be level headed about what he'd done and would have given plenty of thought to getting rid of the bodies and cleaning his yacht.

"I believe he would be very capable of killing this couple."

Alasdair Cassels' view:[69]

"I know Scott Watson and would have known him for approximately 2—3 years.

"Going back to 4 January when we were on our way back from Wellington, we heard on the radio about the missing persons from Furneaux. I knew that Scott had been going to Furneaux to drink on New Year's Eve and when this came across the radio I immediately thought of Scott. It crossed my mind and then when the ketch was described and the suspect boat owner was described, I quickly dismissed it because they were different from Scott and his boat."

---

69 10213 / ST / ALASDAIR CASSELS / RHD188 / 140198

Brian Kinder's view:[70]

"I got quite close to Scott, as close as anyone could get to Scott. He was a bit of a loner. He never hung around in pubs much at all, in fact he spent most of his time working on his yacht. I recognised the yacht straightaway when I saw it on TV.

"Scott was the general hand in the boat yard. He was very good, his dad had taught him well.

"I ended up working with Scott at Careys for about a year. I got to know Scott very well because we worked on two 53 foot boats together. I used to hire windsurfers and he would often come down for a play around. We never went to the pub together or anything like that.[71]

"He definitely had a chip on his shoulder. He was anti-authority and anti-Police. I understood he had a bit of a past with Police and skinheads. He used to be a skinhead he told me, and I gathered they were quite a rough crowd.

"Scott was a very good worker. He worked hard and the quality of his work was reasonably good.

"Scott used to smoke a bit of dope but I never saw him drinking or drunk. He used to make no secret of the fact that he was growing some dope out in the Sounds somewhere.

"He used to be rough looking and unshaven. The only time I ever saw him get shaven and cleaned up was when he appeared at court for pulling a knife.

"Scott told me that he had his dinghy down at Waikawa Bay. A bloke turned up down there and put the boat on the back of the ute. Scott saw him doing it so he yelled at him from his boat I think. Anyway the ute took off and Scott chased him on his motorbike (it was a big old black thing). He pulled the bloke over somehow and said that he pulled a putty knife on the man.

---

70 11038 / JS / BRIAN KINDER / AHD181 / 180198
71 11458 / ST / BRIAN KINDER / DRD506 / 050298

"I doubt whether it was a putty knife because Scott used to carry a flick-blade knife around on his person. He always had it with him and used it for picking out mouldy wood etc from boats. I never noticed him playing with it much, he usually only had it out when he was working. It was a fold out knife with about a 5-6" blade. I really don't remember much more about it.

"Scott never had any girlfriends that I know of. His Dad used to work in the boat yard. He seemed like a real nice guy. His mother worked at the Toot and Whistle. She seemed like a strange bitch. I saw her and Scott have a few yelling matches—she would do most of the yelling and it was usually trivial stuff.

"If I had to say whether I thought Scott was capable of killing the missing couple or not, I'd have to say he is."

That then is the verdict from part one of this book—not from 12 strangers on a jury, not from a coterie of media commentators speculating, but from a collection of people who knew Scott Watson, some quite intimately. He fits the profile of a criminal psychopath. He fantasised about movies where a woman was killed during sex (and expressed those fantasies to three independent witnesses). He is "very capable" of murder.

That does not, however, prove that he did it. But you are about to see evidence that might shake your view of this case.

CHAPTER SIX

Who Was That Mystery Man?

Central to this entire case is one of identification: is Scott Watson the so-called "mystery man" seen in the Furneaux Lodge bar who was later seen by water taxi driver Guy Wallace in the Naiad with Ben and Olivia on their final voyage?

If the answer is yes, then Watson is implicated in a double murder. If the answer is no, then the possibilities become more complicated. Watson could be entirely innocent—it wasn't him, it wasn't his boat. Or, it wasn't him, but it was his boat. A third scenario straddles the options: that it was Watson in the Naiad delivering them to a boat that wasn't his—that the crime took place on a different boat but that Watson was involved.

As sharp-eyed readers will have sussed out, two of these scenarios raise the possibility that Watson had an accomplice.

The defence of Scott Watson, which includes the books *Ben & Olivia*, *The Marlborough Mystery* and *Trial by Trickery*, have all made much of the discrepancies between the mystery man descriptions and Scott Watson. But playing devil's advocate requires a realistic assessment of the similarities in the descriptions.

When *North & South* journalist Mike White published his exclusive interview with Watson, he spent only a handful of paragraphs on the "Mystery Man" issue, but he summed it up in one:

"Many witnesses described a mystery man at Furneaux Lodge who was unshaven and had medium to long hair. Watson was clean-shaven and had short hair."[72] Photos, wrote White, confirm Watson's description. Case closed.

Or is it?

Keith Hunter, likewise, writes:

"The evidential difficulties associated with Scott Watson, suspect, began to emerge immediately. He did not match the description of the mystery man and his yacht *Blade* did not match the description of the mystery yacht."

The problem has been compounded by some idiotic computer-generated identikit sketches released by police very early in the investigation. They were based on Guy Wallace's recollection of the man in the water taxi, and the recollections of bar staff Roz McNeilly and Chey Phipps on a mystery man they saw up at the lodge.

No one is standing by those original identikit pictures today, and they may well have made the job of detectives far more difficult. That's because nearly everyone who'd been at Furneaux was shown the identikits, contaminating the memories and focus of those being questioned.

So let's start at the beginning. Here's how long time family friend Alan Mountford described Scott Watson to police when he saw him a month before the crime:

"Scott is slim to medium build about 5ft 8in tall. He is Caucasian with dark coloured medium length wavy hair. He was reasonably

---

72 *North & South* Dec 2015 p46

clean shaven. He had tattoos on his arms. I can't remember what the tattoos were."[73]

Now, here is how water taxi driver Guy Wallace described the mystery man on the boat:[74]

"The guy that got on board with Olivia and Ben was a male, Caucasian, aged about 32 years. He was about 5'8" tall, wiry build. I think he may have had tattoos on his arms but I can't be sure. His hair was a brownie colour, wavy and medium length. He had about two days growth on his face. He was bourboned up, like his eyes weren't focussing.

"He was wearing a Levi shirt with short sleeves, 100 per cent cotton. It had a collar with a button-up front. I saw the Levi brand on it. It was a short sleeved shirt and the colour was between khaki and very pale green. He was wearing blue jeans and I think sandshoes."

And here is a confirmed sighting of Scott Watson in the Furneaux Lodge bar earlier that evening:

"I would best describe him as male Caucasian, untanned, about 30 years in age, about 165 cm, stocky build, brown short hair, not spiky but not the length you could brush either, facial stubble, he had a professionally made tattoo on his left forearm but I can't describe it. He also had amateur tattoos on the back of his left hand."[75]

"He was wearing blue jeans and a light blue light denim shirt with a colour. It had a red tag or red embroidery writing on top of the left chest pocket. I noticed some chest hair but not a hairy chest as such."

And here's another confirmed sighting of Watson that night:

"He was a male Caucasian, he had a dark lived-in colour. I would say he is in his 30s. He was wearing a blue denim shirt, with a red tag. I thought it was a Levi's tag. It looked new. I think he might have been wearing jeans."[76]

---

73 20354 / ST / ALAN MOUNTFORD / DS........ / 140198
74 10017 / ST / GUY WALLACE / ASD279 / 050198
75 10184 / ST / AMANDA EGDEN / AHD181 / 120198
76 11889 / ST / RAYMOND PADDEN / TFD175 / 260398

"He was about 5 foot 7, 5 foot 8. He had a small frame, but still looked athletic. I think he needed a shave. The reason it sticks out is here is this guy with a new flash shirt yet it looked like he needed a shave and a bit of a clean up. His hair was short dark and not very messy."

And here's a third confirmed sighting of Scott Watson:

"I would describe the guy that I spoke to in the bar as follows. Male, Caucasian, he looked approximately 28 – 30 years but told me that he was 26 years, New Zealand accent, approximately 5'8", medium but strong build, dark brown hair of shortish length with a slightly receding hairline. This guy's hair was longer than mine but didn't cover his ears. His hair was short but not really short. This guy didn't have a beard or anything like that. He had a couple of days' growth on his face."[77]

How can Keith Hunter, or for that matter the rest of us, keep arguing that the description of the mystery man in the Naiad doesn't fit Watson? It's a fustercluck of epic proportions that has distracted the public and frustrated the Hope and Smart families' pursuit of justice for eighteen years.

It all comes back to this issue of false eyewitness memory syndrome and witnesses who discuss their memories with other witnesses, contaminating the recollection of all.

With the best of intentions, witnesses in major murder mysteries are quite capable of overthinking what they've seen as their brains struggle to make sense of it and their minds desperately want to find the crucial memory that will solve the case.

So, if you want to find out how the Scott Watson prosecution train ran off the track, let's start with Guy Wallace.

---

[77] 10055 / ST / CHRISTOPHER BISMAN / BB3624 / 120198

CHAPTER SEVEN

Who Is Guy Wallace?

It's a well-worn cliché that a chain is only as strong as its weakest link, and the case both for and against Scott Watson as perpetrator rests on some very dubious links indeed. One man features both as a star witness for the prosecution, and later the supporters of Scott Watson. That man is Guy Wallace.

Wallace had been employed on general duties at Furneaux in November 1997 and worked there seven weeks, finishing just a couple of days after Ben and Olivia disappeared. He has been arguably the most frustrating witness for police and the defence alike, because his description of what happened keeps changing.

The essence of Wallace's original evidence is this: he dropped Ben and Olivia off at a mystery ketch after they were invited by a mystery man.

We will cover the fateful Naiad journey in detail shortly, but first some background on Wallace.

At the start of this book we covered false memory syndrome,

where witnesses who compare notes with other witnesses to an event end up contaminating their recollection, because of a deeply-ingrained instinct to be part of the herd. No one wants to be the outlier, the only person with a memory of something no one else saw. It makes us feel vulnerable, unsure of ourselves. Yet truth in a criminal justice sense can sometimes come down to something seen by one person in the right place at the right time.

Was Guy Wallace that person? The police certainly wondered whether he had something to do with the disappearance and Wallace felt it deeply.

"[Detective] Tom Fitzgerald, he gave me the grind for I think four hours, and when I could go I could hardly drive, I was that bloody nervous and emotional," Wallace told the Watson defence team in an interview,[78] "and they just look you…, 'you and Scott, you have been mates for years, we know you have been drinking down the Toot 'n Whistle, you are probably going out rooting girls here, there and everywhere, you're a bit of a womaniser, aren't you Guy?' Saying things to me and just keeping on and on and on and on, and he said 'you didn't really drop them on a ketch, you dropped them off on Scott's boat, didn't you. And then he went back in and after you finished your duty, you tied up and went back out there and probably went through both of them, didn't you.' And all that sort of shit. It was just very, very unnerving, I called for a lawyer. I said 'don't you start pinning this shit on me. I want a lawyer present.' He said 'you don't need a lawyer'. I said 'I want one, I want one bloody now, I'm not telling you anything else'."

The police began to collect evidence and opinions about Guy Wallace:

"I employed Guy Wallace to work for me two weeks after I

---

[78] Transcript of Wallace interview with Carl Berryman, February 26 1998

started in October 1997," recalled Charlie Proctor to police.[79] "I employed him to build with me. He started off good but he got hard to motivate. He was a 'know it all' or thought he knew it all. He thought he was always right and he wasn't.

"I knew he had worked for his father. He had helped me with the Toot 'n' Whistle together with his father and Richard King-Turner. That's going back a few years—five years. He was big headed then, a show-off."

Proctor told police other Furneaux staff had found Wallace to be too "sarcastic" towards customers, that he wasn't a people person, and they were allegedly pleased when he quit on January 2nd. "Guy is the type of guy who doesn't like to be proven wrong. I don't suppose anyone does but he takes more offence to it. He's just one of those guys who spouts off and he's not liked for it," Proctor said.

Wallace allegedly told Proctor he was "knocking off" one of the staff at Furneaux, but that didn't stop Wallace from allegedly being suggestive to other women. Proctor's friend Gary Drummond told police Wallace had leaned in and said "you can stay with me tonight" to Proctor's partner Lou, to which she allegedly replied "in your dreams".[80]

For her part, Lou didn't remember: "I can't recall him saying anything on the way out. Guy just seemed his normal self to me."[81]

Another witness, Lee McPhail, remembered Wallace from his time at Float Air when Wallace worked for a car rental company:[82] " I found him mouthy. He thinks he is a lady's man. He is egotistical. He likes to be the centre of attention."

Craig Smith owned a marine business, Southern Sails, and had previously employed Wallace. "During those three years I would

---

79 10335 / ST / CHARLIE PROCTOR / SCC539 / 250198
80 10210 / ST / GARY DRUMMOND / ISD548 / 110198
81 20033 / ST / BERNADETTE OLSEN / ASD279 / 110198
82 10400 / ST / LEE McPHAIL / TFD175 / 250198

describe Guy as being outgoing and friendly in terms of his personality. He enjoyed being the centre of attention and he was the type of guy who had to meet people and chat to them at the pub.[83]

In late 1991, Smith hired Wallace to help bring a yacht from Tauranga to Picton for a client. "The trip back took about 10 days. During that period I found that Guy didn't seem to know anything about yachting whatsoever. He was quite seasick and was like a fish out of water on board the boat.

"I would ask him to do things on the boat like tying knots or something and he would fumble around and say he had done it when he clearly did not know how. Rather than admit he couldn't do it he would try and bluff his way but he wouldn't admit he didn't know how to do it."

They reconnected a couple of times after that when Wallace would talk about his successes.

"He told me he was earning a large amount of money doing what he was doing. I thought he was exaggerating which he didn't do a lot but when he did they tended to be whoppers. I think he did this basically because he enjoyed being the centre of attention again. Guy strikes me as being the type of guy who is very stubborn.

"It surprised me to learn that he was involved in the water taxis at Furneaux because quite frankly I don't believe he has the necessary boat skills to do the job," Smith told detectives.

"In regard to the ketch sighting, I have to say that I am just about adamant that he will be wrong in his identification. I have that assessment on his general lack of knowledge of boats, the height he would have observed the vessel from, the time of day and his pride and stubbornness. By the last point I mean he would rather give Police a description of a vessel rather than admit he is unsure about particular points.

---

83 10536 / ST / CRAIG SMITH / PMC692 / 020298

"I think he is the type of person that once he has given the description he would be very unlikely to back down from it even with the benefit of hindsight.

"I would say that Guy has probably focussed on certain points on some boats and he is genuinely mistaken about the ketch. My experience with Guy is that he will not change his mind and if he was it would have happened a few hours later.

"I thought the sloop that was seized by Police had similarities to the picture of the ketch namely the bowsprit, the sheerline of the boat and the cabin shape."

Smith was probably being a touch unkind. Driving a Naiad wasn't exactly rocket science and did not require advanced boating skills. On the other hand, his observations about the ketch sighting were probably fair.

Wallace by his own admission had been up for 20 hours, it was dark, there were no lights on the boat and he may not have seen as much as he thought—especially if he was mistaking the mast of an adjacent yacht tied alongside as the 'second mast' of a ketch. Scientists are adamant that our brains subconsciously try to put puzzle pieces together, creating false recollections that seem very real.

Ray Jones, five years older than Wallace, had also been at Furneaux that night and told police he too doubted Wallace's claims:[84]

"The moon was out that night at Furneaux but you could really only see outlines of boats. It was certainly hard to tell colours.

"I know Guy Wallace through working at the Federal Hotel in Picton. He used to drink there on occasion. He was pretty much a loner and he drank by himself. I chatted to him when he was there. I don't trust him at all. He thinks he is a bit of a ladies' man and he routinely tried to hit on women whilst I worked at the Federal.

"I have reservations about Wallace's sighting of the ketch and the

---

84 10559/ST/RAY JONES/PMC692/040298

detail he has gone into because it was so hard to see and it would still be dark at 5 am. Unless he has seen the vessel before I don't understand how he could have got so much detail."

Wallace has already admitted police had called him a "rooter", and Keith Hunter writes:

"There were signs of an attempt to link Wallace with Watson as co-rapist/murderer, in a 'two Ws' theory—Watson and Wallace."[85]

Even as detectives were forced to rely on Wallace as one of the last to see Ben and Olivia alive and also the barman who had served the mystery man, they were turning over every rock to see if he was a viable suspect himself. What they discovered emerges from opinions and observations in witness statements:

"Both Steve and Ken made comments about the barman there being a real sleaze. They said he would grab women's hands and make comments to them when he was handing them change. They reckoned he was real strange," recalled Bryan McConkey.[86]

"I went to get a drink from the bar and the barman got me a Midori and milk. He poured in more than a nip and just said, 'Hope you don't mind'. I thought it was very friendly," said Amy Roberts.[87]

On March 24 1998, Detective Jess Bembry of the Los Angeles County Sheriff's Department interviewed ex-pat kiwi nurse Christine Shroll, a former flatmate of Wallace's. This is the report she filed to New Zealand Police:[88]

"Ms Shroll admitted knowing Guy Wallace and to sharing an apartment with him between November 1990 and March 1991. They were only roommates sharing an apartment. When she first met Guy Wallace, her sister, Lisa, who was friends with Guy, introduced her to him.

---

85 *Trial by Trickery*, p33
86 30282 / ST / BRYAN McCONKEY / ?????? / 030298
87 10353 / ST / AMY ROBERTS / SCC539 / 220198
88 12164 / JS / CHRISTINE SHROLL / BEMBRY /

"Christine described Guy as a loner and to her knowledge, never had any close friends. She made several attempts to set him up with girls, as he didn't have a girlfriend. Christine also described Guy as an offensive, loudmouth with a short fuse (temper).

"During the time they shared the apartment, Guy was involved in at least two fights. Christine thought these fights occurred at unknown bars. On one occasion, he came home missing his front teeth. The majority of conversations with Guy would lead to sexual overture by Guy. Christine said Guy was strange and moodier than most people but she never felt like she was in danger.

"Christine described Guy as being possessive around her and her sister, Lisa. She said that when her (Christine's) boyfriend was around, Guy would try to sit between them, as if her boyfriend didn't belong there.

"Christine said that on another occasion, while sharing the apartment with Guy, she came home from work and found him lying naked on the floor inside the front door, with music playing. Guy tried to act like he had fallen asleep, but Christine believed it was staged.

"During the time they shared the apartment, Guy made several attempts to pull Christine's towel off after she exited the shower. He always acted like it was a game or joke. I asked Christine if Guy kept any hard core pornography in the apartment. The only items she saw were *Penthouse* and *Playboy* Magazines. Christine told me there was never anything sexual between her and Guy."

Back in New Zealand, police interviewed Lisa:[89]

"During this time my sister and I became aware of his slightly inappropriate behaviour. I am sure he had designs on my younger sister but she already had a boyfriend. This inappropriate behaviour would take the form of him either bursting into my bedroom or into my sister's room when she was in there with her boyfriend.

---

89 10654 / ST / LISA BADGER / SE8099 / 130298

He would always do a good job of covering it up by pretending to be a larrikin but even so his behaviour was strange. He would take advantage of every situation he could.

"I can remember one time my sister was sunbathing on the deck and he told her that she needed sun screen on her legs and he got the bottle and rubbed it on her legs all the way up and it was clearly inappropriate and not what my sister wanted.

"I am not quite sure of the year it was probably 1990-1991 that my sister moved back to Ohope. She ended up flatting with Guy Wallace in the same place that he used to occupy. My sister was working as a nurse at Whakatane Hospital at that time.

"One evening she finished her shift at midnight and when she got home she opened the front door which went straight into the lounge and she found Guy lying on a lambskin rug completely naked. He was on his back so he was completely exposed—star-fished across the rug. He had obviously set it up so she would walk in on him. He pretended that he had fallen asleep but the tape-deck was on the first song and he had strategically placed the rug and had two or three pornographic magazines lying around.

"Whilst my sister was living with him he would often try to pull her towel off when she got out the shower. Again he would pretend to be fooling around but my sister has told me that he would be pulling really hard and that they were serious attempts to pull the towel off."

Bar owner Kerry Howden told police Wallace struggled to build close friendships.[90]

"When I knew him he habitually had a moustache. When I saw him in the pub he had shaved it off. He used to always wear a black, sleeveless, unbuttoned leather vest. He wasn't wearing it in the pub.

"Guy was a person prone to exaggeration, stretching the truth, to

---

90 10401 / ST / KERRY HOWDEN / SD5025 / 220198

get attention. He was generally on the outside of any group, trying to make friends. He would get mouthy and that sort of thing so he might be accepted I guess. He was always loud.

"He could be offensive to women. Like women would walk past and be on their way to the toilet. Guy might wolf whistle at them and call out just as the door was closing, 'Show us your growler' or something like that. When they came out you could see that the women were offended. I had to tell him a number of times to watch what he was saying but he would take it with a grain of salt."

A Picton woman told police Wallace was working on a building site next door and tried to proposition her while her partner was away:[91]

"I found Guy to be always talking about sex or with inferences to it. It didn't really worry me the first few times. He talked like this, but after a while it became quite over bearing and became a nuisance more than anything.

"One weekend while Graeme was away Guy made a reference to the fact that Graeme was away and we should 'get it on'. I just laughed. I wouldn't have thought that he was serious but I was getting sick of him. I don't recall the exact things he would say but he would yell out sometimes and say, 'Hello gorgeous'."

The builder who employed him on that job, Robert O'Malley, was unimpressed:[92]

"I employed Guy as a labourer working on buildings in Renwick and the Sounds. Initially before we really got to know Guy he appeared to be OK and there were no real problems. Later when we got to know him we realised that he told lies, had a violent temper, and thought he was God's gift to women.

"We found that he had a great imagination about himself and most things that he said seemed to be lies and were very hard to

---

91 30203 / JS / GRAEME METCALF / JPF737 / 150198
92 30983 / ST / ROBERT O'MALLEY / RHD188 / 210398

believe. It was mainly lies about his personal life and not work related, although he initially said that he was really experienced at being a labourer and we found out that he wasn't.

"Sometimes at work he would yell and scream and rant and rave, and it was then that we realised that he had a violent temper.

"He appeared to have a sick attitude towards women and the way he spoke about them. He appeared also to me to be a womaniser. Once when we worked on a job down in the Sounds, he took a fancy to the wife of the building owner and he was always paying her attention.

"Initially when I first saw Guy Wallace on the news about his missing person case in the Sounds, I thought that he had done away with them himself. I really thought that he had done it himself when I first saw it. I don't think that he is the type of person to go and plan something like that but if it was a spur of the moment thing, maybe."

Louise Featherstone, a married reveller at Furneaux, told police she felt a bad vibe from Wallace but she didn't know why:[93]

"He did not say anything offensive to me but his general demeanour made me feel uneasy. As a result when the girls went over to Furneaux I told them to be careful of him as he may say similar things to him [sic, them]. He was the type who always seemed to pass a comment to women."

Louise's husband Harry said the same:[94]

"I didn't know him as a water taxi driver but as the barman. He struck me as being very sleazy because of the way he acted around women and comments he made.

"I remember Guy Wallace behind the bar on New Year's eve. He also appeared to me that he was trying to pick up a girl that night…

---

93 30337 / ST / LOUISE FEATHERSTONE / MK8254 / 070298
94 30336 / ST / HENRY FEATHERSTONE / JSC422 / 070298

He always appeared to me to be on the lookout, on the hunt. I remember one of the first things I said to Louise, Delina and Kristal to watch out for that guy (Guy Wallace)."

The irony is that the two girls with Harry and Louise were hit on by Scott Watson that night.

After Wallace quit Furneaux and went across to his new job at Punga Cove, it appears he rubbed people there up the wrong way as well:[95]

"Guy Wallace, the driver of the Furneaux Taxi that night, came and worked for Dad. I worked with him for a month or about that. I think he is a creep and a pervert as well. He was real sleazy the way he talked about ladies.

"I don't know how Guy could describe the boat to the Police so well because there was just so many of them."

Punga manager Murray Cleverley said much the same to police:[96]

"I also employed Guy Wallace about 10 February 1998 for 4 days doing maintenance. He stayed for 5-6 weeks working. He left just prior to the press release that the ketch was not involved. He said it had got too much for him. He gave one hour's notice and just left.

"Guy's got a violent flare that will just spring up. He has done things like throw hammers and just generally lose it over the smallest thing. This would happen when he's sober. Whilst drinking he was reasonably subdued and had better social skills when drinking.

"I noticed he had an attraction to females. He was a bit creepy, touchy feely around women. He spent a lot of time with couples, married or just partners. He'd always seem to manage to have a drink with them or just be with them. He sort of had the gift of the gab. My staff were wary of him but outsiders loved him."

Cleverley added that he thought the mental stress of being the

---

95 40755 / ST / SHAUN CLEVERLEY / LDC553 / 280398
96 30968 / ST / DONALD CLEVERLEY / JH8914 / 170398

main police witness, and living up to those expectations, was taking its toll on Wallace.

"I don't know Scott Watson," noted Cherie Marshall from Cougarline Water Taxis. "I do however know Guy Wallace and would describe him as an overbearing smart ass. I didn't dislike him but when you tried to get work done he was always there and he was just a bit different."[97]

Another staffer at Punga asked him about the case:[98]

"On the way to Blenheim I did specifically ask Guy, 'How did the Police interviews go?' He said words to the effect of that Police had interviewed him very hard, that they had accused him of murder and that at the end of the interview they were satisfied that he hadn't done it, and that they were just doing their job in asking him the questions.

"During this period he was often nervous—or appeared to be. I think the whole enquiry had him on edge. My own personal feeling is that Guy is an attention-seeker and would do or say anything to make a headline."

"I don't find him a trustworthy person. He has told me a few untruths," added Furneaux Lodge regular Reg McManaway.[99]

And that's exactly what Guy Wallace did—he lied to police and in the process generated headlines as he was forced to make a retraction. Let's start first of all with the police statement that he fabricated. Look at the detail he has created in what is quite an accomplished lie:[100]

"On Friday, 21 January 1998 I went over to Nelson. I travelled over on my own in my parents car. It is a Holden Commodore coloured green. It gets kept at my parents house at … Waikawa Bay.

"I actually told them I wanted it to go to Blenheim but it was always my intention to go to Nelson.

---

97 30399 / ST / CHERIE MARSHALL / SCC539 / 060298
98 13978 / ST / PHILIP CALWELL / DRD506 / 010499
99 10688 / ST / REGINALD McMANAWAY / RMC084 / 110298
100 30380 / GUY WALLACE / DE5136 / 060298

"I think I stayed at home on the Thursday evening. I left with the car at about 10.00am or 10.30am. I drove straight over to Nelson. I went out via Blenheim and the Rapaura Road and then the main highway.

"The car was full with gas. I am pretty sure I filled up at Blenheim on the way home.

"I went to Nelson to have a look for the ketch that I described from New Year's eve. I had heard from a friend. I think her name is Angela. She is a red head and owns (DELETION BY POLICE). Angela told me that her husband or fiance, Fletch, had heard or seen that there was a ketch of the same description over at Nelson. I think it was the previous day, the Thursday, that Angela told me.

"I had called in to the salon to say hello and have a cuppa. At that time I was lying low trying to keep away from the media. Over that day I thought about it and decided to go over and check it out.

"I got to Nelson around midday. I went to a cafe in the middle of Nelson. I had a coffee. I can't recall the name of the cafe but I could take you there. I don't know Nelson that well. It is quite a big place and they do dinners.

"After that I drove out to the first marina you come to as you leave Nelson going to Motueka. It's where some sail makers are. I had a nosy around the marina. There were a couple of ketches in there.

"One of the ketches was called *Waves*. It had a pattern like a thick wavy line along the side. It was tied up opposite the sail makers. I think it is Nalder and Gould, that's their name or something like that. There is the sail makers, the road, then the marina on the other side of the road.

"It was tied to the wharf on its own. It was facing towards Wellington. It is a very tidy vessel. It is blue and white. White is the predominant colour with a thin blue line around the top.

"There was no-one on the boat that I saw. It didn't look to me anything like the ketch I saw at Furneaux.

"I went back into Nelson and used a phone card and went to a phone box in the main street right near the Post Office.

"I rang the Nelson Police Station. A female answered. I told her I was ringing about the missing ketch. She straight away said that the ketch was no longer any part of our investigation.

"That call was definitely made between midday and 2.00pm. I never said who I was.

"As soon as she said that I was taken back and surprised. She said, "Will that be all?" and I sort of said yes and hung up.

"When I saw *Waves* I presumed that this was the ketch Angela had told me about. Thinking about it now I should have gone around to the other marina for a look there. I guess I just presumed that *Waves* was the one Fletch had been talking about. I guess I should not have presumed it.

"I never even got a chance to tell the woman about the ketch I had seen, that is *Waves*. I guess *Waves* is 40-42' long. Whoever it was who talked to Fletch or if it was Fletch himself, must have looked at *Waves* and compared it to my sketch in the paper. I could see there were similarities. For example the size, the set up of the rigging, the blue trim around the top. I knew it wasn't the ketch when I saw it.

"I have been shown a photograph of four ketches. The ketch in the top left of that photograph is *Waves* that I saw at Nelson on Friday, 23 January 1998."

Pretty detailed testimony, but Guy Wallace was lying like a flatfish. Now look at the retraction:[101]

"My full name is Guy Wallace. I am 32 years old...I am talking to Detective Fitzgerald about the disappearance of Ben Smart and Olivia Hope. This statement is to clarify some of the points of my earlier statements.

---

101 10704 / ST / GUY WALLACE / TFD573 / 070298

"On Friday the 6th February 1998 I made a statement to Detective Sergeant Dave Evans in relation to me going to Nelson and seeing a ketch. The ketch was named *Waves*. I had earlier spoken about this in a newspaper article. I told Detective Sergeant Evans that I travelled to Nelson on the 23rd January 1998.

"I would now like to tell the truth in relation to this. I have not seen this ketch, *Waves*, and I never actually travelled to Nelson on the 23rd January. I haven't been to Nelson since September 1997.

"I made up the story of seeing *Waves*, in Nelson, after Don Anderson had told me that he had seen it. I just wanted someone to believe me and this seemed like a good way of backing my story up. I have been under a lot of pressure from the media and things got too much for me..."

Some readers may be reeling in the wake of these revelations about Guy Wallace. That's understandable. But the police investigated him thoroughly. This is not a witch-hunt against Guy Wallace, but there is so much at stake that there is a tremendous public interest in laying all the evidence out so that people can appreciate the complexities. Readers need to understand that unlike some simplistic books and articles, this case is not black and white and the star witness is a man who fabricated false evidence for a police statement.

What we do know is that Guy Wallace's movements on New Year's morning were accounted for, and there were two other witnesses on the water taxi who also confirm Ben and Olivia got off with a mystery man.

The entire "Free Scott Watson" movement hinges on the testimony of Guy Wallace and the bar staff whose memories he may have unwittingly messed with. But as some might say, "If Guy Wallace is the answer, you need to ask a better question".

To work out who the mystery man on the Naiad was, we need to wind back to the earliest witness statements, before memories became corrupted. What we find is surprising.

CHAPTER EIGHT

Who Was In The Naiad?

To get to the bottom of this, we need to reacquaint ourselves with the final Naiad trip of Ben and Olivia.

The narrative is that Olivia had paid for a bunk on the charter yacht *Tamarack*, anchored off Furneaux. She and Ben got a lift out to the vessel, but found it full. In the meantime her older sister Amelia and friend Rick Goddard had arranged a water taxi ride out to *Tamarack* in the company of three other passengers plus the driver, Guy Wallace. When Amelia and Rick arrived, Olivia and Ben seized the opportunity to catch a lift back to shore in the Naiad.

The reconstruction begins with a fax from Gerald Hope to police on 2 January 1998, raising the alarm and setting out a possible timeline:[102]

"Approx 3.00 am (1st Jan)—Olivia and Ben (Smart) arrived on yacht [*Tamarack*]. The yacht was full with original crew members and extras.

---

102 13437 / FAX / GERALD HOPE / .... / 020198

"There was limited sleeping space, she was annoyed at the lack of space and extra people aboard and had an argument with people inside the boat. She was crying and highly annoyed and had been drinking. Ben Smart was also intoxicated.

"They then proceeded to leave the yacht with Ben Smart along with her bag of clothes (red K2 backpack) and a sleeping bag.

"They left the yacht on a rubber Naiad which had 3 other people (not incl. Driver) who were being dropped off at other boats before returning to shore. It was understood Olivia's intentions were to return to Furneaux Lodge and sleep on shore."

On 3 January, Amelia Hope told police:[103]

"When I got to the *Tamarack* it would have been about 3.20 am. There were five people on the boat and two of us got onto the *Tamarack*. Olivia and Ben got off the *Tamarack* and onto this boat. I didn't see her but I heard her get off and heard her yelling that she wasn't going to stay on the *Tamarack* and she was going to go ashore".

Amelia's timing was roughly confirmed by Jeremy Fyfe on *Tamarack*:[104]

"At about 3.15 am they came back down below. There was an argument about no beds being available and then Olivia and Ben decided to go to shore and jumped on the naiad boat from Furneaux which had dropped off Amelia Hope. That's the last I heard of them."

In *Trial by Trickery*, Keith Hunter launched a blistering attack on Crown Prosecutor Nicola Crutchley's opening address to the jury, when she had said "Wallace described him as 32 years old, about. Short brown hair, wearing a Levi shirt with either short sleeves or sleeves rolled up, and jeans."[105]

Hunter was furious: "The 'short brown hair' matched the

---

103 30639 / JS / AMELIA HOPE / ASD279 / 030198
104 40565 / ST / JEFFREY FYFE / WTH454 / 030198
105 *Trial By Trickery*, p91

appearance of the accused man sitting in the courtroom...but the information Crutchley gave to the jury was not true. Wallace did not describe the mystery man as having 'short brown hair' at all. Nor did he ever describe the man in terms that matched Scott Watson. The general thrust of his description of the man excluded Watson altogether."

Now we get to put Hunter's investigative journalist skills and credibility to the test, because on 3 January at 1pm, police interviewed a man named Guy Wallace:[106]

"On New Year's Eve I was working at Furneaux Lodge. I used to be the barman there. I finished work at the bar at about 4.30 am on the 1st January.

"There were about 4 or 5 people on the jetty waiting to go out to their boats and 4 of them were going to *Tamarack* and there was one other guy who was going to another yacht.

"I went to *Tamarack* and dropped the people off onto *Tamarack* and picked up two people from the *Tamarack*. The two people I picked up said that there were too many people on the boat to get any sleep and they got into the tender and I proceeded to this other boat and dropped them all off.

"The two people I picked up off *Tamarack* asked this other guy if he had any room on his boat and he said just jokingly to the girl that she could come on board but she doesn't have to bring her mate with her. This was said as a joke and there was no animosity at all.

"There was a boy and girl picked up off the *Tamarack*. The girl looked about 20. She had blond hair tied up at the back and she was wearing glasses. She had a black handbag with her. She was wearing a black tee shirt with a dark coloured 'v' neck sweatshirt over top. The guy looked about the same age. *He had short dark hair*. I remember he was wearing trousers. The top he was wearing

---

[106] 10861 / JS / GUY WALLACE / ASD279 / 030198

was white. The two of them seemed like real good friends. They had been drinking but weren't overly intoxicated.

"Before I dropped them off on this other yacht I asked both of them if they were okay with that because they didn't know the guy.

"It was a timber ketch with round portholes. It was blue and white and really old. It had a blue stripe on it which was really dark blue. I think it was moored just starboard of the jetty. Looking at the map it would have been next to the *Spirit of Marlborough*.

"The guy on this ketch would have been about 32, about 5'9" tall, wiry build. He was unshaven but didn't have a moustache. *He had short dark wavy hair* and smelled like a bottle of Bourbon.

"It would have been very near 5.00 am or just after when I dropped these people off."

This is the first recorded appearance of Guy Wallace in the police files. As will later be seen, he based his timings on estimates. However, most importantly, his virgin memory of the mystery man is of a guy "about 32, about 5'9" tall, wiry build. He was unshaven but didn't have a moustache. He had short dark wavy hair."

He may not have used the word "brown" in that first identification, but clearly it shows Keith Hunter's book and his arguments are wrong. More than half a million people have been influenced on the Watson case by Hunter's journalism. The irony is that Hunter actually includes the "short dark wavy hair" comment from Watson a few pages later, but ignores the significance, saying it "differed markedly" from prosecutor Crutchley's comments.

At this early stage, Wallace's memory is crucial and he describes the man's hair as "short". Two days' later he would call it "medium". Either way, the description is identical to some confirmed Watson sightings we quoted in an earlier chapter and which described Watson's hair as short to medium and straight to wavy depending on how unkempt it became and the perspective of the beholder.

You'll recall Chris Bisman also made a point of distinguishing between stubble and moustache on Watson: "Male, Caucasian, he looked approximately 28—30 years but told me that he was 26 years, New Zealand accent, approximately 5'8", medium but strong build, dark brown hair of shortish length with a slightly receding hairline. This guy's hair was longer than mine but didn't cover his ears. His hair was short but not really short.[107] This guy didn't have a beard or anything like that. He had a couple of days growth on his face. I don't recall a moustache.

Here is another confirmed sighting of Scott Watson from that same morning in the Furneaux bar from Richard Egden:

"He was asking them if they wanted to go on his yacht.[108] He said he would give them a Prozac t-shirt if they did. He said that he was going to Tonga or the islands. He said he was from Wellington. He said he was a druggy. I had a conversation with him at one point. He said to me that at our age he was on acid and stuff like that.

"He said he didn't go to school. I asked him his name. I think he said it was Scott. He said he was 26 although he looked older than that. I would have spoken with him for about 5 minutes.

"I would describe him then as: Caucasian, approximately 30 years old. He was short, between 5 foot 6 to 5 foot 8 tall. He had short straight dark brown or black hair. He may have had some stubble. He was of average build, athletic, and he had muscly arms. He had tattoos on his arms. There was one large tattoo on one arm and some smaller ones around his hands.

"He was wearing a blue denim shirt which had a collar. I think it was a long sleeved shirt which he wore uncuffed. He pulled the sleeves up to show the tattoos. He was a wee bit drunk and smoked. He would have stayed with our group for an hour or so in the lodge bar."

---

107 10055 / ST / CHRISTOPHER BISMAN / BB3624 / 120198
108 20043D / RICHARD EGDEN

OK. We've seen Guy Wallace's very first description at 1pm on 3 January.

A short time later Anna Cunliffe, one of Olivia's friends on *Tamarack*, revised her and Ben's departure time on the Naiad from roughly 3.20am to between 3.30am and 4am, saying the Naiad arrived around then.[109]

The next major development is at 7.45pm that evening, after police evidently played video of assembled boats to Guy Wallace to try and trigger his memory.[110]

"I have just seen a video of boats at the Furneaux and I'm pretty sure the boat I dropped the people off on is next to the *Spirit of Marlborough*.

"The guy off the boat was not the owner. I remember asking him and he said that he was just crewing.

"The people that came off the *Tamarack* asked if there was any place to stay and the other guy said they could bunk down with him and that's how they got to be on his ketch.

"It would have been about 5.00 am when I took these people out to the boat because after I dropped them off I went back to the bar at Furneaux and had a few drinks and then we noticed the sun coming up and that was probably about ¼ to 6.

"I'd say the ketch was about 38-40 ft long. I'm pretty sure it had two masts. It had quite a low cabin in the middle. I remember the side had a very thick railing on it. It was white on the bottom then through the middle it had a very dark blue strip and then it was white on top. I remember there were a lot of ropes hanging around by the cabin. I'm not sure how many portholes there were but they were round."

Wallace is evidently estimating a 5am Naiad trip based on working backwards from a 5.45am sunrise. In fact it was much earlier

---

109 10982 / JS / ANNA CUNLIFFE / RR5348 / 030198
110 10859 / JS / GUY WALLACE / ASD279 / 030198

and we know this because one of his eventual passengers, Hayden Morresey had a watch:[111]

"When I was in the lodge bar I remember looking at my watch and it was about 2.45 am. I had had enough and I knew it was late and I was getting tired. Sarah was with me and there would have been 20-25 people in the bar who were mostly Christchurch people that Sarah knew.

"Fifteen to twenty minutes after I looked at my watch [ie, at 3am] I left the bar with Sarah. We had intended to walk home. We walked down towards the wharf and along the beach to the left of the jetty to take a short cut on to the track to go back to my parents' bach. We got about 10 metres in on the track in the bush before we decided to stop because it was so cold and dark. We lay down off to the right-hand side of the track. Sarah was sleeping for a while, but I didn't—I just lay there awake.

"There was no noise at all really. It wasn't windy, but it was very cold. I have stated that we lay down for about 45 minutes. This is an approximate time, and a rough estimate—I didn't look at my watch. When Sarah woke up we walked back down to the jetty."

This confirms the timing of the fateful Naiad trip between 3.30am and 4am.

The next day, things quickly gathered speed. In *North & South*, Mike White claims Scott Watson continues to be mystified "why Picton cops immediately fingered him as a likely suspect...even before Rob Pope arrived to take over the investigation on January 6."[112]

Newsflash. It wasn't hard to find out if you actually read the police files.

On 4 January Picton police received a phone call from teenager Amanda Egden:[113]

"I was at Furneaux lodge celebrating New Year with a group of

---

111 20616 / ST / HAYDEN MORRESEY / SCC539 / 080298
112 *North & South*, Dec 2015 p42
113 13794 / AMANDA EGDEN / 040198

friends. We arrived at Furneaux about 10pm. There were 30 of us in our group.

"About 2 or 3am on 1.1.98 a man came up to me and Richard Egden, Millie Savill, Cara Brosnahan, Ollie Perkins, Chris Bisman and Clive MacFarlane plus a few others. He said to me about a "PROZAC" T-Shirt if you come on my boat you can come to Tonga and around the islands.' We asked how big this yacht was he said 30' or 34' long. My friend Millie Savill asked him what his yacht was called he said "He said whatever you want sugar."

"We were saying we can pull ropes on yachts or whatever. He was saying about sexual favours, we were saying no thanks. He said he was from Wellington and was 26 yrs old but I reckon he was older.

"Later on he was causing trouble. I think this guy said to Ollie Perkins I hope your sister dies of cancer and Ollie's sister does have cancer. I think he actually punched Ollie, Chris Bisman told him to apologise as Ollie's sister did have cancer, I think he did apologise. The conversation with Chris went on for ages.

"This happened in the bar at Furneaux by the pool table. We left soon after that, that's the last we saw of him.

"I would describe him as: Male Caucasian, Approx 28-30 years, Short, Stocky, Short brown hair No. 4—all spiked up. Stubble only, Small eyes, Nose pointed/hooked, Tattoos up left arm—little one by thumb. One on left arm was a large tattoo. Possibly wore earring.

"Clothing: Jeans Blue, Blue denim shirt lighter than jeans colour, Possibly boots, A smoker/drinker. Quiet talker, seemed seedy and weird.

"He said his yacht was out there so I think he meant in Furneaux Bay. We first saw him about 2 or 3am. We walked out after that."

The description was as obvious as dog's proverbials to Picton police. Elementary, you might say. Scott Watson. Well known to the local constabulary.

Meanwhile, Amelia Hope was moving her headspace away from

the physical search for her sister and instead trying to wrack her brain to remember more about the Naiad passenger:[114]

"The single guy that was on the boat with us that took us to the *Tamarack* was white but I didn't really take much notice of him. He was slim and quite tall. He was in his late 20s."

She told detectives she was sure they'd caught the water taxi between three and three-thirty in the morning.

Olivia's friend Kirsty Sutherland was lying on *Tamarack*'s deck and says she heard Ben and Olivia get onto the Naiad:[115]

"I haven't got a clue as to how many were on it or who apart from Ben and Olivia were on it.

"Amelia and I started to sleep on top of the boat. I hadn't taken any notice of where the boat with Olivia and Ben went. Amelia and I looked at the time at some stage on top of the boat where we were trying to sleep and it was four something. I didn't really sleep at all."

On 5 January, police managed to track down one of the other passengers in the Naiad. Sixteen year old Sarah Dyer and her very tall boyfriend Hayden Morresey would feature strongly in the later mythology surrounding the case, Sarah didn't see the mystery man's face, but nor did she see a two-masted ketch:[116]

"When we got into the water taxi we seemed to motor out to the right of the wharf, then when we got to the yacht that was full, the other guy's boat was over in the opposite direction so we seemed to go over to the left hand side of the wharf. It was pitch black.

"When we got to the other guy's boat they all hopped out. I didn't notice anything at all of the other boat, not even the colour."

Dyer timed the trip at 3.45am.

Detectives moved swiftly to chase up the Scott Watson lead.

---

114 30648 / JS / AMELIA HOPE / ASD279 / 040198
115 10051 / ST / KIRSTY SUTHERLAND / RR5348 / 040198
116 10026 / ST / SARAH DYER / ASD852 / 050198

They spent most of the afternoon of the 5th looking for him, finally locating his father Chris Watson.[117]

"I believe that Scott went to Erie Bay in Tory Channel for New Year's," said Chris Watson. "I'm not positive that's where he was but that's where he said he was going. He certainly never said that he was going to Furneaux. He came home on the Saturday after New Year's and then both he and his sister (Sandy) got back on his yacht and headed towards Nelson. I don't know when they are due back".

Watson was probably just trying to protect his son by trying to deflect the police with his comment about Furneaux, because the files appear to show he was well aware by 5 January that Scott had been there.

"I knew he was going over to Furneaux Lodge," mother Bev Watson told the family's private defence lawyers. "I told him to be good, and that was the last I saw of him before New Year's Day."[118]

Chris Watson also told Scott's legal team: "I know Beverley saw him refueling his yacht on New Year's Eve morning and I later heard that he had gone up to Furneaux Lodge for New Year's Eve."[119]

Watson added that he'd seen Scott when he returned home on January 3.

"There was no real discussion about his trip up to Endeavour Inlet. I may have asked him if he got drunk—I'm not sure. I did not notice any injuries on Scott at all. I wasn't aware that he may have been assaulted while at Furneaux Lodge.

"On Monday 5 January, I returned to work. After work that day, I was home mowing my lawn when a Police car stopped outside. The Policeman, who was local, approached me and wanted to know where Scott was and where he had been over the New Year period.

---

117 30925 / JS / SCOTT WATSON / MLD886 / 050198
118 Statement of Beverley Watson, 23 February 1998
119 Statement of C J Watson, 23 February 1998

"I told him that I thought he had been up to Endeavour Inlet for New Year's Eve and probably stopped off to see his mate in Erie Bay on the way back. I told him that he was currently sailing to Nelson with his sister. The Policeman noted down the details and left."

There's something amiss with Chris Watson's statement to the private investigators. Perhaps he forgot what he really told police on 5 January. There can be little doubt that the police version of events is correct, because on 5 January the cops would have given their first-born children for the slightest sniff of evidence down to the molecular level that Scott Watson was at Furneaux.

January 5 also saw Guy Wallace give a more extensive statement with this description:

"The guy that got on board with Olivia and Ben was a male, Caucasian, aged about 32 years. He was about 5'8" tall, wiry build. I think he may have had tattoos on his arms but I can't be sure. His hair was a brownie colour, wavy and medium length. He had about two days growth on his face. He was bourboned up, like his eyes weren't focussing.

"He was wearing a Levi shirt with short sleeves, 100 per cent cotton. It had a collar with a button-up front. I saw the Levi brand on it. It was a short sleeved shirt and the colour was between khaki and very pale green. He was wearing blue jeans and I think sandshoes."

No wonder police were honing in on Watson even before Rob Pope arrived.

On the morning of January 6, detectives caught up with Rozlyn McNeilly, who'd been serving behind the Furneaux Lodge bar on the night. She'd noticed someone sitting in "Reg's Corner"—the usual perch of bar regular Reg McManaway.

"He had brownish hair and dark skin and was aged 28-30. He had a scruffy appearance and his hair was longer and scruffy. He had a weather beaten experience [appearance?]".[120]

---

[120] 30753 / JS / ROZLYN MCNEILLY /—/ 060198

In that very same bar that night, Scott Watson had been making an impression.

"At about 9.30-9.45 pm I was drinking with our group that was Nick, Brent Newton, his girlfriend Teresa and Tania. There were locals near us.[121] This male person came over and started speaking to me. He said that he had built his boat and that it was in the bay.

"He asked me if I had any drugs. I said no. I said 'Look I don't know you, you could be a cop; anyway I don't take drugs'. He then said 'Dog on a chain bro'," remembered Ray Padden.

And we all know whose signature phrase that was.

"He was in my face for a good amount of time even up to half an hour. The main conversation was about his yacht and the drugs but apart from what I've said I can't be more specific. In the end I had to tell him to f**k off because he was being a pain.

"He was a male Caucasian, he had a dark lived in colour. I would say he is in his 30s. He was wearing a blue denim shirt, with a red tag. I thought it was a Levis tag. It looked new. I think he might have been wearing jeans.

"He was about 5 foot 7, 5 foot 8. He had a small frame, but still looked athletic. I think he needed a shave. The reason it sticks out is here is this guy with a new flash shirt yet it looked like he needed a shave and a bit of a clean up."

Lawrence McKay, a passenger on *Mina Cornelia*, met Scott when Watson tied up *Blade* alongside *Mina Cornelia* on the afternoon of New Year's Eve.

"Scott looked about 5.10 tall, 75 kgs, Caucasian, slim build, unshaven, a couple days' growth, scruffy appearance.[122] I noticed he had tattoos on him.

"He had brown straggly hair. It wasn't long, but it wasn't short either, possibly to his collar."

---

121 11889 / ST / RAYMOND PADDEN / TFD175 / 260398
122 20286 / ST / LAWRENCE MCKAY / MBD353 / 150198

The varying descriptions of Scott's hair from different witnesses probably result from the fact his mum cut his hair.[123] Perfectly brushed, it would look short, neat and tidy, but with a bit of wind or running his hands through his hair the amateur cut would start to look messy with long bits and short bits—just like the photos of Watson show.

The important take home point from all this is that despite what Keith Hunter and others have said, so far we have seen no inconsistency between those all-important first descriptions of the mystery man by Guy Wallace and Roz McNeilly, and confirmed sightings of Scott Watson. They could easily be the same person.

McNeilly did *not* say the mystery man's hair was "long", she said it was "longer"—a term of relativity. Larry McKay said Watson's hair "wasn't long, but it wasn't short either, possibly to his collar... straggly...scruffy".

On 7 January, Amelia Hope remembered more of the Naiad trip. She was waiting with friend Rick Goddard (who remembered virtually nothing).[124]

"We waited on the jetty for about five minutes. Then I saw three people come down from the Lodge area. One appeared to be on his own and the other two were together. There were two males and a female. The female looked about 20 years. She was Caucasian, short, quite petite—little and she had blondish hair in a ponytail. I can't remember what she was wearing.

"The guy with her was tall—about 6'1", Caucasian and skinny. He looked in his early 20's He had short dark hair. I can't remember what he was wearing."

Amelia Hope has just described 16 year old Sarah Dyer and her tall boyfriend Hayden Morresey. But on 7 January here's what she now recalled of the mystery man:

---

[123] "Scott's hair is always cut by mum at home. I think Scott last had a hair cut by mum before he went to Whangarei. This would have been in November." 10163 / ST / SANDRA WATSON / DH6260 / 120198
[124] 10085 / ST / AMELIA HOPE / ASD279 / 070198 / F

"The other guy had short hair like a crew cut. It was dark brown. He was Caucasian—about 25 years plus. He was shorter than the other guy but not by much—two inches. He had a medium build. I can't remember what he was wearing."

Again, male Caucasian, 25 plus, short dark hair, medium build, shorter than other men.

"The three of them got into the yellow Naiad which was the biggest of them. I asked if we could get a lift out to the "*Tamarack*" and he knew where it was.

"Initially when the couple came down to the jetty the Naiad driver was with them and then we got on and then the guy on his own came down and got on.

"The driver was a male, Caucasian, about 50 years old, about 5'7" tall. He was medium build and he had tattoos on both of his lower legs. He had shorts and a shirt but it wasn't a Furneaux shirt."

32 year old Guy Wallace was probably horrified that young women thought he was 50, but it just goes to show how descriptions can be wrong on more subjective details. When you are 20, arguably anyone aged over thirty looks decrepit.

"When I got on the Naiad I was sitting at the front left and Rick was at the front right. The guy on his own was sitting right at the front point of the Naiad. The other couple were behind us but I'm not sure which side.

"We went out to the "*Tamarack*" first. There was no conversation from anyone. We pulled into the back and I think I got off first. Maybe Rick did—I'm not too sure. I got on to the "*Tamarack*" at the back on the left side. I'm not sure about Rick.

"As we were pulling up to the "*Tamarack*" I could hear Olivia. She was saying that there was too many people aboard and she must have seen us coming and she said something along the lines, "We'll get this boat back to shore". As I was getting on she was getting off on the right side.

I remember her asking the driver if they could get a ride ashore. The driver said, "Yeah".

"The guy on the Naiad that was on his own and didn't appear to know anyone. I don't recall seeing him at any time during the night. I can't recall anyone on the Naiad saying anything to Olivia."

The police net was starting to turn up "Scott" everywhere. Random revellers being tracked down and interviewed by police in these early days were frequently mentioning their encounters with "Scott", and detectives by now had a very good idea who that was. They'd been interviewing boat owners as well and struck gold on 7 January when they located Dave Mahony, skipper of the *Mina Cornelia*. Police knew of Watson's boat as "Raha", the Maori name painted on the windvane at the stern.

The initial information came in a phone call early that morning:[125]

"Rafted next to them was a Raven 26 ft yacht with a young couple whom he thought were from Auckland. This may be a local boat having been chartered.

"On the port side of their yacht was a 30 ft steel yacht which was predominantly white. This was skippered by a guy Scott Watson whom the Police have knowledge of in relation to a knife fight incident. His father works at Carey's as an engineer and the boat is normally moored at Shakespeare Bay (is this the yacht "Raha"?)

"Mahony said he didn't go ashore over the evening of 31 December 1997 but his group did. He took them in and they caught water taxis back. At various times during the afternoon he did go ashore but that was to take his dog for a walk.

"Mahony said that at about 4.00 and 5.00 am Scott Watson came on board and woke him up saying something about nobody wanted to be with him or something like that. It was shortly after that that Watson slipped his lines and left the area.

---

125 12256 / JS / PROFILE "MINA CORNELIA" / BM6952 / 070198

07.01.98[126]

1015 HRS Re: Locating Scott WATSON and Yacht "RAHA".

Constable RACKLIFF—Picton briefed to interview Dave MAHONY at Picton and to make enquiries regarding whereabouts of "Raha" and WATSON.

Details also passed to him regarding EGDEN and conversation re Tonga in bar at Ferneaux.

At the formal interview, Mahony revealed he knew Watson personally and that Scott had rafted up alongside him at 4pm on New Year's Eve. He told police Scott had been smoking cannabis and drinking heavily before going ashore.

Mahony, a charter skipper, waited for his own passengers to return from shore as the celebrations wound down.

"We stayed up until about 2.00 am socialising and then went to bed."[127]

"At around 4.00 am, although I'm not exact on the time—that's what one of my passengers told me—Scott stuck his head into the cabin. He was drunk and wanted someone to get up and socialise with him. We all ignored him and I heard him go across to the Raven and try to get them up as well.

"One of the passengers called Ernst—I think his surname was DERYSER(?)—said to me that Scott had muttered about nobody wanting to know him and he chucked the lines off and left in his boat.

"Scott left one of his tethers still attached to my boat.

---

126 13791 / JS / LOCATION SCOTT WATSON & YACHT "RAHA" / RR5348 / 070198
127 10084 / ST / DAVID MAHONY / RRC196 / 070198 / W

"When I saw Scott he was by himself and I didn't hear any other noises."

This is the first confirmation in the police file that Watson had been positively identified at Furneaux. Not just that, but police had him returning to his boat around 4am—the same time as the mystery man journey.

Then came a bombshell. One of the other passengers on the fateful Naiad trip, Hayden Morresey, remembered enough of the nights events to give police a valuable briefing:[128]

"About 3.00 am me and my girlfriend left the bar in the lodge. There would have been about 30-40 people left in the bar at that stage."

This is important. It tells us not only the time but also that in this latter phase of the evening there were not hundreds of people, just dozens.

"We tried to walk home but it was too dark. We mucked around for about 45 minutes trying to get back to our bach and in the end we just headed back to the lodge."

So it is now around 3.45am. Morresey and Dyer asked at the jetty for a ride to the bach and were told 'no'. As they headed up to the lodge to get a torch so they could walk the track home, another Furneaux staffer, Guy Wallace, offered to take them in a Naiad.

"The three of us started walking down to the jetty. As we were walking down to the jetty, there was a guy walking in front of us [the mystery man] and another guy already at the jetty [Rick Goddard with Amelia Hope]. They wanted a ride also.

"The guy that was giving us a ride got the yellow Naiad that was tied to the jetty. I untied the front rope and someone else untied the back rope. We all got in the Naiad and there would have been the driver, me, Sarah and two other guys.

"I already told the driver we wanted to go to Solitude. I can't

---

[128] 10031 / ST / HAYDEN MORRESEY / ASD279 / 070198

remember anything the other two guys said but I'm pretty sure that they didn't know each other.

"We left the jetty and we headed out to our right [*Tamarack* was moored out to the right]. We were going quite slow and we had to weave for a couple of boats heading out to where one of the other guys was going.

"We went out to a white yacht. We came into the back of the yacht and one of the guys on the Naiad got onto the yacht I can't remember anything about him.

"I remember seeing a girl on the back of the yacht getting ready to jump onto the Naiad [Olivia Hope]. I remember that she was wearing glasses and had straight hair which went down to her shoulders at the back. I think she had a bag with her.

"She got off the yacht with a guy [Ben Smart] and they both got on the Naiad. I can't really remember anything about him.

"My girlfriend and I were sitting at and she was on the left.

"I can't remember anything the girl said but I can remember the guy on the Naiad inviting her and her friend to stay on his boat.

"We then headed back towards the jetty but further out to sea. When we got to the guy's boat, I looked back towards the jetty—the right side of it looking at it from the sea. [which indicates they were somewhere to the left of the jetty if you were standing on the shore]

"I can't remember anything being said on the way out to this guy's boat. We pulled up alongside the boat, and the guy who owned it jumped off first and then he helped the other two up. The boat was facing inshore and we pulled up to the left side of it.

"I only thought the guy owned it but nothing was said that he did own it.

"I would describe the boat as a yacht. I can't remember the colour but I think it was white. When we came up to the boat I can remember seeing a bit of white at the top of the side and then another colour and then white again. I can't remember what the middle colour was. I can't remember a lot about the yacht other than it having heaps of ropes. I can remember a mast near to the back and there was heaps of ropes coming off that.

"I can only remember seeing the back of the guy that I thought was the owner of the boat. I'm not sure of his race. I would put his age at between 25 and 35 yrs. His hair was quite scraggly looking. By that I mean it was quite wavy It went down to just before his shoulder line. I think it was brownish in colour. He had long pants on and I think he had a long sleeve shirt on but I can't remember anything about it.

"I didn't take that much notice of him or the other couple that got on his boat...I'm not positive but there could have been another girl on the Naiad when we first left the jetty. The driver was getting pissed off about something cause we were having trouble finding the first yacht.

"I cannot remember whether or not there was any other boats around the yacht we dropped the people onto."

Unlike Guy Wallace, nowhere in that first statement does Morresey call the boat a ketch. It is just a yacht with some ropes hanging off. There are no descriptions of portholes or a blue stripe. He doesn't remember whether it was rafted against any other boats but this is not surprising either—it was pitch dark and depth of field for viewing would have been limited.

Dave Mahony, the *Mina Cornelia* skipper, said of Watson's yacht: "The deck area looked a bit cluttered. Other than the 4 lines we had tying the boats together there was other line and rope lying there or tied to the rails. I can't be specific but there were all the lines associated with the sails. There were lines tied to the rails but again I can't be specific."[129]

Significantly, Morresey says the mystery man's hair was brown and "quite scraggly looking. By that I mean it was quite wavy. It went down to just *before* his shoulder line." [author's emphasis]

---

129 10669 / ST / DAVID MAHONY / DE5136 / 080298

Where have we heard that before: "He had brown straggly hair. It wasn't long, but it wasn't short either, possibly to his collar," said Larry McKay when he shared a beer or two with Watson on his boat eight hours earlier.

"He is Caucasian with dark coloured medium length wavy hair," said long time Watson family friend Alan Mountford.

So Morresey's testimony is highly relevant. It sounds like Scott Watson. It doesn't prove Scott Watson is the mystery man, but it sure as heck does not rule him out.

In *The Marlborough Mystery*, Mike Kalaugher claimed Watson could not be the mystery man because Watson had "straight, dark brown, very short hair…not wavy or scraggly looking, same length all over."[130]

As you can see, that claim is simply not sustainable, not if you are looking at the evidence objectively.

Here for example, is yet another confirmed sighting of Scott Watson in the bar two hours before the disappearance:[131]

"I would describe Mr 'Prozac' as: Male Caucasian—reasonably tanned. Generally messy, untidy, unshaven. Looked like he hadn't showered for a year. Approx 5 ft 8" height. Average build. Approx 3-4 days growth (unshaven). Shaggy dark brown short hair."

That is definitely Scott Watson—even Watson's lawyers agreed it was a confirmed interaction with him. Yet that description also fits his evil twin, the 'mystery man'.

So what has Keith Hunter written in *Trial by Trickery*?

"Two more people qualified as witnesses to him. They were bar manager Roz McNeilly and barman Chey Phipps. Both had served the man, both remembered him and both described him. Their descriptions were consistent with that given by Guy Wallace. They were not consistent with Scott Watson," insists Hunter.[132]

---

130 *The Marlborough Mystery* by Mike Kalaugher, Tandem Press 2001 p128
131 11417/ST/SEAN THOMPSON/MRF086/240198
132 *Trial By Trickery*, p31

Oh really? You've read the descriptions given by Wallace, McNeilly and Morresey, and as you've discovered they are eerily close to known confirmed sightings of Watson that night. But let's take up Hunter's gauntlet and check his bold claims further against the fourth witness.

The final piece of the jigsaw falls into place when detectives roll around to barman Chey Phipps. Of all the hundreds of potential mystery men at Furneaux on New Year's Eve, he remembered only one:[133]

"The only person that really stood out to me was a guy drinking at the bar in the area of Reg's corner or that side of the bar. I noticed him because he was kind of getting in the way of other customers, trying to get served, because he was leaning on the bar and not shifting out of the way.

"As different girls were coming up to the bar to get served, this guy would start chatting away to them. I can't remember any conversations but his body language was suggesting 'come on baby, how about it' type of thing.

"One girl looked at him with a look of disgust and she then turned to some guy that was probably her boyfriend. I can't recall anything about her other than she was fairly attractive.

"There didn't seem to be any girl taking advantage of his advancements.

"I did talk to him at some stage because I was serving him. I think I recall him asking for doubles—probably.

"I'm fairly sure he was a spirit drinker."

That point just there is also crucial. It would later be said that the mystery man was exclusively drinking bourbon, but Phipps doesn't specify this in his initial statement. He "thinks" he "recalls" the man asking for doubles, and is "fairly sure" he's a spirit drinker.

This is evidence of a memory gap vulnerable to being contami-

---

133 20250 / ST / CHEY PHIPPS / ASD279 / 090198

nated through talking to others. Phipps is not certain what he remembers. However, look at who he initially describes:

"He didn't have any distinctive accent to suggest he was from overseas. My opinion of him was that he looked like an Aussie surfie or a younger West Coast miner.

"He was Caucasian, aged between 26 years and 32 years. His height was about 5'7" tall. I am about 5'5" and he was a couple of inches taller than me. I would describe his build as wiry—he wasn't real skinny and he wasn't real built either. He had mousy brown hair and I think possibly brown eyes. I would describe his eyes as sleepy in that they were half way droopy. I think his eyes were naturally that way.

"His hair wasn't styled or anything like that. It was about shoulder length, just at the back. His hair wasn't straight but it wasn't curly either, it was somewhere in between. I think he was slightly unshaven probably 2—3 days worth.

"His eyes were the most distinctive thing about his face because they looked like sleepy eyes. This could of been because he was drunk. My opinion was that he had had a fair bit and was pretty well intoxicated."

This next part of Chey Phipps' description of the mystery man is also highly significant. He says the man is wearing a jersey over his shirt, which is a new twist:

"He was wearing a neutral coloured jersey. The colour could have been something like tan/grey. I thought he was wearing a jersey with a collared shirt underneath and that may have been a neutral colour also. I can't be sure on that. I'm pretty sure the jersey was long sleeve."

"This guy appeared to be drinking on his own."

So here we have a short, wiry 'Nigel No-mates' drinking at the bar with a grey or tan jersey over his collared shirt to keep warm.

Did Scott Watson even have a jersey? Let's find out from the man himself.

CHAPTER NINE

Conflicting Descriptions?

Keith Hunter argues that the first four witnesses had "a distinctly common feature...the hair. Wallace, McNeilly, Phipps and Morresey all gave him long or medium length hair."

Actually, no they didn't. Wallace called it "short, dark wavy hair".[134] McNeilly said his hair was "longer and scruffy"[135], key word being longer rather than the definitive long. Phipps called it "about shoulder length, just at the back. His hair wasn't straight but it wasn't curly either, it was somewhere in between".[136] Morresey stated the hair was "quite scraggly looking. *By that I mean it was quite wavy. It went down to just before his shoulder line.*"[137]

Arguably, Keith Hunter is spinning the long hair story in a Star-Warsy kind of 'these are not the droids you are looking for' kind of way.

---

134 10861 / JS / GUY WALLACE / ASD279 / 030198
135 30753 / JS / ROZLYN MCNEILLY / —/ 060198
136 20250 / ST / CHEY PHIPPS / ASD279 / 090198
137 10031 / ST / HAYDEN MORRESEY / ASD279 / 070198

Nothing in the initial descriptions differs from known sightings of Scott Watson on the night. Except for that jersey.

Forget the *North & South* interview. Let's see what Watson told the police at the time of his very first statement on 7 January 1998:

"I own a 26 foot steel yacht called "*Blade*". At about lunchtime on New Year's Eve I arrived at Furneaux Lodge on my yacht. I was the only occupant.

"I rafted alongside a charter boat, a blue and white yacht. From photos I have been shown it appears to be the "*Micro-Cornelia*". I rafted up against the yacht because Dave Arnie, who was skippering the boat, yelled out to us.

"We were also close to another friend of mine, Warwick (?) who was skippering the "*Unicorn*".

"I talked to Dave for about an hour. Then I saw Warwick, his wife and another couple from Gisborne row out from Furneaux to their yacht. They yelled out to me so I went over and spent some time with them on their yacht. I had spent the rest of the afternoon there.

"Between about 7.00—8.00 pm, Warwick and the others took the water taxi to Furneaux Lodge.

"I went over to my boat and finished drinking a bottle of Rum, put my shoes on and went and saw Dave on the "Micro Cornelius". He had some charter people with him.

"I was pretty pissed by this stage. At some stage we got the water taxi to Furneaux. I can't even remember that. I think there might have been some "pot"—I can't really remember.

"I remember going into the bar and some guy tried to pick a fight with me. There was some pushing and shoving and then some big guys came over and told him to "piss off" and he did.

"I remember talking to lots of people.

"Later on I remember speaking with Rick McLeod who owns Furneaux Lodge. He owns the yacht the "*Clansman*".

"I can't really remember speaking with anyone else.

"I have seen the photos of the two missing people Ben Smart and Olivia Hope. I cannot recall seeing them at all.

"I have read the description of the suspect and can't recall anyone like that being there.

"I have seen the picture of the ketch and cannot recall seeing another boat like that. There was a ketch—a cream coloured, steel, square transomed. It was seaward to us. I remember talking to Warwick about it. It was about 35 foot. I think it had an aft cabin. We didn't take that much notice of it. It might not have even been a ketch. It's not in the photo montage that you have shown me. This was about 3.00 or 4.00 pm. I can't remember if it was there afterwards. It didn't look like the picture. It looked like a Bruce Roberts' design. I used to be a boat builder. I still sort of am. I take quite an interest in boats.

"I was wearing blue jeans, white and black Bianchi shoes. I was wearing a grey jersey with two red stripes across the chest. I also had a grey t-shirt. It had "Ocean Spirit" written on it.

"I remember seeing the "*Tamarack*" come in. It was about 4.00 pm. I was with Warwick then. We mentioned all the pissed people on it. They dropped their anchor about 300 to 400 yards away near the wharf.

"At about 2.00 am I took the water taxi back to my yacht. It was a Naiad, yellow. It was driven by an old guy with a hat on. I was the only passenger. I remember he wouldn't let me on until he had parked the boat. He kept telling me to wait. I don't think I spoke with him.

"He dropped me at my boat and I cooked up a feed of eggs and bacon. Just before eating I jumped back on the "Micro Cornelius". They were all asleep. I remember waking someone up and being told that the party was over.

"After that I cooked up the eggs and bacon and then went to sleep.

"I left Furneaux at about 7.00 am. I sailed to Erie Bay in the Tory Channel. I visited my boss's house. I spoke with *Keating [his name was suppressed, this is a pseudonym]. His nickname is "Zappa". He is the caretaker out there. The house is owned by Alister Cassels. I think he is a property developer. He collects rent. He owns a couple of big boats," concluded Scott Watson.

That's the key detail of Watson's first statement to police. We'll return to the overall narrative in a later chapter, but let's look first at the issue of the jersey. The mystery man was reportedly wearing a grey/tan jersey at some point in the night. Watson says "I was wearing a grey jersey with two red stripes across the chest. I also had a grey t-shirt. It had "Ocean Spirit" written on it."

There are serious doubts about Watson's story. Photos show he was wearing a plain white t-shirt at Furneaux, not the grey Ocean Spirit one. Watson does not mention at all the blue denim shirt he actually wore, and not once was he photographed wearing the grey jersey. None of the clothes Watson was seen wearing on the night have ever been found. Curiously, like Ben and Olivia, they're missing—except for the Bianchi shoes.[138]

We know Watson spent time on Warwick Eastgate's yacht *Unicorn*, but then Watson says he returned to *Blade* and put his shoes on. He does not mention having a shave, which is significantly more time consuming.

In a second statement dated 12 January, Watson elaborates on this, and specifically says he returned to *Mina Cornelia* after getting changed and grabbing a jersey:[139]

"I went back to my boat. Had another drink. I put some shoes on. I remember that I had some in the bottle and I spilt it somewhere. I got changed—put some jeans on, kept my teeshirt on, grabbed a shirt or jersey. A jersey I think—a grey one.

"I went over to *Cornelius*. I started giving them all shit, like just

---

[138] Statement made by Rob Pope, published in *Silent Evidence*, p117
[139] 20029 / ST / SCOTT WATSON / JMD684 / 120198

talking with the guys. I think I took my rum. Smoked some drugs. It was dope. I had a couple of tokes. I don't know who's the dope was. It wasn't mine."

That appears to have been a lie. Numerous witnesses on *Mina Cornelia* saw Watson pull out a joint and offer it around. Skipper Dave Mahony disapproved and flushed it down the sink.

The important point however is that Watson admits he took a jersey with him to shore. We know this because he himself says so. We don't know if it was light-grey or the kind of darker-grey or navy sometimes confused for black. We know Watson had both kinds of jerseys. He did not leave it behind on *Mina Cornelia* because he claims to have kept it with him:

"I don't think I had my jersey off—I still had it the next day."

A 15 year old girl from the ketch *Alliance* ran into someone by the toilets soon after the time we know Scott Watson arrived onshore:[140]

"I do recall a guy who looked a little like this. That was about 10.15. Dad took us into the bar toilets first. There was this guy standing just inside the main bar doors. He was to the right of me. He was standing on his own with his arms folded. He looked like he was giving everyone the evil eye.

"I'm sure he wasn't a bouncer. The bar was full of people. He was about 5 foot 8. He had dark brown messy oily hair. He was unshaven. His hair was straight, it was medium length, really messy and sticking up all over the place. He was sort of wiry looking but not skinny.

"He had on a black or dark grey machine knitted round necked jersey on. He didn't have anything in his hands because they were folded. I think he had dark coloured jeans on. I noticed him because he was mean looking. He was on his own. The jersey was long sleeved."

Again, it doesn't prove that Watson was the mystery man wear-

---

140 10457 / ST / ALISHA KENNEDY / HMG150 / 160198

ing the jersey over a collared shirt in the bar, but it sure as heck does not rule him out. Watson's admission that he had a jersey also neutralises the argument over the so-called "two-trip theory", where it was suggested Watson may have returned to *Blade* to get a jersey then come back to the bar. Such an explanation isn't necessary if Watson is on record saying he took a jersey with him on the only ride into Furneaux that we know about, the one with Dave Mahony.

Also significantly, Guy Wallace never described the mystery man in the Naiad as having a jersey.

Witness "Zappa" at Erie Bay told police: "On the 1st of January 1998 Scott was wearing blue jeans and a dark coloured jersey. I think he had a cut foot and might of been in bare feet. He had a bit of shadow of growth on his face. He wasn't clean shaven."[141]

Which brings us to another point. A mythology has built up that Scott Watson was "clean shaven". It was a myth created by Watson's defence lawyers, for good reason, but we in the media did not do a good enough job cross checking it.

In *Ben & Olivia*, we reported this example:[142]

"The witness was drinking orange juice all night so his recollection wasn't affected. Defence counsel Mike Antunovic asked what Watson was wearing, the witness replied a blue shirt and dark trousers and that he was clean shaven."

The witness was Murray Knowles, and what is not clear from that passage from the book is that Antunovic asked leading questions, which he was allowed to do.

"Did you see your wife and her friend Phillipa talking to a male who was wearing a blue shirt and some darker trousers?"[143]

" … yes I did."

---

141 20066 / ST / BARRY GREEN / TFD175 / 140198
142 *Ben & Olivia*, p108
143 Trial Notes of Evidence p254

"Would you describe him that evening as you saw him as being tidy in appearance?"

" ... yes I do."

"And clean shaven?"

" ... correct."

It's a subtle thing, but Antunovic was planting cues in Knowles' mind that played down comparisons between Watson and the mystery man. A blue shirt and dark trousers sounds respectable. The adjectives "dark trousers" and "clean shaven" were the lawyer's phrases to which the witness politely agreed. It is a commonly-employed tactic of cross examination.

But what Knowles had actually told the police in his statement was slightly different:[144]

"When I got there I saw the girls were talking to a man who was wearing blue denim jeans and a blue denim shirt, as I recall...He was definitely wearing denim jeans that were darker blue and his denim shirt matched or appeared to match the colour... I would describe him as being tidy in appearance and if he was unshaven I did not pick that up."

He wasn't making a positive claim that Watson was clean-shaven, he was just saying he didn't notice. Yet by a cunning question, the sting of his evidence was manipulated at trial.

The *Ben & Olivia* book bought into the clean-shaven manipulation, largely because we didn't have access to the original witness statements. Lacking the files and relying only on court testimony filtered by skilled lawyers, we made bold statements back in 1999:

"Initially described as 32 and unshaven, the suspect eventually arrested was 26 and clean shaven on the night of the vanishing."[145]

Waiheke yachtie Mike Kalaugher built on this theme, going so

---

144 13984 / ST / MURRAY KNOWLES / PMC692 / 270499
145 *Ben & Olivia*, p21

far as to say that not only was Watson "clean shaven—he shaved eight hours earlier".[146]

There is actually no hard evidence supporting this. Watson himself never said he'd had a shave. While it is true a handful of witnesses in the original police statements described him as "clean shaven" that night, by far the majority of confirmed Watson sightings described him as having one or two days' growth, or even "clean shaven, BUT..."

Which is exactly how bar manager Roz McNeilly described the mystery man at the bar in her second briefing to police on 8 January:

"A male, Caucasian, between 30 and 35 years, clean shaven, although his face gave the appearance of two days growth or hadn't shaved that day, thin, scruffy, almost unkempt as if he hasn't seen a hairdresser for a while. What I mean by that is the hair was uneven and different lengths. The hair roughly parted down the centre and fell over his ears. The nose was skinny to bony. His face was weather-beaten and well tanned, almost olive in colour. Was sitting in Reggie's corner on his seat.

"He had a leather complexion a sea person sort of look, like he had been in the sea or worked out doors. He had brown hands like tradesman hands, definitely not an office worker. His hands were fairly skinny but not soft.

"I could not recall his clothing but it was dark in colour. I have to comment that I am left with the impression that he was unkempt and scruffy in appearance."

Compare McNeilly's description once again to a confirmed sighting of Scott Watson in that very same bar by Sean Thompson who said Watson was "reasonably tanned, generally messy, untidy, unshaven. Looked like he hadn't showered for a year...Approx 3-4

---

146 *The Marlborough Mystery*, p128

days growth (unshaven). Shaggy dark brown short hair."[147]

Imagine—what are the chances of two identical looking men, both psychopaths, being in the same bar at the same time and attracting the same attention from different witnesses?

Roz McNeilly continues: "He bought a few drinks and I think bourbon and coke was his drink.

"I got the impression that he was alone as he never had anyone standing around him for long.

"When I say that though there was a female, Caucasian, between 18 and 20 years, no make-up on, blonde hair tied back but not neatly, no glasses, wearing dark top but had bare arms which suggests a sleeveless top, I recall seeing in the corner.

"She was standing behind him for about 15 minutes. I recall her being drunk and leaning on or over him. When I say leaning on him I recall seeing her putting both her arms over his shoulder and giggling and talking to him.

"I got the impression that they may have been together but then she later left him while he stayed.

"While they were both together I recall him appear to be buying her bourbon and cokes. It was sort of strange in that he ordered the drink and he paid for it or at least handed the money over, then passed the drink to her.

"I couldn't say how many he bought for her but it got to the stage where I was going to say something to him about me not being prepared to serve her any more drinks but the next thing is she has left the bar. He stayed though.

"I then thought, well, they weren't together, perhaps she was using him for drinks together."

There's a possibility then that the man at the bar wasn't buying bourbon for himself but for a woman behind him, or alternatively

---

147 11417 / ST / SEAN THOMPSON / MRF086 / 240198

that in an attempt to attract her he was 'mirroring' her in an "I'll have what she's having" way.

For his part Scott Watson actually never outright denied drinking bourbon, instead using the curious turn of phrase:

"I think I was probably drinking rum and Coke at Furneaux Lodge. I don't think I would drink bourbon. I'd drink rum if it was there."

In *The Marlborough Mystery*, a definitive Mike Kalaugher writes Watson "had definitely not been drinking bourbon as he never drinks it."[148]

Really? If he ain't a Jim Beam drinker, you'd think Scott Watson would have been much more direct with police in that case. Surely he knew whether he would drink bourbon whiskey or not? Perhaps Watson didn't want to lie to police about this in case a witness positively identified him. After all, he had been seen drinking whiskey during an eight week stint working on *Galerna*:[149]

"He drank a little bit of whiskey on the boat from time to time but not much really."

Keith Hunter may have missed that when he wrote: "No one ever spoke of Watson buying or drinking bourbon."[150]

The woman standing behind the mystery man has never been found by police. The description is similar to Olivia Hope, which could explain why she was never found. Perhaps she agreed to go on the yacht with him because she'd already developed an alcohol-fuelled superficial 'trust' of him at the bar. Even Roz McNeilly conceded it could have been Olivia:

"I have viewed the photograph of Olivia Hope and I cannot specifically recall seeing her but her description and style of hair if

---

148 *The Marlborough Mystery*, p128
149 12884 / ST / GREGORY CURLING / PMC692 / 220798
150 *Trial By Trickery*, p74

she had it pulled back and removed her glasses, it could have been her drinking with the male in Reggie's Corner."

Gerald Hope told police his daughter was "a young 7th former at 17 years and in some respects she was ahead of her years, but not quite an adult, possibly more trusting than she would be wise to be."[151]

Significantly, he also confirmed Olivia was a bourbon drinker. She was technically underage so using an intermediary to buy drinks might not have seemed strange. According to her friend Hamish Rose she was scrounging for bourbon because she didn't have any money left by midnight. They went up to the Lodge, and Olivia decided to look for her friends while Rose went down to the garden bar. He never saw her again.

Roz McNeilly remembers the mystery man shared another similarity with Scott Watson, who'd been carrying "a packet of Port Royal cigarettes in his top pocket" according to another witness[152]. McNeilly said of the mystery man:

"I remember him smoking 'rollies', that is roll your own cigarettes. He was sitting there with a skinny rollie in his mouth.[153]

"I remember someone fell over in that corner. I asked someone if he was alright and they said yes, that's when I noticed the guy had moved from that corner. I'm not sure if it was him that fell over but I presumed it was because he had gone after that incident. If it was him that fell over in that corner he would have got wet because there was a lot of beer on the floor."

Which is interesting, because we know Scott Watson fell over in that exact corner and got spillage all over his arm.

"The next thing I remember was some guy saying I had spilt my drink. I was in the back of the bar. There are double doors with glass

---

151 10034D / GERALD HOPE
152 11399D / THOMAS DALE
153 40330 / ST / ROZLYN McNEILLY / TFD573 / 020498

in them. I remember being at the bar hanging around somewhere there," Watson told police.

Sarah Kernick definitely had a run-in with Watson, and she noted both hair "longer at the neck" and a wet sleeve:

"I would describe this person as a male, Caucasian, aged about 30 years, very pale, dark brown hair average length longer at the neck. I don't think he was clean shaven, but he didn't have a moustache or beard. He was taller than me, possibly around 5 ft 7". I think his eyes were brown/hazel[154]...I couldn't recall any jewellery on him, his clothing long sleeve shirt (right sleeve wet), it was a dark colour, it appeared to have a collar & he had a dark coloured t-shirt underneath. He had jeans, coloured black or blue/black."

Millie Savill told police Scott Watson "had thin, squinty eyes. He was quietly spoken and appeared to have thin lips. I would say he was about 30—35 years old. He had a round face with a big hooked nose, it was quite pointed. He hadn't shaved but had stubble. He was wearing a blue denim shirt, it was a pale blue. It could have been a long sleeved shirt which was rolled up. He was wearing dark jeans, the shirt was collared. He had tattoos on his left arm definitely."[155]

Like Savill on Watson and McNeilly on the mystery man, Amanda Egden distinctly remembered Watson's eyes and nose:[156]

"His eyes and nose are the features that I can identify and recall about him. I recall his eyes as being squinty and small and his nose kind of hooked and big."

It seems pretty clear from the hard evidence that regardless of what earlier books on the Watson case have reported, there are overwhelming similarities between the description of the mystery man, and confirmed sightings of Scott Watson that night.

With the two most recent books, Mike Kalaugher's 2001 *The*

---

[154] 20079 / ST / SARAH KERNICK / RMC084 / 130198
[155] 20214 / ST / CAMILLA SAVILL / SID741 /120198
[156] 11918 / ST / AMANDA EGDEN / JH8914 / 020498

Marlborough Mystery and Keith Hunter's 2006 *Trial by Trickery*, the continued adherence to the impossibility of a link is arguably inexcusable, because the record shows both those authors had access to the police files.

So what are they basing their argument on?

A photo. An image that purportedly shows Watson tidy and clean shaven. The entire defence case for Scott Watson has come to rest on that photo. Let's see if it can stand the pressure of real scrutiny.

ELEMENTARY

CHAPTER TEN

The Camera Never Lies— Or Does It?

One one-hundredth of a second. That's the average shutter speed used on the average photo. By definition, your face can move into 100 slightly different positions and expressions over the space of one second. Which one of those 100 possibilities will define your life for that second?

Star witnesses Guy Wallace and Roz McNeilly became unsure of their identifications of Scott Watson as the mystery man after they were asked to view different photos of the man. We reported it in *Ben & Olivia*:

"Wallace agreed with Mike Antunovic that after being shown an police identikit of the man he had described to police he asked for a pencil to make the facial hair stand out more.[157]

"But Guy Wallace appeared uncertain on the point. At an earlier

---

157 *Ben & Olivia*, p128

depositions hearing he had dropped a bombshell, when shown a photo of Watson by defence lawyers, Wallace had to agree based on the photo that Watson was not the man he dropped off with Ben and Olivia. Until that time Wallace had been adamant, he had dropped the pair off at a ketch with Watson. Wallace agreed with the defence that at that hearing, after a series of questions, he had ruled out Watson as the man.

"As the jury in the trial watched, Wallace was shown the photo taken aboard the *Mina Cornelia*, sometime after 9:00pm on New Year's Eve. Wallace agreed with the defence that Watson appeared to be clean shaven.

"That would rule the man out from the start, wouldn't it?" queried Antunovic. Wallace agreed.

"Also under defence questioning, Wallace agreed that the photo of Watson in the police montage needed to have longer hair and more stubble to resemble the way he remembered the man on New Year's Eve."

North & South's Mike White writes, "photos of him at Furneaux Lodge confirm he was clean-shaven, with short hair."[158] Well there you go, case closed. We can all go home. Except, if White had actually read the witness files, he would have known his statement was vacuous.

We know that Watson arrived onshore at Furneaux just on 10pm, because of his fellow passengers on the *Mina Cornelia* inflatable went straight to Furneaux's EFTPOS machine to withdraw cash, and the receipt is time at 9.58pm.

Just before they left to come ashore, the *Cornelia* passengers and Watson gathered for a photo. You can see it for yourself. As Keith Hunter says, it shows Watson with "a freshly shaven sheen".

Or does it?

---

158 *North & South*, Dec 2015, p46

The woman who took the photo was Brigette Radford. She recalled that "when Scott first arrived and rafted up to our boat, he was wearing a pair of shorts only. At that time he appeared to have a couple of days stubble on his face then and he appeared quite scruffy then."[159]

Scott had gone away for several hours to the *Unicorn*, and when he returned to *Cornelia* Radford stated, "it appeared to me that he had tidied himself up and had a shave at that time."

This is where Kalaugher and others base their claim that Watson had shaved.

However, it appears that Radford's own photo subconsciously influenced her, because as fellow passenger Marcel Rutte told police,[160] "in this photo his stubble is not as noticeable but I still believe he had not had a shave.

"Larry McKay who is also in the photo had stubble that night as well but it does not show up much in the photo as well."

In fact, as witness after witness who met Watson later that night has described him, he still had one or two days' growth on his face. Some confirmed sightings even described it as 3 or 4 days' growth. He could not have truly had a freshly shaven "sheen", no matter how much a low resolution image taken with a flash might suggest. This point can't be overemphasised. A photo is only as good as the camera and lens it was taken on. If the lighting was dim or the focus wasn't sharp enough, fine detail like whiskers simply won't appear—it's the same principle of soft-focus beloved of movie stars to hide wrinkles. When high-definition HDMI TV came along it provoked panic attacks amongst a generation of actors who'd never had their flaws exposed to such a degree.[161]

---

159 10667 / ST / BRIGETTE RADFORD / JSC422 / 050298
160 20287D / MARCEL RUTTE
161 "I'm A Celebrity poser Helen Flanagan branded worst HD horror by TV fans—with Darcey Bussell, Tulisa and Victoria Beckham also named and shamed: Tulisa's 'covered in moles' while male HD horror

In simple terms, photos can and do lie, and the photos being waved around to show Scott Watson "clean shaven" fall into that genre. There are simply too many different witnesses, using high definition eyes, who each independently testified to Watson being unshaven that night. If Guy Wallace and Roz McNeilly recanted their testimony on the basis of these photos, they've been had.

There's a reason for the saying "five o'clock shadow". The phrase describes how fast whiskers grow after a 7am shave. By 2am the next morning you've added a further nine hours on top and it's a whole new grade of shadow.

The words "clean shaven" also mean different things to different people, as we've seen in "clean shaven—but".

A re-analysis of the court testimony shows Guy Wallace—never the strongest witness in the world—was simply bamboozled by clever lawyers waving a photo around, and a prosecution team who evidently lacked the image manipulation experience to expose the flaws in the argument. To be fair, the *Ben & Olivia* book bought into that particular trickery as well.

But the photo, and another one taken onshore, show how carefully you have to consider images against the bigger picture. Many witnesses reported Watson's hair was "longer at the back", almost touching his shoulders. Not so, argued Hunter and the Watson defence team, pointing to some low resolution supermarket surveillance footage from earlier that day.

Look at the supermarket photos more closely, however, and you will notice something: Watson's head is tilted forward in all the shots that matter, which has the effect of raising his hairline at the back to well clear of his collar. Put your own finger on your hairline

---

Simon Cowell looks like he's 'overdone the Botox' say viewers—Darcey Bussell and Victoria Beckham also big HD disappointments" Daily Mail, 15 November 2012, http://www.dailymail.co.uk/femail/article-2233319/Im-A-Celebrity-poser-Helen-Flanagan-named-worst-HD-horror--Darcey-Bussell-Tulisa-Victoria-Beckham-too.html

The Camera Never Lies—Or Does It?

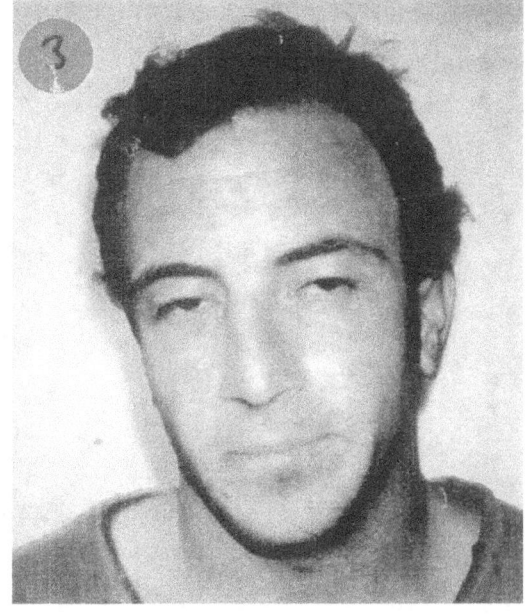

ABOVE: Two versions of the *Cornelia* photo found on the Defence database. The main one is the official evidence photo. The inset version has been lightened and is softer focus than the already low-res main shot. It is not known who edited the photos.
RIGHT: Montage 3, the so called 'blink' photo

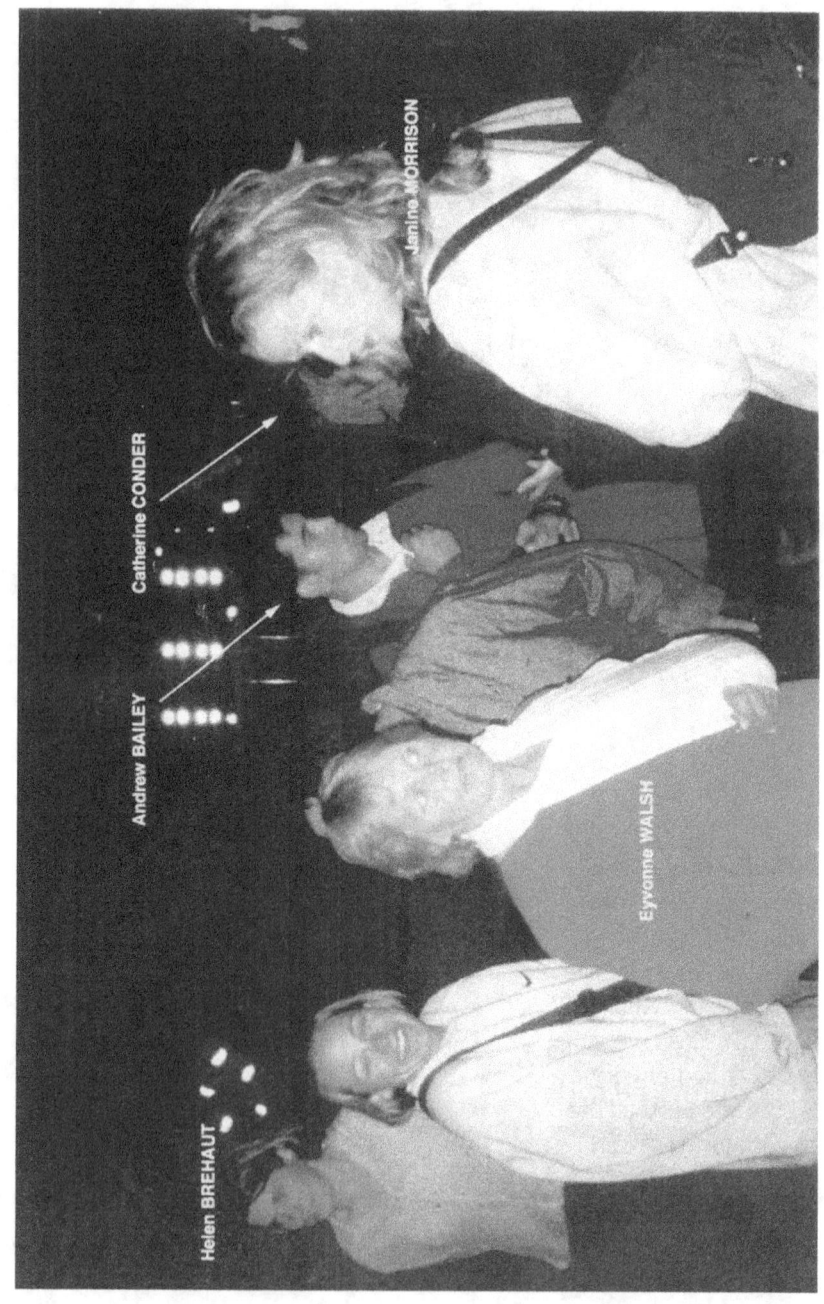

at the back, then tilt your head forward or back: your hairline will alter by up to six or seven centimetres relative to the arc of your neck and the collar of your shirt.

Now think about the implications of that: one witness who sees you tilting your head back while you swig a beer might describe you as having long hair falling to your shoulders. Another seeing you gazing down at your toes a few minutes later will say your hairline was well above your collar. We generally dredge up our memories of what strangers look like from first impressions; we take a mental snapshot and file it away. We could spend ten minutes with someone but when asked to remember them we access that split second first impression when we were mentally sizing them up.

Now look at the second photo taken onshore showing a partially obscured Watson. This photo clearly shows his hair virtually at his collar, in sharp contrast to the supermarket surveillance.

In short, reliance on snapshots without explanation of their technical limitations is crazy.

When Wallace had doubts, the process of comparing notes meant his friends developed them too, as police files indicate.

"Phone enquiry with Rozlyn McNEILLY. Initially contacted at her home address but advised she is working at Furneaux until the weekend.[162] McNEILLY is asked questions regarding her most recent contact with another witness Guy WALLACE.

"She advised that she has had no contact with him since approximately the first weekend in February 1998. On that occasion she finished work at Furneaux she thinks Waitangi weekend (7 8.2.98). She rang WALLACE from her home on the Monday 09.02.98 and he was at Punga Cove at that stage.

"She said it was a call to see how he was doing. McNEILLY said the call was after she had been shown a series of photos by the Police

---

162 40780 / JS / ROZLYN McNEILLY / BM6952 / 210498

and this topic was mentioned in the phone conversation. She said that she had trouble picking out the particular guy.

"McNEILLY states that she has had no contact with Guy WALLACE since that Monday phone call in early February.

"NOTE—Impress upon McNEILLY that as the investigation is entering a critical phase that it is vital that she not compare notes, as it were, with other witnesses. She understands the importance of this and is not expecting any future contact with WALLACE.

"FURTHER NOTE—McNEILLY was shown Montage B by me on 20.03.98 and a statement taken to that effect at the Nelson Police Station."

In fact, in McNeilly's new statement, her second in the case, she identified a picture of Scott Watson as either "that male" or very similar to:[163]

"I have viewed a series of 8 photographs titled Montage B and I identify photograph 3 as being that male or very similar to. The most noticeable thing about him from memory was his eyes which were slanted as appear in the photo. When he was sitting in the bar his eyes were as they are in the photo, slanted and drooping as if he was pissed or stoned.

"The nose appears the same but the hair shown in the photo is shorter than I remember. His lips appear the same—thin as opposed to the other photos.

"I think that the first time I noticed the guy I have described was after midnight. I certainly served him more than five times—it was like he was constantly getting drinks. There was a girl that was near to him that he seemed to be buying drinks for also. She was sort of standing behind him.

"He was drinking doubles and always paid by cash. I've been asked about his voice but I can't recall it. It got to a stage where he

---

163 40587 / ST / ROZLYN McNEILLY / BM6952 / 200398

didn't even have to ask for what he was drinking because I knew.

"I can remember that his hands or fingers were skinny like long and thin. I don't remember seeing his forearms and thought that he had on a dark V necked jersey. I remember thinking that he must have been hot in it.

"He pretty much stayed in the same area while I noticed him in the bar. It was about an hour and a half that I saw him in the bar. After that I didn't see him again."

In 2006, Roz McNeilly retracted her identification of Watson in a dramatic affidavit:

"The police never showed me the photo of Scott Watson that was taken on the yacht named *Mina Cornelia* before he went ashore that evening. The first time I saw this photo was in the book "*Silent Evidence*". The police told me that the man I saw sitting at the bar was Scott Watson. So I believed them. If they had shown me the photo of Scott Watson taken on the yacht *Mina Cornelia* I would have said it was not the same man. I assumed that Scott Watson must have had long hair that night at Furneaux Lodge and must later have cut it short. After the trial I saw for the first time the photo taken on *Mina Cornelia* and realised that the man I saw could not have been Scott Watson.

"I feel used by the police. They have betrayed my trust in them to help convict an innocent man, and it's wrong. I know now that the man I saw at the bar was not Scott Watson and there is an innocent man sitting in gaol."

Roz McNeilly, like all Crown witnesses in a criminal case, was not permitted to see the descriptions other witnesses had given of Watson; for her, like the rest of them, giving evidence was a very lonely place from which it is easy to succumb to doubts. This book is actually the first time since the murders for witnesses, jurors and the public to see the real weight of identification evidence.

It's true Roz was conned, but probably not by the police.

Cameras—and photographs—can lie. They are only as good as their technical limits. The photos of "shaggy" Watson that she identified him from were taken only a week after the disappearance—his hair had not grown three inches in that time, it was just unkempt instead of brushed like it had been on the boat. He was more "clean shaven" because—hello!—men shave every few days when the summer stubble gets scratchy. That's why we have shavers: the whiskers grow back every day.

Nowhere was this simple biological truth ignored more forcefully than when Watson's defence counsel got witness after witness to agree that the mystery man differed from the police mugshots of Watson because the mystery man had more stubble. The mugshots were taken a week after the murders—Watson's state of stubble when the photos were taken is utterly irrelevant as he could have gone through several 'stubble/shave' cycles in that time.

Thus, the *Mina Cornelia* photo falls away as a foundation for an innocence claim. It was one moment in time, one hundredth of a second out of 86,400 seconds that day. If you'd pointed a camera at Watson and shot continuously, that's more than 8.6 million possible images for that day. Which single image best defined him? The one on *Cornelia*, or the one in the bar, drunk and tousled, that nobody took?

Or maybe the one on *Blade* as he sailed away at 5am.

Now, what about the mystery ketch...

CHAPTER ELEVEN

The Mystery Ketch

Perhaps the most perplexing stumbling block in the debate over the Scott Watson case is the existence of the "mystery ketch".

While there are numerous witnesses who saw the "mystery man", there is only one man whose testimony is definite about dropping Ben and Olivia off at a "mystery ketch". Unlike the *Marie Celeste*, this ghost ship described by Guy Wallace has never turned up.

The real question is, was it there? The police infuriated the public across New Zealand with an insistence that a distinctive old fashioned ketch did not exist, despite many people saying they'd seen one. That denial, with no further attempt at explaining their reasoning, allowed a head of steam to build up around this case that has lasted nearly two decades. Surely you cannot find a man guilty of double murder *beyond reasonable doubt* when so many people saw the mystery ketch sailing off into oblivion with a blonde resembling Olivia Hope on the back?

So far the books on this case have given you—especially in the case of *Trial by Trickery*—a carefully edited version of events. Now, you are about to see a different construction of the evidence; one, that, instead of posing questions, answers them.

Officially, four ketches were at Furneaux Lodge for New Year's Eve. Only one matches the description.

The *Alliance* was a 52 foot (16m) old style scow, ketch rigged, with round portholes. Part owner Peter Kennedy told the court the vessel is of steel construction with a white and dark blue hull—the portholes are inside the blue stripe.

"It has the name *Alliance* in gold on both sides of the front bow[164]…The vessel has a distinctive squarish wheelhouse right at the stern. On 30 December 1997 I took the vessel from its Waikawa Marina mooring with a group of mainly family members. We went to Endeavour Inlet on 31 December 1997 arriving at Furneaux Lodge at about 3.00 pm."[165]

This arrival time is consistent with a description given by two witnesses on the launch *Yolande* who saw a ketch heading up Endeavour Inlet towards Furneaux a little after 2pm:[166]

"We had just rounded the corner past Marine Head into Endeavour Inlet," skipper Greg Taylor told police. "The boat was heading into Furneaux the same as us. It was on our left and travelling slowly by motor. It didn't have its sails up.

"I cannot recall if it had two masts but the colour sketch the Police have shown me is a very good likeness. It is the shape of the hull with the wide blue stripe and portholes. It was an older style wooden boat, it was 35 to 40 feet long.

"The shape of the hull is an old design with the stern as a round double end as shown in the Police sketch. The instance that I saw that boat on TV, I knew it was the same one I had seen. I didn't see the boat again after passing it that day. I have never seen the boat

---

164 20344 / ST / PETER KENNEDY / GFD687 / 160198
165 20344D / PETER KENNEDY
166 20188 / ST / GREGORY TAYLOR / CHC045 / 140198

The Mystery Ketch

ELEMENTARY

The Mystery Ketch

before. It was very distinctive to me as it's the old sailing ship design."

Another on *Yolande* who saw it was Bruce O'Malley:[167]

"I can recall seeing an odd looking boat that was in Endeavour Inlet. I can't recall what time it was. I would describe this boat [as an] old antique looking yacht. It was white with blue. It had big huge portals which drew my attention.

"I cannot remember how many masts it had but it definitely looks like the sketch of the boat the Police have shown me. I only noticed that boat the one time."

A police note of their interview of O'Malley adds, "he says it had a blue stripe and some gold on it as well...he said the ketch was at Furneaux for a couple of days."[168]

There was a reason O'Malley saw gold on the mystery ketch—he was actually looking at the gold lettering of *Alliance*, which was indeed at Furneaux for the 31st and the 1st.

It is possible O'Malley not only saw it from *Yolande*, but also from his helicopter. It was an old Army Iroquois with a distinctive 'thwump' from its blades that ricocheted through the Sounds. He had whizzed out of Furneaux to Picton to uplift the rock band for New Year's Eve. Then he had flown out over *Yolande* while it was fishing in Queen Charlotte Sound and buzzed Greg Taylor.

"At about 1.15 pm Bruce came overhead in his helicopter and signalled to me. I knew he wanted me to head back to Furneaux and pick him up," Taylor told police.

For their part, passengers on *Alliance* saw O'Malley's chopper flying over them:

"There was a helicopter coming and going from different parts of the Sounds."[169]

---

167 20182 / ST / BRUCE O'MALLEY / MK8254 / 140198
168 10582 / JS / BRUCE O'MALLEY / 11 JAN 1998
169 30106 / ST / SUSAN CARLSON / DAC529 / 170198

This is a key sighting for both Keith Hunter and Mike Kalaugher, who say *this* was the mystery ketch that police failed to investigate. Hunter makes a huge deal of it, implying police foul play in not calling Taylor or O'Malley to give evidence at trial about the mystery ketch:[170]

"The Crown only called two of the *Yolande* complement to give evidence. They were two of those who had not seen the ketch. The two who saw it, O'Malley and Taylor, were not called by the Crown."

Just as well, for their own sakes. Apparently "veteran investigative television journalist" Keith Hunter[171] did not do his homework with a proper review of the police files. He should have been able to join the dots.

In case there is any lingering doubt that O'Malley and Taylor were watching *Alliance* saunter into Furneaux between 2pm and 3pm on New Year's Eve, consider this. The men only saw one unusual blue and white ketch with portholes and gold lettering. They didn't see another one coming in at the same time. As Sherlock Holmes might say, a process of elementary deduction leads us to conclude that if they only saw one distinctive boat coming in, and we know the *Alliance* arrived at the same time, then what they saw had to be *Alliance*.

Peter Kennedy added that he certainly didn't see a twin of his boat drag-racing him into Furneaux. "For the whole time I was down there I did not see any other boat that resembles ours in either era, style or colour."[172]

Keith Hunter would argue that because the men saw a double end ketch, these must be different boats. It's unlikely for reasons just discussed, and also because the double-ended identikit had been given huge media prominence on TV for a week already and would have influenced hazy recollections. Think back to that car

---

170 *Trial By Trickery*, p130
171 *Trial By Trickery*, back cover
172 20344 / ST / PETER KENNEDY / GFD687 / 160198

or boat you noticed going past last week—what did it really look like? Again, the research shows that where our memories have blank spots the power of suggestion will rapidly fill in the gaps.

Proof that the double-ender issue is a red herring comes from Guy Wallace himself. In a video interview with Mike Kalaugher about the different sketches of the ketch he admitted he hadn't seen the stern and was guessing:

> MIKE KALAUGHER: Right. OK. Um, now, the other thing that changed in the two diagrams was the shape of the stern?
> GUY WALLACE: Yes.
> MIKE KALAUGHER: Now you described how you approached um, approximately from forward, from a forward direction anyway aiming towards amidships approximately.
> GUY WALLACE: Correct.
> MIKE KALAUGHER: And that later on you reversed away and turned around and went around the bow.
> GUY WALLACE: That's right.
> MIKE KALAUGHER: So with your impression of the stern does that denote that you're uncertain about the stern or one or the other is…
> GUY WALLACE: That's right.
> MIKE KALAUGHER: Correct?
> GUY WALLACE: If you have a look at both of them, they are both very different.
> MIKE KALAUGHER: Yeah.
> GUY WALLACE: Um, I've been through it in my mind plenty of times and I can't actually say it was either one or the other.
> MIKE KALAUGHER: Right.

Boatie Peter Thompson was aboard the launch *Hoani* out of Punga Cove in Endeavour inlet when he saw what can only have been the

Alliance. Again, he did not see two such vessels at this time, and it is a matter of record that *Alliance* followed this route to arrive at 3pm:[173]

"At about 2.30-2.45 pm on the 31st of December 1997, my wife, Judith, and I left Punga Cove with Derek and Heather Jones on Derek's boat, the "*Hoani*", a 45 foot launch, to go to Furneaux Lodge. We motored out from the cove towards Furneaux Lodge and I was driving the boat inside the cabin and everyone else was in the cabin with me.

"We were keeping on the left side of the channel as we approached Furneaux and were doing between eight or nine knots. As we approached the area marked on the charts as a reserve, I could see that we were coming up on a vessel which was on the starboard side of us hugging the inlet on the Tawa Bay side.

"I didn't take much notice of it, but Derek pointed it out and said, 'that was that boat that was on TV at Christmas that had just completed a voyage sailing around New Zealand'. We all looked over towards it and there was some conversation about the fact that none of us would feel particularly safe going anywhere in it, let alone right around New Zealand.

"The vessel resembled a Chinese style junk and was a twin-masted ketch with a banana shaped hull and a cabin at the back. It appeared to be mainly black and white in colour. I couldn't see how many people were on board. We passed it still on the left side of the channel, and we pulled up out from the jetty at Furneaux and didn't see it again after that, but by this stage it would have been well amongst the vessels tied up at the head of the inlet."

The boat's deep royal blue stripe probably looked black if the sun was behind the ketch, which it could have been.

As explained repeatedly in this book, the best evidence is usually that collected closest to the event in question. Over months

---

[173] 20781 / ST / PETER THOMPSON / DM7851 / 040298

and years, memories fade or witnesses damage their memories by discussing the case with others or reading other people's accounts to try and put their own fragile recollections in context. That's why in a cold case like this modern memories are usually unhelpful. It's highly likely the witnesses to this day genuinely believe they saw the mystery ketch; the hard evidence however suggests they didn't.

One of *the* key "mystery ketch" sightings of *Trial by Trickery* and *The Marlborough Mystery* thus collapses. Let's have a look at some more.

Another of Hunter's star witnesses on the mystery ketch is Ted Walsh. Walsh was a local.

"On 31 December 1997 about 2.45 pm, returning from Gem Resort, which is in the Bay of Many Coves [just down from Endeavour Inlet]. I passed a ketch coloured white and blue. The blue was a line and was a royal blue colour with round portholes possibly right down the boat and in number 6 to 8. The portholes were within the blue strip.

"I have seen a picture of the boat and I would say that the boat I saw and this are the same, although I saw a lot of roping dangling between staunchions. The blue I saw was darker and wider but other than that similar as the picture.

"I got the impression that there were a lot of people on it and it was coming to Endeavour Inlet.

"I have spoken to other people and the boat that arrived with a lot of people on may have been another one but saying this I saw a number of boats that day and these two were two that stuck out so I can't be certain whether there was one or two.

"Anyhow, when I came back into Endeavour Inlet I recall seeing the ketch I had earlier described just entering the Inlet. I can't recall much about it other than it was the same ketch."

You've probably guessed by now—this was the *Alliance* entering Endeavour Inlet between 2pm and 3pm. It's blue was a deep royal blue, almost mauve, and just like Walsh said the strip was wider than the sketch suggested. The *Alliance* had spent the day fishing in various locations between Gem Resort and as far north as Motuara Island by Ship's Cove. There were eight people on board.[174]

Now watch how Ted Walsh's "mystery ketch" sighting—one we also promoted heavily in *Ben & Olivia* based on the courtroom testimony—crumbles just like the previous one when you examine the original fresh statements instead of relying on the court transcript.

Here's what Ted told police:

"While I was taxiing across the Inlet I noticed the ketch anchored outside Furneaux Lodge. I have viewed a photograph and would describe the anchoring as on photographs 3 and 4. It was a way out on the outer edge.

"I passed the ketch a number of times but can't remember seeing anyone on the ketch moving. I stopped doing the crossings and went home at 02.45 am.

"I suppose I came back over to Furneaux around 10.30 am. I don't recall the ketch being anchored there. If it had been I would have seen it."

Now here's what *Alliance* skipper Peter Kennedy told police about his time of departure:

"We arrived at Furneaux at 1500hrs on the 31.12.97 and left at 1000hrs on the 01.01.98."[175]

And here's what he said about its location:

"There were about 100 other boats there when we got there. We had to drop anchor. We did this about 200 m straight off the jetty."

The same rules of deduction that demolished the Gray/O'Malley sighting also apply to this one. Ted Walsh's mystery ketch was the *Alliance* as well. No one saw two of these vessels arriving at Furneaux in the same time window.

Another witness relied on by Keith Hunter is David McNoe

---

174 20344 / ST / PETER KENNEDY / GFD687 / 160198
175 30686 / JS / WAIKAWA MARINA / RRC916 / 030198

who, while staying at the Pines, took his daughters waterskiing near Furneaux that afternoon:

"While we were doing the water skiing during the afternoon was when I noticed the boat with the portholes along the side. It was the sort of boat that took your eye. I noticed it because it was the only one that had portholes along the side.

"I cannot say positively if it had one mast or two. I remember that it had heaps of rigging on it. It was a predominantly white boat but I couldn't say what other colour was on it. I remember it mainly because of the portholes. It was the only boat that had portholes out of the heaps that were tied up around the area.

"I would describe the boat with the portholes as moored more or less straight off the end of the jetty for Furneaux Lodge. There were a great deal of boats tied up around the area but as I say the one with the portholes sort of stood out."

Straight off the end of the jetty is where *Alliance* was, 200 metres out. McNoe's sighting, mid to late afternoon, corresponds with the scow's known location at that time.

Eyvonne Walsh, Ted's wife, had been physically stationed on the Furneaux Jetty from 4pm onwards. She says around about 8pm or 9pm she happened to notice a distinctive old ketch:[176]

"I stayed on the jetty between about 4.00 pm to 2.30 am or 3.00 am. The only time I left was to go to Furneaux to get a cup of coffee for myself or Ted.

"I remember amongst other things that night seeing an unusual looking ketch in the Inlet. This boat was on anchor, near the Pines area but not that close to the coast line. It was anchored by itself and it looked to me to be in line with the point in the inlet which sticks out and leads to the Pines area. You can see this point clearly from the main Furneaux jetty looking back towards the Sounds.

---

176 20235 / ST / EYVONNE WALSH / JSC422 / 300198

"I would have noticed this boat between 8.00 pm and 9.00 pm. I can't really be sure of the time.

"What made me notice the boat was the back of it. It had old fashioned type rope work which went to a point at the top of the masts. It was clearly visible from the back as you looked at it. I had a white hull with a thick dark blue stripe around it."

Again, the Pines was about a kilometre away. Middle-aged Eyvonne Walsh could probably not have distinguished ropework at anywhere near that distance....but her line of vision from the jetty across to the Pines would have put *Alliance*—200 metres out from the jetty—smack-bang in her view. The boat had pivoted on its anchor in the face of the incoming tide, making its stern visible. Yes, just like the mystery ketch she thought she was describing, the *Alliance* was "anchored by itself".

To argue that she was seeing a second, "mystery ketch" further out, one would have to explain why she would notice the much smaller ornate 'junk' in the distance as opposed to the closer, bigger one which certainly had those same features. In the absence of contrary evidence, that boat she saw was *Alliance*. This will be confirmed shortly, as you will discover.

It is easy to see why this mystery ketch issue developed such a head of steam, however. When detectives were asked in court about these Walsh sightings, instead of doing the donkey work and showing it was *Alliance*, they simply denied the ketch existed:[177]

"The court has heard evidence from Mr Walsh about a boat that he saw in the vicinity of Furneaux Lodge when he was making trips to and from Punga Cove to Furneaux and referred to a large vessel off to the right of this track seen during one of his return journeys around evening, did you have information from Mr Walsh and did you seek to identify a vessel such as that in that area?"

"... yes Mr Walsh was spoken to by the enquiry team and did

---

177 Bruce McLachlan, Trial Notes of Evidence

The Mystery Ketch

indicate that there was a boat of that nature in perhaps the vicinity of either 3-400m to the south of Furneaux jetty through to BBQ point. There were various, the locations seemed to change a wee bit. We concentrated our efforts in that area in speaking with people who had boats of their own in that area and with people that had passed through that area and no other person talked of seeing a boat of that nature."

If the police had gone through the exercise this book does, they could have put the sightings in a proper context. By suggesting no one had seen this ketch, instead of explaining what it clearly was, they left a credibility hole large enough to sail the *USS Nimitz* through, and fuelled public discomfort about the case for nearly two decades.

Alliance had spent every day since 30 December motoring around the Sounds, fishing right as far out as the entrance to Cook Strait. It will have been seen repeatedly by hundreds of different people in different locations. Prior to 3 January when word of the missing couple got out, *Alliance* was irrelevant to most people. Then people began to remember strange places they'd seen it.

"I was wondering whether they are confusing the wanted ketch with mine," *Alliance's* Kennedy told police.[178]

Ted Walsh's sighting is really important to the free Scott Watson campaign, because the argument goes that this ketch has never been identified by police. More significantly, Walsh and some others on his boat saw what he believed was the "same ketch" two days later on 2 January, heading out towards Cook Strait with a blonde teenage girl on the back.

This has become *the* iconic mystery ketch sighting, encapsulating the haunting possibility that it was the last sighting of Olivia Hope alive, heading out into the great unknown. Because of the

---

[178] 40008 / JS / PETER KENNEDY / SM7883 / 090198

courtroom evidence, we treated this sighting uncritically in *Ben & Olivia*. The witnesses thought it was a different boat to *Alliance* and we had no basis for challenging that:[179]

Unlike Ted Walsh, who was skippering *Sweet Release*, Ries doesn't recall seeing anyone aboard. While up on the flybridge, Ries' attention was drawn to the vessel, which he described to the court as an older style yacht, with twin masts.

> He thought to himself it was a pretty old vessel, with the hull having an old sweeping design and a wheelhouse cabin[180] at the rear. The police showed Ries a sketch of a ketch, based on water taxi driver Guy Wallace's description of the boat that he delivered Ben and Olivia to. Ries said the sketch was quite similar to the boat he saw on January 2.

Prosecution lawyers, sticking to the *Alliance* theory even though the *Alliance* was not in that area on that day, showed Ries a picture of *Alliance*. The witness said the boat he saw was different.

In contrast to Ries, Greg Feek who was also fishing on *Sweet Release* can remember seeing wavy blonde hair that looked like that of a woman blowing in the wind. The All Black, just back from a win against South Africa, told the court he was fishing off the stern of the launch, while, "some girls were trying to learn how to fish."

His attention was drawn to the boat by Ted Walsh, and Feek glanced up. He remembers the blonde haired person, but he's unsure now whether it was a male or female. He didn't see anyone else on the vessel. Feek can't remember many details about the boat, and couldn't tell the court if it had masts, or what colour it was.

---

179 *Ben & Olivia*, p140
180 Which is exactly what *Alliance* has, a wheelhouse cabin at the rear.

He does remember a series of holes along the side of the vessel, but with no knowledge of boats or sailing, he was unsure what they were. One of his fishing colleagues asked him what they were, he replied that he thought "they must be for fishing when it was raining". This comment produced a roar of laughter in the court, with most people at least smiling, all except for Scott Watson, who sat staring straight ahead in the dock, his facial expression not changing.

Prosecutor Mark Davies went on, "I don't want to sound like *Playschool* here, but were the holes in the side round or square?"

Feek replied with a smile on his face that they were round and big enough to fit a fishing rod through them. There was also a smile on Feek's face when defence lawyer, Mike Antunovic, asked about the fishing that day, the All Black replied that the fishing was really good, with the blue cod almost jumping into the boat. At end of his evidence Mark Davies wished Feek all the best for the upcoming tri-nations match against Australia.

Here's what Ted Walsh actually told police on 8 January—six days after the sighting:[181]

"We cruised out to the north tip of Ship Cove which is the next bay around. We were anchored up around 10.30 to 11.00 am—the same ketch went past. The range was 50 to 70 metres.

"The ketch was the same one I had earlier seen. The ketch was motoring.

"I observed in the port of the cockpit a female, Caucasian, young-ish—being 15—30 years, long blonde hair—free but very blonde. Clothing unknown. Sitting next to a male, Caucasian, 20—30, short cropped hair. Clothing unknown. Possibly with no shirt on. Both were in a cockpit which appeared to be very small."

---

[181] 10058 / ST / EDWARD WALSH / DH6260 / 080198 / W

Look at the photo of the *Alliance* again:

"There was another male, Caucasian, age unknown but 20 to 35 years," Walsh continued. "Clothing unknown but possibly no shirt on. Walking along on the area forward of the cabin. He was bending over periodically and seemed busy doing something.

"The roping was very heavy and stood out. The male could have been doing something with the ropes.

"The ketch was heading towards Cape Jackson and between Ship Cove and Motuara.

"The swell was about 12 metres and a 25—30 knot northwester and the sea was fair rough. The ketch appeared to be handling it okay through.

"The ketch going by was very distinctive because all the males on my boat commented about wishing they could be on the other because of the blonde. I have viewed a photograph of Olivia Hope and can't say that the female is her. The hair is definitely similar.

"I wrote on the sketch the name 'Astrix', thinking that might have been the name but the more I think about it the more I am not sure it was in fact that.

"The picture is slightly wrong with second mast in front of the cockpit. The cabin went back further and was very small," said Walsh in his 8 January statement.

His wife, Eyvonne, concurred:[182]

"On the boat I saw the cabin port was at the back of the vessel."

You'll recall she had seen a so-called "Chinese junk" at Furneaux while on the jetty:[183]

"I'm pretty sure this boat was the same one I had seen at Endeavour Inlet on New Year's Eve which I have previously described in this statement.

---

182 30627 / ST / EYVONNE WALSH / JFD014 / 050298
183 20235 / ST / EYVONNE WALSH / JSC422 / 300198

"I had a closer look at the boat then. I guess it would have been 50 metres from us.

"It was a ketch, would have been 40 or 45 feet long, bargey looking, the front was quite pointy and the back of it was squarish but not really squared. I would say the back was a bit tapered. It had a cockpit at the back which gave it a Chinese Junk look to me. I could see clearly then that it had a deep blue stripe on a white hull. In the stripe were maybe 5 or 6 round port holes. I noticed the old fashioned rope work on it. The rope work around the hand railing went around the boat in a zig zag pattern. It appeared to be real rope. I noticed the ropes which secured the masts ended by hanging over the hull a small length. It gave it an old fashioned look.

"I guess I would be 90% sure that this yacht was the yacht I saw at Endeavour Inlet on New Year's Eve. It was definitely a sea going vessel. I can't remember a name on the boat but I feel it could have had gold writing on it. I can't be sure of that however.

"The yacht was coming from the Queen Charlotte Sounds, I don't know where it had come from. It was heading towards Cape Jackson," said Eyvonne Walsh to police.

Now, let's deconstruct this sighting based on what a proper analysis of the police files actually reveals. You'll recall that in *Ben & Olivia* we reported the claim made in court that the *Alliance* had not actually been in this area on 2 January. Take a look at this piece of evidence from a police discussion with skipper Peter Kennedy that contradicts that:[184]

"He stated that on 2 January 1998 the *Alliance* left Punga Cove and it was decided to go fishing in the area of Long Island."

Long Island is alongside Motuara Island and Ship's Cove.

"We motored out into Queen Charlotte," police record Kennedy as saying, "and it was a rough lumpy sea and the girls on board did

---

[184] 30945 / JS / PETER KENNEDY / KM5725 / 100398

not like the conditions that much. On the map you have faxed me we travelled out of Endeavour Inlet and headed towards Long Island.

"We would have got out just past the point of Resolution Bay to a point where the letter Q is in the word Queen on the map you have faxed me. At this point we turned around and motored towards Blumine Island. We spent about an hour at the southern tip of Blumine Island fishing."

This is crucial. It reveals *Alliance* began the day steaming to the area where Walsh and his passengers saw "the same ketch", and it is consistent with a 10.30-11am sighting in that location. What are the chances of two identical ketches being in the same small area?

"I only really looked at the boat for a second or two," passenger Kyle Ramsay told police,[185] "and that's when Eyvonne Walsh (wife of skipper) said, 'Oh, look at that Chinese junk'.

"The boat had a big mast at the front and a smaller mast at the back."

Now go back and look at the photo of *Alliance* again: big mast at the front and a smaller mast at the back.

"The raised back was squared off and because of the high back it definitely looked like a junk."

Kyle Ramsay also shoots down those clinging to a rounded "double end" style of mystery ketch like the original identikit:

"I've seen the photograph in the paper of the double ended boat and the one that passed us definitely had the raised Chinese junk style back and not the double ended look."

Passenger Kevin Ries added that the boat was,[186] "about 40' long. Twin masted ketch rear mounted cabin. Was under power, the unusual part was where the cabin was placed at the rear, and the shape of the gunwales. Very old style—like a Chinese junk."

---

185 10433 / JS / KYLE RAMSAY / MR8667 / 220198
186 10763 / ST / KEVIN RIES / GDD779 / 170298

"I only glanced at it briefly. I cannot remember there being anyone on board, or seeing anyone on the deck. My mind was elsewhere."

All Black Greg Feek recalls the direction of the vessel, which is consistent with the *Alliance* testimony:[187]

"This boat came from Scott Point and headed up to Motuara Island. I don't know whether it went between Cannibal Cove and the Island or whether it went the other side of the island.

" I recall seeing a few port holes on the boat. I also saw what I thought was a girl at the back of the boat. The person had long blonde hair, it was quite windy. The boat was at least 100-150 metres away."

For anyone who understands statistical probability, it's probably becoming very clear that it was *Alliance* that Walsh and his passengers saw. For those who don't understand the math, here's why: We've already had the Gray/O'Malley/Walsh sighting of the mystery ketch going into Furneaux mid-afternoon on New Year's Eve. While it is technically possible that an identical boat was heading in at exactly the same time, the odds against that are high. The odds against a *replay* of the same two identical ketches of this type being in the *same* place at the *same* time on a different occasion—so that you end up with a twin-set of sightings but everyone only ever sees one of the boats—are so astronomically high that you probably have a higher chance of being hit by a meteorite.

A principle called Occam's Razor is used to point towards the most likely possibility. William of Ockham was a medieval philosopher who argued that when there are competing scenarios, the one that is simplest, with the least need of extra suppositions, is more credible. In this case, one incredible coincidence of two identical yachts of this description being in the same place is believable, just, but to say it happened twice is not.

No one reported seeing a rounded double-ender stern, they all

---

187 20148 / ST / GREG FEEK / TV8075 / 110198

reported a Chinese junk style boat with a high back and a wheelhouse cabin at the back. The boat had a bigger mast at the front and a smaller one at the rear. They were describing *Alliance*. Ben and Olivia were not on *Alliance*.

Peter Kennedy, the *Alliance* skipper, confirms he recognised Ted Walsh's boat:

"I have also looked at a fax of a boat called the *Sweet Release* you have sent me. I can recall seeing this boat in the Sounds but cannot put a time or date when I have seen this boat."

Kennedy also offers up evidence of who the mystery blonde was that Walsh and his passengers may have seen:

"On board the *Alliance* was my daughter Alisha's friend Hollie Pickering. She is blond haired and aged 14 years. She is very mature looking and looks like a 17 year old girl.

"There were also two other women with blond hair. My sister Debbie who is aged about 40 years and my brother's wife who is aged about 41 years. There were no young males aboard except my brother and myself who are aged 43 and 45 years respectively.

"I cannot recall who was outside on the *Alliance* when we were motoring on the Sounds on the 2nd…I do not recall seeing any other ketches in the area when we were out on the water," Kennedy reported.

Now, Ted Walsh mentioned above that he thought the mystery ketch's name might be *Asterix*. This is a further clue that he was looking at *Alliance* because he had confused its gold lettering with *Asterix* in a previous statement:

"The scow had two masts I think, with a flat back. It was named *Astrix* [sic] with the name written in gold at the back of the scow. The scow had a blue line around it and I believe it is usually moored behind the fuel jetty (Castrol) at Waikawa Bay. The scow was in the inlet from 4.00 pm onwards on 31 December 1997 but I don't know when it left. I never saw anyone on board it".

Walsh had originally said the mystery ketch had gold on it, we know the name *Alliance* was in gold, Walsh says it was the "same ketch" he'd seen at Furneaux, Walsh has transposed *Asterix* in gold, and he recalls the ketch at Ship's Cove being possibly named "*Astrix*". Eyvonne Walsh remembered gold lettering on the back of the "bargey…Chinese junk". This is not rocket science. It was *Alliance* they were all staring at. If this sighting is the strongest evidence of Scott Watson's innocence, God help us.

After fishing at Blumine Island, the *Alliance* began heading for Picton on the afternoon of 2 January. Numerous people appear to have witnessed the distinctive vessel and they all described it as a "Chinese junk" because of its back end:[188]

"On either 1 or 2 January 1998, late in the afternoon, I saw a ketch come into Blackwood Bay. It wasn't under sail. It made a deep sweep through the bay, coming in from the eastern end of Queen Charlotte. We lost sight of it as it went behind Te Huahua Point. I didn't see it leave the bay.

"It stood out. The boat looked a bit like a Chinese Junk ship. It had a lot of rope and washing hanging."

It did leave the bay however, because Penelope Zohrab saw it heading towards Picton further south of Blackwood.

"I did see a ketch that looked like an old Chinese junk. I saw that on the 1st or 2nd of January at about 4pm in Queen Charlotte Sound southwest of Blackwood Bay."[189]

Every sighting of a "Chinese junk" in the police files (and they have all been checked during research for this book) can be reconciled with the known movements of *Alliance*, regardless of what Keith Hunter and Mike Kalaugher have published in their books and documentaries.

Those of you who doubt the logic can take comfort from the

---

188 10352 / ST / JOHN BEATTIE / TFD175 / 210198
189 20651 / ST / PENELOPE ZOHRAB / DCC611 / 020298

advice of Keith Hunter himself, about a sighting of *Blade* at the entrance to Tory Channel. Hunter said you can't have two similar boats in the same place at the same time and only one seen. He was arguing the vessel was actually *Dau Soko*, known to have been in the exact spot at the same time. "The two witnesses on the ferry would have seen them both. They did not. This indicates there was only one boat out in Cook Strait...*Dau Soko*."[190]

As talk of a mystery ketch dominated the media in that first week of 1998, everyone began comparing notes, talking about boats they'd seen, and second-guessing their original recollections. In other words, they muddied the waters beyond recognition.

Proof of this comes from another Ted Walsh statement on 30 January, a month after the disappearance. By this time Walsh has seen pictures of the *Alliance*, talked to others and convinced himself there must have been a different boat.

Walsh returned to his New Year's Eve sighting in the afternoon, telling police he now remembered three boats, not one:[191]

"As I approached Kurakura Point there seemed to be a sea of boats heading the opposite way to me. They were still in Queen Charlotte Sound. Amongst these boats were three distinctive boats which in previous statements and phone discussions with the Police I may have merged their descriptions and confused things.

"One of those boats was the *Alliance*. It has been in the area of the Sounds for awhile and has two masts. It also has round portholes, is painted blue around about six inches above the water right up to the gun whale. It does not really have a cabin, it's more like a strange box on the end of it and I think it is painted white. It is definitely not the ketch I have previously referred to seeing on the 2nd of January 1998.

---

190 *Trial By Trickery*, p193
191 10786 / ST / EDWARD WALSH / JFD014 / 300198

"In a statement I made to the Police over the phone I referred to a boat called the *Asterix* with its name written in gold, having a blue line around it and being moored at the right of another boat called the *Nugget*. This statement was made (J/S 08.01.98) in response to the Police asking about ketches moored at Furneaux. At the time I spoke with Police I didn't know the name of the ketch. Having more information available to me now I believe this ketch was in fact the *Alliance*.

"The second distinctive boat I saw off Kurakura Point was one that I have previously referred to as having 20-30 people aboard (J/S 7.1.98). All I remember about this vessel was that it was mainly white, there was something about it that made it stick in my mind. I can't tell you whether it had one mast or two and I don't know its name. I assumed because of the number of people, that it was going to the celebrations at Furneaux but I don't recall seeing it again or where it moored. It was just another boat. This boat was not the vessel I have previously referred to sighting on 02.01.98."

There are two boats entering Endeavour Inlet at that time that had large numbers of young people on. One was white, carrying Olivia Hope and her sister. It was named *Tamarack*. It arrived at Furneaux after the *Alliance*. There was also the large blue and white yacht *Frenzy* which had more than 30 people on board which motored out to Endeavour Inlet at this time.

"We stopped at a bay on the way for the kids to have a swim then continued on.[192] We then did a circle around the yachts at Furneaux and past the jetty before dropping the kids off at a bay a short distance away from Furneaux. Once we had dropped the kids off we went over to Punga Cove."

Sighting explained.

Now returning to Walsh's new claims, here's where Walsh tries to

---

192 11269 / ST / JOHN EGDEN / MK8254 / 230198

convince himself that there were indeed two virtually identical old style ketches, when he starts talking about a "third" boat:

"The third distinctive boat I saw off Kurakura Point was similar to *Alliance* but older, not with a flat bottom. It was similar colour to *Alliance* but the blue line did not go all the way up to the gun whales. It had similar portholes, it had a little cockpit at the back which was not a cabin. Just in front of the cockpit was a very low lying dodger, the opening where people would walk down below. I can't say how many masts it had but I seemed to have the impression of two, although I can't remember two booms. There was a handrail all around this boat which had thick rope hanging from it. The rope appeared to be old. There was also rope hanging from a mast. This rope gave me the impression that someone knew what they were doing, it also made it distinctive. I can't remember anything about any people on board.

"I previously had told Police that I thought this boat moored at Furneaux around 4.00 pm on the 31.12.97. I now can't say exactly when it came in but it definitely was there at 7.00 pm. I passed it on my first trip out, it was moored up on the Furneaux side of Barbeque Point. I can't think or remember anything more about this boat other than thinking "it's arrived". My wife Eyvonne has since referred to this as the 'Chinese junk' and I believe this is an appropriate description.

"In my earlier statements to Police these three boats have merged and the descriptions I have given were confused. However the 'Chinese junk' was definitely the boat I saw on the 02.01.98.

"When I passed these three boats I would have been relatively close between 50–100 metres.

"I have just been shown again the artist drawing of a ketch. I can't say yes or no if this is the boat I refer to as the 'Chinese junk'. Similar things include the blue line and portholes under the gun whale and the heavy handrail.

"Things that are different include the fact I can't say for sure there were two masts, the dodger was further back, the cockpit was a lot smaller on the 'Chinese junk' and there was more ropes on it. I am unsure about the rounding of the back but the artist's impression of a long boat whereas my thoughts of the 'Chinese junk' was being shorter."

Asked to compare the 'Chinese junk' he'd seen anchored at Furneaux, which we now know to be *Alliance*, and the boat that went sailing past near Motuara Island on 2 January, Walsh was certain:

"This was definitely the boat I have referred to earlier in this statement as the 'Chinese junk'. I admit that when I previously spoke with Police I may have confused and merged descriptions regarding boats I saw on the 31.12.97 but I am definite on the sighting on 02.01.98.

"The 'Chinese junk' was travelling at about 6-7 knots, slowish and had no sails up. It was at a distance where you can see a person but not make detail out…The boat went past and we carried on fishing, it was just another boat.

"I have just viewed a photo of two boats one red/brown before 1 January 1998 and one blue after 1 January 1998 [*Blade*]. This was definitely not the boat, which I have referred to in this statement as the 'Chinese junk'."

No, it definitely wasn't Scott Watson's *Blade*, it was *Alliance*, just before it rounded and went back because of the rougher seas coming in.

It follows as elementary that the "blonde" Walsh and everyone saw from between 80 to 150 metres away was either 14-going-on-17 Holly Pickering or one of the two blonde 40 year old women on the boat.

It follows as elementary that the most celebrated "mystery ketch" sighting of all turns out to be innocent and irrelevant, and if you are still struggling to believe that then please consider one last piece of circumstantial evidence: let's assume it *was* the mystery ketch with Ben and Olivia on the stern, or even just Olivia. It is 36 hours since you have been abducted. You have a policy of always letting your mum know where you are. If you are in danger, you would be looking for opportunities to escape and raise the alarm. So you are acutely aware of another big vessel nearby. Why would you not simply leap off the side with a scream, knowing you would get the attention of a powerful launch more than capable of outrunning the ketch you are on?

Alternatively, if you are the kidnapper, why in God's name would you have your hostages up on deck in plain sight of other vessels in broad daylight? Surely the risk would be immense.

No, for all of the above reasons, no one jumped or screamed because it wasn't Olivia and Ben. If the prosecution had sold this better at trial and spent time really nailing this down, they could have avoided three major books based on this mystery ketch sighting.

One of those books, however, is built on the premise of a different mystery ketch. Could it be the one?

CHAPTER TWELVE

Another Ketch Bites The Dust

In his 2001 book *The Marlborough Mystery*, Mike Kalaugher makes a huge deal of a mystery ketch parked out beyond a vessel called *Sea Shanty*. Mike is not an investigative journalist by trade, he's a yachtie who after hearing the evidence at trial had the same doubts we had when we published *Ben & Olivia*.

Given his lack of professional investigative training, he cannot be subjected to the same level of criticism as Keith Hunter, who arguably should have done a much more professional job than has been displayed in *Trial by Trickery*.

In Mike's case, he bases his thesis on the evidence of a passenger on *Sea Shanty*, Yvonne Lloyd. Let's see what she actually told police:[193]

"On New Year's Eve we arrived in Endeavour Inlet at about 4.00 pm. There was the four of us on our boat/launch (it's diesel powered) called the *Sea Shanty*.

---

193 20510 / ST / YVONNE LLOYD / AJ7598 / 010298

"On the *Tamarack* there were lots of idiotic things going on. They all appeared to be drunk. Girls were screaming out and guys yelling. Guys were swinging from the beam that goes across between the masts. The language was less than desirable. A couple of guys were thrown overboard.

"They had this contraption where beer would be poured through a rubber hose into a drinking bowl at the end of it. It appeared that they had to drink as fast as they could before it exploded. As soon as it exploded and sprayed everywhere it was the next person's turn.

"There were complaints from other boats. I heard someone from another boat yell out "Watch your language". *Tamarack* then pulled up their anchor and moored further out past the boats because they were upsetting people.

"After the *Tamarack* had moored we decided that we would pull up anchor too. We just cruised very slowly up and down through the boats while my husband got the anchor ready. We finally dropped it quite a way out. I have been shown a photo montage which shows the final resting place of the *Sea Shanty*. We could see the *Tamarack* but we were quite a way from it. We had distanced ourselves.

"At about 10.30 pm, I remember that because someone looked at their watch and said, "It's 10.30 pm already—we better get to Furneaux". Everyone got tidied up—they called up the water taxi from Furneaux.

"After everyone had gone it left me and my two grandchildren on board. I put them to bed and started to clean the boat up.

"I could hear the midnight countdown from Furneaux. It was so loud. I knew that it was midnight. After the countdown there was a whole lot of fireworks let off and lots of boat horns. After midnight I listened to some music and watched the fireworks and just watched what was going on in other boats. There were parties on other boats.

"I had a watch on and we have clocks on the boat. Robin and

the others had said that they would be back by 1.00 am and to keep the music going. I remember knowing that it was 1.00 am either by my watch or clock and thinking that they hadn't come back yet. I was kind of disappointed.

"I made myself a cup of coffee. I turned the music off and also turned off the boat lights except for a navigation light. I then sat on the back of the boat. The boat had turned around on the anchor and the back of the boat was facing Furneaux Lodge.

"I sat there in the dark. It was quite dark because we were quite a way out.

"I just sat there and listened to the music from the other boats and from Furneaux Lodge. There was some songs being played from Furneaux over and over again. I can't remember what that song was.

"I was sort of getting a bit drowsy at this stage. I was sitting in a chair with my feet up on the table.

"At about 1.30 am I heard a noise in the water. I was facing Furneaux and the noise came from behind and to the right-hand side of me. I had a feeling that it was another boat and I was just making sure that it wasn't too close to us. I wanted to make sure that he could see us.

"I looked around the side of *Sea Shanty* and I saw in the water not far from us a big boat. To me it looked like a big launch. It was all in darkness except for what appeared to be lights that went up across and down a mast. They were like an arch. From what I could see it was quite a big flash boat. There were no other lights on the boat. It was all in darkness. The portholes were in darkness. I'm pretty sure they were round portholes.[194]

"There was no noise coming from the boat at all. The portholes were quite high and that made me think that it was a boat with a cabin on it.

---

194 It wasn't a ketch, it was *Swift n Sure*, 20350 / ST / DEAN BENSON / LC8773 / 070298

"It was dark and I could see the boat. I do remember that I went and got my glasses to have a closer look because I remember thinking what a lovely boat. It was pitch black out there.

"While I was still looking at the boat, that's when I heard the water taxi start up at the jetty. I saw the water taxi come out from the jetty. I don't know what water taxi it was. The water taxi went past the back of our boat while I was sitting there. It went over in the direction of where I saw the boat. I didn't get up and have a look.

"It was only a matter of minutes later when I saw it go past our boat again towards Furneaux. I saw it go in the direction of the Furneaux jetty.

"As it went past our boat I heard two distinct male voices. I assume that there were only two people on the dinghy because I only heard the two voices. I couldn't hear what they were saying. There was nothing unusual about the voices I heard. I didn't notice any accents or anything like that.

"After the dinghy had gone past I thought it was strange that only one person had got off such a big boat assuming that he had come from that one.

"Being nosy like I am I got up and had another look. That's when I saw a second boat there. By there I mean over where I had seen the other one, behind and to the right. It was very close to the other one. It could have been rafted to it.

"I got quite a surprise when I saw it there. It was on the other side of the big boat away from our boat.

"I can't really describe it except that it was a long and low boat. It would have been a yacht not a launch. It was long and low. I could just see it behind the other one. I got the impression that they were rafted together because when the big boat moved so did that one. They seemed to move together.

"The water taxi could have gone to the second boat. I only saw it go in the direction of the boats and didn't see it after that. I remember thinking that they had picked the person up quickly as though the person had been waiting. I thought that he must have radioed ahead.

"There were no lights on the second boat that I could see.

"I then went to bed and left the back of the boat open for my husband. I had a reading torch and I was laying in my bed reading. Then I heard my husband's voice and heard him coming on board. I looked at my watch and it said 1.45 am.

"Robin got back to the boat not that long after the two boats had arrived. He came in a water taxi. I said to him did you see the people going in on the water taxi. He said he hadn't. I told him that two boats had come in while he was away and that it was an odd time for them to come in after all the festivities were over."

Yvonne Lloyd's sighting is interesting. She had not been drinking, so she had an instant advantage over some of the other people floating around Furneaux. However, there's room for confusion. Behind and to her right was actually a chartered fishing boat called *Swift n Sure*, which arrived at Furneaux just before midnight and radioed for a water taxi. The jetty was too busy to send a taxi out, so the people on *Swift n Sure* used their own dinghy to row ashore in two trips, past *Sea Shanty*. They didn't get to the Lodge until closer to 1am.

Lloyd does not mention the arrival of *Swift n Sure*, but it was in the position she claimed to have seen the vessels. Behind it and further out was not a yacht but a launch called *Aquareen II*. Neither of these vessels report seeing any other craft in their immediate vicinity.

Now, according to Guy Wallace, Roz McNeilly and Chey Phipps who'd been working the bar, the "mystery man" had been at the bar since shortly after 10pm. Ergo, he cannot have arrived on any boat that arrived late at Furneaux Lodge.

According to Yvonne Lloyd, the boats she was talking about pulled in around 1.30am. That makes it even less likely that they had any connection to the mystery man. Secondly, she described one as a launch and the other as long and low, probably a yacht. We can't be certain because it was pitch black. Was she really looking at a yacht in the distant darkness, or just the silhouette of *Aquareen II*?

It is possible that she misapprehended what she was seeing in the dark, so that when she awoke she did not recognise *Swift n Sure* or *Aquareen* as the vessels she had actually glimpsed.

By the time it reached trial, Yvonne Lloyd had revised her feelings about two vessels:[195]

"Could you see this boat particularly well?

"... No, we were quite a way out and it was pitch black. I could see the outline of the boat and I couldn't tell you the colour but I could tell you a few descriptions about it."

"Was this boat just on its own?"

"... No."

"What was in association with this boat?"

"... It had another small boat rafted up to it."

"When you say another small boat rafted up to it can we take it from that this 2nd boat was smaller than the other boat?"

"... Lower in the water."

Yvonne Lloyd said the first boat was definitely a launch, and it had a row of mast lights running up and down:

"There would have been probably about, looking at about 20 maybe, 10 up one side and 10 down the other," she told the Court.

"As I understood your description that you gave then and give now, a launch type boat with this mast type arrangement?"

"... Correct."

"There was nothing to suggest to you for example a 2nd mast?"

"... I did not see a 2nd mast."

"You told us your impression of the 2nd boat with it, but you

---

195 Yvonne Lloyd, Trial Notes of Evidence

couldn't tell us anything about that other than there seemed to be something there with it or behind or beyond it in some way?"

"… that's correct."

Lloyd confirmed she saw a "small low boat rafted up to it" on the launch's starboard side.

Of course, maybe a yacht did slip in under cover of that early morning darkness, but the odds against it being a ketch (based on the statistical distribution of ketches to other vessels at Furneaux) were 25 to 1. Additionally, it would have to be crewed by one—at most two—people, and the latter option would require conspiracy. Thirdly, they would have to have a criminally psychopathic personality, at odds of around 100 to 1. Fourthly, even if all these unlikely ducks lined up, you couldn't get past the hurdle that put the mystery man in the Lodge long before midnight. Fifthly—and this is what kills the relevance of Yvonne Lloyd's sighting, the "small low boat" was on the wrong side to have been the vessel approached by Guy Wallace. Wallace, Morresey and Dyer all reported approaching a yacht on its port side, but this one's port side was occupied by a hulking great launch.

The mystery ketch out beyond *Sea Shanty* theory bites the dust like all its predecessors.

Murder cases are nearly always based on probabilities. The civil test in court is actually called "balance of probabilities"—is it more likely than not that "X" happened? Criminal cases require a higher burden of proof than a mere 51/49 balance. Building a defence on the basis of a mystery boat not even properly seen, coming in after 1am, is such a longshot that you'd have a much better chance of picking a Melbourne Cup winner by throwing a dart at the names of horses on a board.

Now, for reasons which will also become abundantly clear, you are going to see why there was actually no "mystery ketch" at all—it was a figment of Guy Wallace's tired imagination. There's no need to run through any more ketch sightings (although for the sake of research we did look at all of them), if the ketch story is actually a distraction.

This is where the rubber hits the road: why did Guy Wallace tell everyone he saw a ketch when he actually did not?

CHAPTER THIRTEEN

Wallace Waffles

It's all very well having huge numbers of ketch sightings, but they are only relevant if in fact Ben and Olivia were dropped off at a mystery ketch. If they weren't, then all of those ketch sightings and discussions on Facebook pages are meaningless.

They can also soak up unwarranted attention and resources. There was a statement taken from one witness for example, right at the very end of February, eight weeks after New Year's Day. He told police this, and it was an example raised by Watson's defence lawyers of a ketch never traced:[196]

"At about 8.00am on New Year's day I was the only one up having breakfast. I noticed a boat leaving the inlet [Tawa Bay, just down from Furneaux and across from Punga]. It was a double-masted boat but was a light green colour with a white cab. It was low to the water and towing a white dinghy. I noticed it as it looked junkie. I

---

196 30504 / ST / STEVEN MARSHALL / ST / JRD703 / 270298

don't remember anybody on the deck.

"At about 10.00am we left Tawa Bay and went to Ship Cove. It took us until about 1.00pm. It was very windy."

At first glance this looks exactly like a mystery ketch—albeit the wrong colour—sneaking out of Furneaux on New Year's morning, unaccounted for by police. Watson's lawyers beat up police officer Bruce McLachlan over the failure to identify this ketch.

The clue to this sighting being wrong however is in the second paragraph. New Year's day was fine and the sea calm, with a breeze between five and 15 knots according to a meteorology report.[197] It was 2 January that high 30 knot winds howled in making it hard for the *Alliance* to sail out towards Cook Strait, meaning it was probably 2 January that this Tawa Bay sighting took place.

"I remember that the 1st of January was a nice day and there were plenty of boats around," *Sweet Release* skipper Ted Walsh told police, "but the 2nd was a not so good day and there wasn't many boats around at all."[198]

In fact, the *Alliance* had been in Tawa Bay on 1 January, had spent that night just across the inlet at Punga Cove, and had slipped out of Punga past Tawa Bay early on the morning of 2 January heading out into the sound.

You could chase ketch sightings till the cows came home in this investigation, but to what purpose?

When push comes to shove, *only one witness has insisted from the outset that a mystery ketch is involved.* That witness is Guy Wallace. He, and he alone, is responsible for the ketch theory. If he is wrong, then the free Scott Watson campaign loses its biggest weapon.

Let's reacquaint ourselves with the evolution of Guy Wallace's thought process regarding the boat he took the couple to.

---

197 13565/LTR/CHRISTOPHER WEBSTER/RR5348/301098
198 20473/ST/EDWARD WALSH/PMC692/140598

GW, 3 JANUARY 1998, statement one[199]

Before I dropped them off on this other yacht I asked both of them if they were okay with that because they didn't know the guy.

It was a timber ketch with round portholes. It was blue and white and really old. It had a blue stripe on it which was really dark blue. I think it was moored just starboard of the jetty. Looking at the map it would have been next to the *Spirit of Marlborough*.

GW, 3 JANUARY 1998, statement two[200]

"I have just seen a video of boats at the Furneaux and I'm pretty sure the boat I dropped the people off on is next to the *Spirit of Marlborough*. The guy off the boat was not the owner. I remember asking him and he said that he was just crewing.

"The people that came off the *Tamarack* asked if there was any place to stay and the other guy said they could bunk down with him and that's how they got to be on his ketch.

"I'd say the ketch was about 38-40 ft long. I'm pretty sure it had two masts. It had quite a low cabin in the middle. I remember the side had a very thick railing on it. It was white on the bottom then through the middle it had a very dark blue strip and then it was white on top. I remember there were a lot of ropes hanging around by the cabin. I'm not sure how many portholes there were but they were round."

So, in the first 48 hours, when his memory is freshest, Guy Wallace reckons it was a timber ketch, white hull, blue stripe, white cabin.

---

199 10861 / JS / GUY WALLACE / ASD279 / 030198
200 10859 / JS / GUY WALLACE / ASD279 / 030198

Lots of ropes hanging by the cabin. Round portholes. But although he calls it a ketch he is not certain it has two masts. If it only has one mast, it's not a ketch.

The problem for Wallace is that his memory of this boat is too detailed. It's as if he's plucked it out of a memory bank from another occasion. Here's why: it was pitch black, around 4am. Although witnesses talk of seeing the moon, they may as well not have—lunar charts show only a tiny sliver of the moon was visible on the morning of 1 January 1998.

In terms of lighting, Furneaux staffer Rachael Veitch told police that the jetty the water taxis were operating from had the kind of lights that made it impossible to see colours properly,[201] which could explain why Wallace thought the mystery man was wearing a "light green" denim Levis shirt. More to the point, however, the light did not travel very far:

"In darkness, once the Inflatable was approximately 10ft off the end of the "floater" [floating jetty] you couldn't see it and the inflatables weren't showing any lights. Veitch advised that during the night most boats had left on their mast lights and when people would call up asking to be picked up from their boats she would tell them to turn on their navigation lights, which were on either side of the vessel."

Wallace is expecting people to believe that in pitch darkness, with virtually no moon, and no light on board, that he could tell this boat was a ketch, that it had not just a blue stripe but a dark blue stripe (instead of green, red or black) and that it had lots of rope around its cabin area. He was also able to determine a length of 38 to 40 ft, when visibility even with light was only a few metres.

If Guy Wallace had a photographic memory, you might cut him some slack. But he doesn't. In fact, his memory throughout this investigation was appalling.

20113597 / JS / RACHAEL VEITCH / BM6952 / 121098

The only credible explanation for such a ketch description at the absolute darkest point of the entire night, is that Wallace was mixing up his memories of another vessel he had seen in daylight, superimposing a real ketch onto his memory in the dark.

How could that happen? The power of suggestion. What if the mystery man had in fact said to him, "Any chance of a ride out to my ketch?"

Funnily enough, it's exactly the kind of thing Scott Watson had been saying in the Furneaux bar only a couple of hours earlier:

"The guy told me he had a yacht. He said it was the only double-masted ketch yacht at Furneaux. He didn't say much more about it to me," Ollie Perkins remembered Watson boasting.[202]

Geoff Hall, who spent New Year's Eve afternoon drinking with Watson on the *Unicorn* also recalled:

"He said he was a boat builder, and that he had built his own ketch."[203]

Amanda Egden, accosted in the bar by a drunk Watson wanting her to come on a trip to Tonga on his yacht in exchange for sexual favours, also said he boasted of having a ketch—pretty close in size incidentally to the mystery ketch:[204]

"Milly asked the guy what his yacht was called in front of me. He said 'Whatever you want sugar.' He told us the yacht was 30-40 foot, but I don't recall exactly what length. he said it was the only double-masted ketch in the bay that night. He also said he was from Wellington…he said his name was Scott, he didn't say his last name."

So what are the odds? We have a psychopath prone to violence, and rape and murder fantasies, drunk and on drugs, with a Jekyll and Hyde personality, matching the description of the mystery man, and boasting to all and sundry that he had "a double-masted

---

202 10120 / ST / OLIVER PERKINS / AHD181 / 080198
203 20088D / GEOFFREY HALL
204 10184 / ST / AMANDA EGDEN / AHD181 / 120198

ketch" in the bay. And we have a very suggestible water taxi driver convinced in pitch darkness that he went to a "ketch" where a rape and murder played out.

We'll return to the evidence shortly that proves Guy Wallace is prone to having his memories manipulated, but first let's continue with the evolution of the story. Although Wallace is doing media interviews all over the place, his next statement to police is two days later. New detail is called [NEW] while added detail to comments made in earlier statements is called [EXTRA]:

GW, 5 JANUARY 1998[205]

Ben was pretty quiet. I can't recall him saying much. He thanked me very much for getting them off the boat. [NEW]

When Olivia got on the Naiad the other passenger I had told her to come and sit by him. [NEW] That was just for balance of the boat.

Olivia asked me about accommodation, words to the effect, "Is there anywhere left to stay?" I told her there wasn't and this other guy piped up and said, "You can stay on my boat but he can't". It was said jokingly with no malice.

By that stage we were well on the way over to the ketch.

When we left the "*Tamarack*" I kept asking this guy where he was going and he said, "To the ....". I can't remember the name he said. [NEW]

He kept saying, "Over that way, over that way". It was straight ahead in the direction the boat was going and that was back towards the jetty. [EXTRA]

As we were getting closer to where the boat was, this guy pointed to it and there was a group of four or five boats rafted up. [NEW]

---

205 10017 / ST / GUY WALLACE / ASD279 / 050198 / W

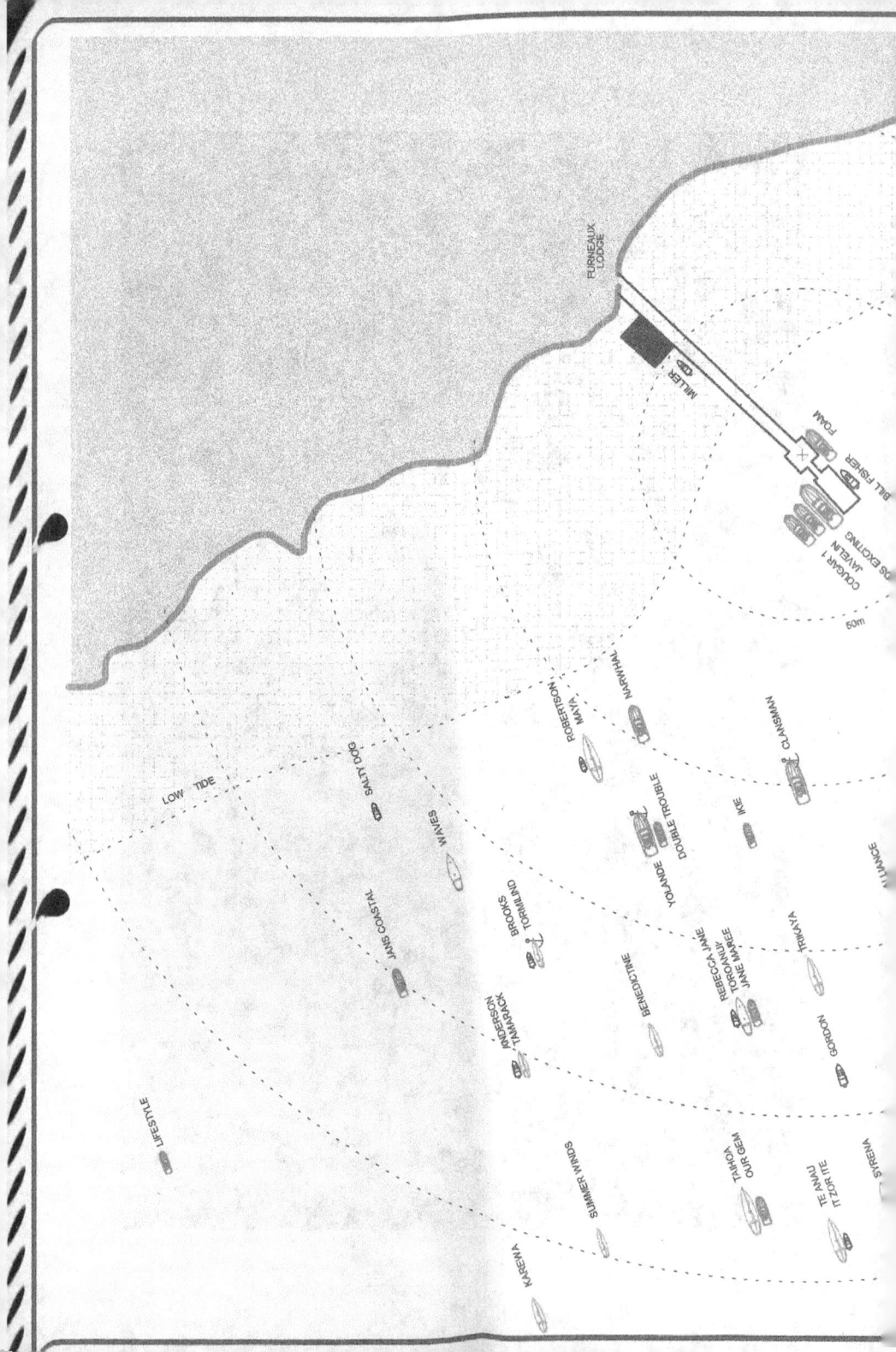

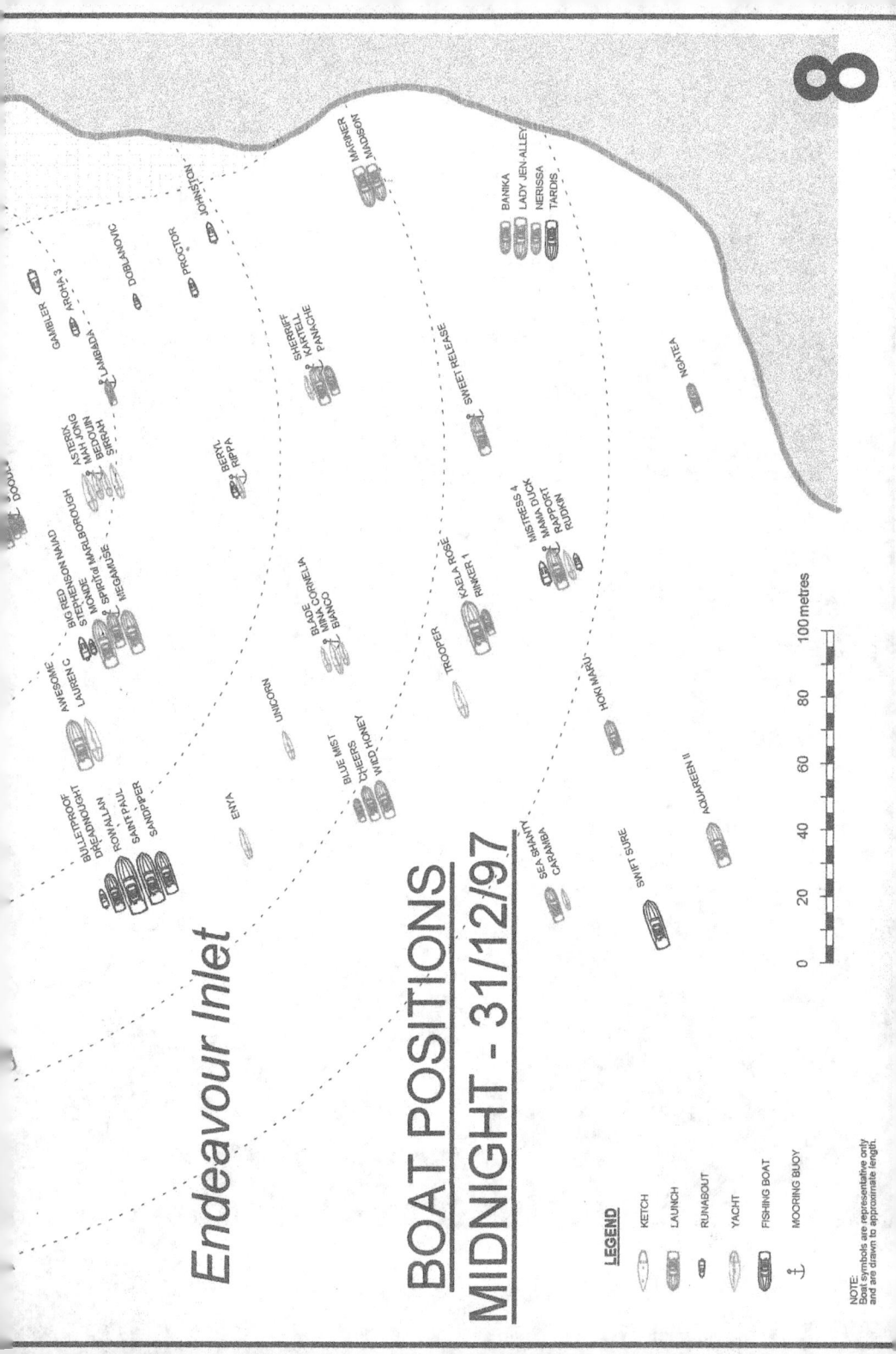

#	Name	#	Name	#	Name
1.	N/A	21.	ENYA	41.	BILL FISHER
2.	N/A	22.	BIANCO	42.	N/A
3.	N/A	23.	MINA CORNELIA	43.	N/A
4.	N/A	24.	WINSOME	44.	N/A
5.	N/A	25.	DREADNOUGHT	45.	TAIHOA
6.	N/A	26.	ROWALLAN	46.	KAREWA
7.	RUDKIN	27.	SAINT PAUL	47.	SUMMER WINDS
8.	RAPPORT	28.	N/A	48.	JANE MAREE
9.	MAMA DUCK	29.	N/A	49.	TOROANUI
10.	MISTRESS 4	30.	SYRENA	50.	BENEDICTINE
11.	TARDIS	31.	N/A	51.	TRIKAYA
12.	NERISSA	32.	AWESOME	52.	ALLIANCE
13.	LADY JEN-ALLEY	33.	LAUREN C	53.	ORANUI
14.	BANIKA	34.	RIPPA	54.	NUGGET
15.	BLUE MIST	35.	THE SHERRIFF	55.	BEAU DOR RELL
16.	WILD HONEY	36.	KARTELL	56.	N/A
17.	CHEERS	37.	PANACHE	57.	MONDE
18.	KAELA ROSE	38.	MARINER	58.	SPIRIT OF MARLBOROU
19.	RINKER	39.	N/A	59.	N/A
20.	SWEET RELEASE	40.	N/A	60.	TITIRANGI

KEY TO INDEX:

BLACK: Vessels present 6 a.m. 01/01/98 – as recorded in Photo Exhibit 52

YELLOW: Vessels departed prior to Photo Exhibit 52

- 61. WET MINK
- 62. ANNA
- 63. DICKSON RUNABOUT
- 64. STROPHE
- 65. MOONSHINE
- 66. TAUTANE
- 67. LIFESTYLE
- 68. JANS COASTAL
- 69. WAVES
- 70. YOLANDE
- 71. DOUBLE TROUBLE
- 72. CLANSMAN
- 73. IKIE
- 74. TAMARACK
- 75. TORMILIND
- 76. N/A
- 77. MAH JONG
- 78. BEDOUIN
- 79. N/A
- 80. CAPPY
- 81. STEPPING STONE
- 82. DOODLUM
- 83. LAMBADA
- 84. SALTY DOG
- 85. N/A
- 86. N/A
- 87. FURNEAUX NAIADS x 3
- 88. FOAM
- 89. N/A
- 90. THE GAMBLER
- 91. LJ
- 92. JOHNSTON RUNABOUT
- 93. TROOPER
- 94. BERYL
- 95. REBECCA JANE
- 96. ANDERSON RUNABOUT
- 97. STARKEY RUNABOUT
- 98. BONIFACE RUNABOUT
- 99. STEPHENSON NAIAD
- 100. BULLET PROOF
- 101. MADISON
- 104. PROCTOR RUNABOUT
- ENDURA
- 108. REVENGE
- 109. PROCTOR RUNABOUT
- 110. RB
- 111. MEGAMUSE
- 112. BLADE

ELEMENTARY

#	Name	#	Name	#	Name
3.	HOKI MARU	25.	DREADNOUGHT	50.	BENEDICTINE
15.	BLUE MIST	26.	ROWALLAN	52.	ALLIANCE
17.	CHEERS	31.	GORDON RUNABOUT	54.	NUGGET
18.	KAELA ROSE	32.	AWESOME	69.	WAVES
21.	ENYA	33.	LAUREN C	70.	YOLANDE
23.	MINA CORNELIA	49.	TOROANUI	71.	DOUBLE TROUBLE

#	Name	#	Name
72.	CLANSMAN	85.	ROBERTSON RUNABOUT
73.	IKIE	86.	MAYA
74.	TAMAiTACK	87.	FURNEAUX NAIADS x 3
75.	TORMILIND	88.	FOAM
76.	ASTERIX	93.	TROOPER
83.	LAMBADA	95.	REBECCA JANE

96.	ANDERSON RUNABOUT
97.	STARKEY RUNABOUT
113.	NGATEA

OP TAM Photo Exhibit 52 - BAMFORD

Furneaux moorings at 0600 hrs on 01.01.98   #26

I remember Ben saying, "Please say that's it". [NEW] Ben was referring to a big Markline that was there. [NEW] This other guy said, "No, but it's tied next to it if that helps". [NEW] Ben said something like, "No worries, that's cool". [NEW]

The bow of the ketch was pointing to the shore and I came port side on. I was pulling up at his port side—port to port. I was facing away from the shore. [EXTRA]

Olivia got on first, then Ben and he got on last. [NEW] I remember Olivia saying, "This is really nice of you. Are you sure there's enough room?" [NEW] His reply was something like, "Yeah, heaps". [NEW]

That's when I asked if Ben and Olivia were all right with this and they said, "Yeah". Then it was Happy New Year and away I went back to the jetty.

I saw Olivia and Ben and this other guy get on the ketch but I didn't see them go down below. [NEW]

The "*Tamarack*" was anchored about 80—100 m portside of the jetty. I refer to the port as being the side when you face the jetty from the water. It was probably 50—60 m out from shore. [EXTRA]

The ketch was just on the starboard side of the jetty. It was close to the jetty but I wouldn't want to say how close. [EXTRA]

From the jetty to the "*Tamarack*" would have taken me four to five minutes and from the "*Tamarack*" to the ketch would have taken me about the same time. [NEW]

The ketch I would describe as a timber ketch, about 38—40 foot. It's what I would describe as a typical old ketch design. I'd say it's designed in the '60's era. It was white with a dark blue stripe running along the side above the waterline. It had round portholes which were below the deck. I'm not sure how many but I think 5—7 per side. [NEW] I'm not sure if the portholes went through the blue stripe. [EXTRA] It had a bulbous transom (refer sketch). [NEW] A transom is the stern of the boat—where the stern leaves the water. The ketch had heaps of ropes on it. Even though it was old it was very well maintained. It had a flexi side rail with staunchions running along the side. [NEW]

The buffing strip was blue and was chipped. [NEW]. This runs along the length and is located above the deckline.

There were brass surroundings on the portholes. [NEW] There appeared to be no activity on board. [EXTRA]

After I dropped them off I went back to the jetty and I tied up. Two guys came down to the jetty and I took them out to a private vessel that was moored by the fishing trawlers. It was a yacht with an unusual name. I remember laughing about the name.

I then went back to the jetty, tied up, pulled the fuel tank out. I saw a guy standing on the floating jetty and he asked to go out to the fishing trawler built in Bluff.

GW, 6 JANUARY 1998[206]

When I took Olivia and Ben and the other guy out to the ketch I noticed that the ketch was in a group of about five vessels. The ketch was on the port side of the group and all the boats were pointing to shore. The boat next to the ketch was a big Markline. These boats were sprung together (rafted up).

I don't really know what the other boats were next to the Markline because I went straight to the ketch from the "*Tamarack*". I have heard that the Markline was the "*Nugget*" [NEW] but I didn't see the name and can't confirm that.

The Markline was grey and white [NEW] and that is typical of a Markline. It is very similar to a Markline I know as the "*Nova*". [NEW]

---

206 10016 / ST / GUY WALLACE / ASD279 / 060198 / W

The Markline has a flybridge at the top, then a second storey below and then it comes down to deck level. The second level was weathered in with clear and white plastic fitted covers. [NEW]

I knew there were about four or five vessels in the group because I had been past them earlier when I went to the Pines. [EXTRA]

Further back from the ketch on the port side was a vessel that kept spotlighting me while I was out taxiing people. [NEW] I believe this boat was the "Squadron". [NEW]

I can recall that on the way to the ketch I remember when Ben had said, "I hope that's yours", referring to the Markline and the other guy said, "No, it's tied up next to it but I don't own it, I only crew on it". [EXTRA]

The guy from the ketch didn't have any accent. He just sounded like your average Kiwi guy. [NEW]

When I said yesterday that the portholes were below the deck, I mean they were below the deckline and above the waterline.

I have just seen photographs of Furneaux taken on 1 January 1998. I can see the Markline in the photo but the ketch is gone. [NEW]

GW, 9 JANUARY 1998[207]

Once Olivia and Ben had got on the boat and we had started away from the *"Tamarack"*, Olivia asked me if I knew of any accommodation. I said, "No, this is New Year's Eve. We are fully booked". [EXTRA]

The male said, "There is room in my boat". Olivia said, "That's nice". Then he said, "You can come but he can't". Again Olivia didn't even acknowledge him. [EXTRA]

I asked the male where he wanted to go. He told me the name

20710081 / ST / GUY WALLACE / TFD573 / 090198 / W

of his boat. I remember thinking "I don't want to know the name, I want directions". I can't remember what the name was but it was something like "The Manz". [NEW] He told me the name two or three times I think, then he said, "It's over there" and pointed towards the end of the jetty. I started going in that direction. I remember asking one of the people up the front to put their head down or move so I could see where I was going. [NEW]

It would only have taken about one to two minutes [NEW] to get from the "*Tamarack*" which was on the right-hand side as you look from the jetty. It would have been in line with the Lodge in the second line of boats.

The ketch the unknown male pointed to was about 20—30 metres to the left-hand side of the jetty in about the second or third row of boats. [EXTRA]

We were about 15—20 metres from the ketch when he said, "That's it there". At this time of the morning it is very dark in the inlet. When he pointed to it initially I could make out it was a yacht but I couldn't tell what it was.[208]

When the male pointed to the ketch and said, "That's it", Ben said, "Please tell me it's that one". He was looking at a boat very similar to or a Markline which was rafted next to it. I'm not sure if any of the boats which were rafted to the ketch were attached to a buoy or anchored.

He said, "No but I'm next to it if that helps".

I don't know how it came up but I know that he said he was crew on a fishing boat.

I pulled up alongside the ketch and remember thinking, "this is a nice old boat". It looked very tidy and extremely well kept. I can't add any more to the description I gave in the first statement.

---

[208] Contrast Wallace's admission about how dark it was with what he told the *NZ Herald*: "No. Crystal clear, stars in the sky, calm conditions. There was lighting from the nearby boat sheds. It wasn't pitch black or anything."—reprinted in *Ben & Olivia*, p53

The ketch did not smell of fish at all. It was very tidy. The ropes at the back made me believe it was used for fishing. I have seen ropes like that before on other fishing boats. We had one very similar at Ohope Beach where I grew up. They use the ropes for tying marker buoys to long lines.

I pulled up next to the ketch with my port side against the port side of the ketch. I would normally go to the stern to drop people because there is normally a ladder or steps to get on, which makes me think there must have been a dinghy on the back of the ketch but I can't remember.

Olivia stepped on to the ketch first. Ben was holding the boat. Once she was on the ketch, Ben handed her something. It could have been a sleeping bag or handbag. It was something similar. Ben then got off. Then the unknown male got off.

Once they were on the ketch I said, "Are you guys all right with this?" I just had a feeling it wasn't right. They were both facing me and said, "Yes". They walked towards the rear of the boat as if they were going to the cabin.

I backed away from the ketch, went to the bow and carried on to the Doctor's Jetty to drop off the other young female and male on the boat.

I didn't see whether Ben and Olivia went into the cabin or not. That was the last I saw of them.

The ketch was rafted on to the port side of the Markline or a boat similar to a Markline. I think there was another three boats rafted to the Markline. There seemed to be a big group there. I can't remember any of the other boats.

I remember a launch that kept spotlighting me as I was driving. It was yellow and brown. I thought it was called "Squadron". The people on board were still partying. I could hear the music playing and laughter. They were just behind the ketch. I'm not sure how far but the spotlight was really bright.

That was about the only boat that I remember with any life on it at that time of the morning.

It was very quiet in the inlet and on very still nights you could hear a noise from a great distance. Certainly any scream or loud noise would have been heard by most of the people in the inlet. I don't think you would hear it at the Lodge but you would definitely hear everything on the water.

I left the ketch and carried on to drop the other young male and female off at the Doctor's Jetty. It took me about four to five minutes to get there. I was going really slowly because the young girl was really cold. I dropped them off. They were really grateful for the lift and headed back to the jetty.

I got back to the jetty and took Charlie Proctor, his partner Lou and their mates to Charlie's Bonito boat. One of Charlie's mates fell in the water. Lou and I helped him back in. They were all pretty drunk. I dropped them off at the Bonito. He was anchored on the starboard side of the jetty, very close to the shore, close to the old jetty.

I remember when I was on the way out to Charlie's boat I saw the guys that had been causing trouble in the bar all night coming towards the jetty with the security guards behind them. I remember thinking, "I better get Charlie out of here". He is a real troublemaker and I thought he would start something.

When I got back to the jetty they were there—three of them waiting for a lift to their fishing boat. I took them out to their boats—three trawlers. They were moored straight out from the jetty, behind all the other boats. One of the guys, the ringleader, was bleeding. They were all drunk and very agitated.

I got rid of them on to their fishing boat and came back into the jetty.

I was standing on the jetty having a smoke, talking to the security guards when the Andersons came down and asked for a lift to their boat. There was Karen Anderson, her father Ian Anderson and his wife.

I have spoken to Karen Anderson since and she told me it was 4.15 am when I took them to their boat. It's a launch, about 27 foot, called "*Panache*". It was moored next to their son's boat, "*Beryl*". "*Beryl*" is a small speed boat. They were moored about 80 metres on the left-hand side of the jetty, close to the shore.

It's at this point one has to start asking hard questions of Guy Wallace. Not only is he saying it's a ketch, but now it's rafted up to four other boats (which he sees in the inky darkness), and what's more he, Ben Smart and the mystery man are having a blokey, hail-fellow-well-met, three way conversation about the Markline-style launch the ketch is supposedly rafted up against.

Ben Smart was wasted, not to put too fine a point on it. According to the other witnesses in the water taxi, Ben didn't have the energy to say 'boo' to a goose:

"I can't remember anything about the guy at all or even if I heard him speak," said Sarah Dyer.[209]

"When we got into the water taxi we seemed to motor out to the right of the wharf, then when we got to the yacht that was full, the other guy's boat was over in the opposite direction so we seemed to go over to the left hand side of the wharf. It was pitch black.

"When we got to the other guy's boat they all hopped out. I didn't notice anything at all of the other boat, not even the colour."

Dyer's then boyfriend, Hayden Morresey, didn't hear any of this excited chatter about Marklines and ketches either.[210]

"I can't really remember anything about him. I can't remember anything the girl said but I can remember the guy on the Naiad inviting her and her friend to stay on his boat.

---

[209] 10026 / ST / SARAH DYER / ASD852 / 050198
[210] 10031 / ST / HAYDEN MORRESEY / ASD279 / 070198

"We then headed back towards the jetty but further out to sea. When we got to the guy's boat, I looked back towards the jetty the right side of it looking at it from the sea.

"I can't remember anything being said on the way out to this guy's boat. We pulled up alongside the boat, and the guy who owned it jumped off first and then he helped the other two up. The boat was facing inshore and we pulled up to the left side of it. I only thought the guy owned it but nothing was said that he did own it."

So where on earth did Guy Wallace's suddenly detailed recollections of fishing and 'I'm just crewing on it' come from? Morresey and Dyer remember a silent trip and Ben saying nothing. Neither of them describe seeing a Markline launch, let alone hearing Ben's joyous exclamation at the possibility and the mystery man's convoluted explanations about simply being tied up to the launch and the ketch isn't really his. None of it took place, according to independent witnesses. So was Wallace hearing voices in his head, or gilding the lily to make his tale seem more believable? And if he was lying to make his story sound better, why should we believe it was a ketch rather than Watson's *Blade*?

Morresey didn't even call it a ketch.

"I would describe the boat as a yacht. I can't remember the colour but I think it was white. When we came up to the boat I can remember seeing a bit of white at the top of the side and then another colour and then white again. I can't remember what the middle colour was. I can't remember a lot about the yacht other than it having heaps of ropes. I can remember a mast near to the back and there was heaps of ropes coming off that."

So far, 17 year old Morresey's description is consistent with *Blade*. It too was white, with a reddish-brown strip below the deckline, white deck and superstructure and a reddish-brown cabin with a white roof visible. Others had described seeing lots of rope on *Blade*.[211]

---

211 20288 / ST / MONIQUE RUTTE / SHD080 / 150198

"I remember Dave saying at the time that Scott built the boat himself," remembered Monique Rutte from the *Mina Cornelia*.

"There was a lot of rope on board his boat, particularly down the back of the boat. These ropes were wounded up in coils but loosely lying around the deck."

"I can remember that there was rope on the deck," added Marcel Rutte.[212] "I don't know if it was an excessive amount for a yacht because I do not know much about boats. The rope was light in colour. I don't recall any of it hanging over the side, however I only saw one side of Scott's boat. That was the side parked up beside us."

"I recall the deck being quite cluttered with ropes and stuff. I think the deck was wooden," Deborah Corless remembered of *Blade*.[213] The deck at the back of *Blade* was indeed wooden.

Something very important—something that every author and all relevant police officers appear to have missed—was said by Morresey in his first formal statement. The mystery yacht was pointing towards shore. The Naiad was approaching it from its front left quarter. If Morresey was looking at a mast "near to the back end" he was arguably looking at "the" mast, remembering visibility was nil and he makes no mention of passing any other mast first as the Naiad came in from the front. This suggests the yacht was a single-masted sloop.

Although Guy Wallace talked above of ropes coming off the stern that made him think of a long-line fishing boat, and drew a sketch of the "ketch" with a "bulbous transom" (rounded rear), his evidence states he *never* went around the back of the boat to see. He had nursed the Naiad in from the front to the front mid-section of the mystery yacht (about the same position as *Blade*'s mast incidentally)—far enough forward that he watched Ben and

---

212 10653 / ST / MARCEL RUTTE / MK8254 / 060298
213 20284 / ST / DEBORAH CORLESS / MMG072 / 150198

Olivia walking along the side towards the rear where he assumed the cabin entrance was. Then, what did he do next?:

"I *backed away from the ketch, went to the bow and carried on to the Doctor's Jetty* to drop off the other young female and male on the boat."

He reversed his Naiad backwards so he could take a beeline past the bow of the yacht for Doctor's Jetty on the mainland. His trip wasn't taking him around the back of the yacht.

It appears Guy Wallace has inadvertently allowed his mind to make up things he never saw and, in what he himself acknowledged was pitch darkness, arguably could never have seen. Seeing the whole of the eight metre *Blade* from a front three-quarter approach on a basically moonless night would have been impossible, and seeing the whole of a 12 metre ketch down to the detail of chipped paint and "brass" portholes would have been a magnitude more unlikely. In a bid to fill the void his brain has dredged up a daylight image of a ketch he *has* seen.

Is he prone to doing that? You bet, and you're about to see proof.

Worse, however, Wallace appears to have invented conversations with Ben Smart and the mystery man that never happened. They couldn't have! None of the launches at Furneaux were tied up to the mystery ketch, therefore Ben could never have commented on it.

It's one thing to have a false memory about something you've seen. It's harder to think of a subconscious scenario that accounts for fictional conversations in support of something else we know did not happen. These appear to fall into the category of either deliberate fabrications which, as we have seen, Guy Wallace has form for—having deliberately lied to police about the ketch *Waves*—or snippets of conversation taken out of context as they passed other boats along the way. If they were approaching *Blade* from the direction of *Tamarack*, they would have passed close to *Monde*.

There are other areas where you can see Wallace appears to have drawn on different memories from other Naiad trips. One is his trip to a Markline launch, *Panache*, close to where *Blade* was moored. Then there's his memory of being spotlighted from a big Squadron launch. That was *Megamuse*, and it was the next boat towards the jetty from *Blade*, albeit maybe 30 to 50 metres away. *Megamuse* was tied up to *Spirit of Marlborough* which in turn was rafted to the launch *Monde*. This was the group that Wallace initially insisted the ketch was part of, which shows how confused he was.

The confusion gets even murkier, however. According to a search of police and defence files and boat profiles, the only Squadron launch at Furneaux was *Megamuse*, and it departed for Picton at 1.30am, two hours before Guy Wallace began his stint on the water taxis. *He cannot have been spotlighted from a Squadron.* He cannot even have seen that Squadron in his travels on that night.

The two teenage girls on the ketch *Alliance*—Alisha and Holly—were operating a spotlight to look at fish, but according to skipper Peter Kennedy they were all in bed asleep by 2am, 90 minutes before Wallace took to the water. *He cannot have been spotlighted from Alliance.*

There was a spotlight being operated, but that was way over the other side of the jetty, between *Maya* and *Tamarack*. It was nowhere near the alleged mystery ketch. Additionally boats leaving the moorings would use spotlights as they left to ensure they didn't collide with another vessel.

However, sharp-eyed readers will have noticed in Wallace's 9 January statement that he suddenly offers up a name for this mystery ketch: "The Manz". This is the hard evidence that Wallace's memory was fundamentally vulnerable to the power of suggestion, in this case to a name planted in his head. You are about to see how.

CHAPTER FOURTEEN

Diversions

On January 8, the day before Guy Wallace's "The Manz" statement, Furneaux staffer Ron 'Rippa' Farrell gave a statement to police that seemed to put a name to an unidentified ketch:[214]

"I remember seeing two boats moored in this area—one was the "Mae NZ" and the other was the "Bin Tang". There was also an older type of boat that was similar to the boat you are interested in. It was moored in this general area.

"It was a large boat and I'm sure it would have been a two mast boat just because the type of boat it was. I didn't see two masts but that's the impression it gave me.

"I may be getting a bit confused here. If the "Mae NZ" is a large white yacht with a blue line then this is the older boat I saw. The name "Mae NZ" sticks in my mind and this makes me think it could be the older boat.

---

214 10064 / ST / RONALD FARRELL / TFD175 / 080198 / W

"I didn't see any movement on the boat, however I only glanced at it as we sped past."

Where on earth had Mae NZ come from? It seems more than coincidence that Guy Wallace the very next day offered police the name "Manz", when previously he'd remembered nothing. Wallace by this time was working over at Punga Cove so this presumably did not result from a discussion around the water cooler.

Detectives went back to Farrell to seek more details.

"I saw a vessel matching the description of the ketch you are looking for moored in Furneaux in the inlet (I've spoken to Tom Fogarty).[215]

"At the time I was on a tender and this ketch was moored around *Bing Tang* and a party boat called *Double Trouble* (26' Cresta craft). *Bing Tang* was a plastic yacht.

"I don't recall much about the ketch, other than the name MAE NZ, which was written in black on the bow. The letters MAE were in block letters and the NZ was in letters about quarter of the size. I can't recall whether the last two letters were NZ or AZ but it was something like that.

"The hull was white and it had a blue stripe through it, below the water line. The stripe was about 8" thick and was about the same distance down from the top of the deck, as it was wide.

"I was low down in the water and didn't really get to look at how many masts it had. I think it was on 31 December 1997 I saw it."

Curiously, also on the 9th, a routine file note was passed to Operation TAM revealing Ron Farrell had first tipped off Picton Police three days earlier, and back then he'd called the boat *Mea NZ* and said it was tied up alongside *Oranui*.[216]

"Obtain notification notice through operation correspondence

---

[215] 30814 / JS / RON FARRELL / MR8667 / 090198
[216] 20035 / JS / MEA NZ / WS5242 / 100198

of a notification from "Ripper" FARRELL from the vessel *Ripper*, moored at Furneaux on New Year's Eve.

"Notification originally made to the Picton Police on 06.01.98.

"FARRELL states that he remembers the vessel *MEA NZ* rafted to the outside of *Oranui* on New Year's Eve. States that the vessel is similar in description to the one sought by police."

It appears odd that Farrell had originally remembered the name as MEA NZ then changed it to MAE NZ in his statement two days after first telling police, although that may have been attributable to uncertainty on his part or the fact that Detective Sergeant Wayne Stringer, who authored the quoted file note, somehow knew by 6pm on the 9th that the boat was called MEA.

In the book *Silent Evidence*, author John Goulter writes:[217]

"Wayne Stringer reported that 75 of the 82 boats seen in photos and videos had now been identified. He was most interested in a boat called something like *Mea New Zealand*, he said. 'This looks like our vessel. It was described by the water taxi people as being in about the same position as Wallace describes, so it all seems to tie in'. Stringer told the briefing his team was alerting Maritime Safety, Customs and Interpol about the boat to try and pin it down."

Regardless of Keith Hunter's criticisms about a lack of interest in ketches or other suspects, police had earlier that day scrambled to find this mystery ketch, asking Customs Intelligence for any info on "MAE.NZ or variations of this:

MAE.NZ, MEA.NZ, MAE.AZ, MEA.AZ, MEANZ, MAENZ

By 7pm on the 9th, police had received a phone call from Kevin Kershaw at Customs.

"Name provided doesn't ring a bell. We are still doing further

---

[217] *Silent Evidence* by John Goulter, Random House, 2000, p91

checks for you, however a vessel by the name of "MIZ.MAE" arrived in November 1993 and departed 1994. It came from Road Bay, Alaska. Will call you back with other details".[218]

By 8pm on the 9th, detectives had tracked down Ted McDonald, a Dunedin man skippering the other yacht Farrell mentioned, *Bintang*.[219]

"When asked about the name 'Mea' or 'Mae' he is aware of a similar vessel which he's had dealings with in the last two weeks. he describes it as being a big wide 47' concrete yacht and they have seen this vessel in and around the Picton wharf where McDonald is presently moored. He has had dealings with the occupants of this vessel because he said they basically stood over them to get their berth. he has seen it on more than one occasion at this location and thinks the last time he saw it was either the previous day or two days previous.

"He said the occupants of the vessel looked fairly rough. There may be a female name Katherine on board and there is another slim guy with tattoos and possibly a bit of Maori in him. He thought it was a guy in his 40's that had control of the yacht and they may have originated from Auckland and be returning to there via the Mana Cruising Club."

By 10 January, police found the yacht—ironically—at Furneaux Lodge. It was named MEAnz and it was a single-masted sloop, not a double-masted ketch:[220]

"We were not in Furneaux Inlet on 31 December 1997," the owner told police. "On 3 January we headed to Furneaux Inlet for the first time. We saw the Police around Furneaux that day. From that and the notices we saw around Furneaux we found out about the missing couple. We were not aware of it until then.

"On 4 January 1998 we travelled across to Punga where we remained for the night.

---

218 20032 / JS / KEVIN KERSHAW CUSTOMS / SCC539 / 090198
219 20629 / JS / PROFILE "BINTANG" / BM6952 / 090198
220 10147 / ST / MEA NZ / KY7541 / 100198

"We are just at Furneaux for the day and will be staying near Punga tonight. We are returning back to Wellington tomorrow and the "MEA" will be moored back at Mana.

"During our travels in the Sounds we have not seen any ketch similar to that you are seeking. I think the ketch may even be American design."

Guy Wallace could have seen MEAnz at Punga Cove, but it doesn't look like the picture of the ketch he was trying to sell so there'd be no ultimate gain for him. And if he'd seen MEA on the 4th, he could have used it as a reference in his statements on the 5th and 6th if that was his intention. He didn't, so the alternative remains on the table: Rip Farrell has seen the boat at Furneaux, assumed it could be the ketch, and the jungle drums got word through to Wallace, who altered the name to "Manz".

To add to the confusion, Furneaux staffer David Furneaux said this:[221]

"I never went onto the water as such. My wife went out on the "*Yolande*" though. From what she has told me, the only thing she saw of interest was the name of a boat which was similar to "Meanza". I haven't seen that name on your boating list in the paper though."

Why on earth would the name "Meanza", out of more than a hundred exotic boat names, attract attention? And again, it was a sighting tracked back to Furneaux staff. MEAnz was reportedly not at Furneaux on New Year's Eve, although it was on 3 January and again on 10 January.

Meanza sounds awfully close to Manz.

The mystery over MEA deepened however, when the skipper of *Nugget* which had been rafted on one side of *Oranui*, told police he'd seen MEA leaving on New Year's Day, although he did not say it was part of the *Oranui* raft:[222]

---

221 10560 / ST / DAVID FURNEAUX / PC4625 / 150198
222 10133 / ST / *Nugget* / SM7883 / 100198

"I saw a vessel named "MEA NZ" (MEA in capitals, NZ in small letters). I first noticed it on New Year's Day when it was leaving. It is a ferro (concrete) boat coloured white with a green stripe. I have subsequently seen it and socialised with the crew around the Sounds. It is not like the boat you have described. For a start it is sloop rigged. The skipper is from Auckland. I can't recall his name."

Sherryl Hanna, who with her husband Gordon in their converted fishing boat was also tied alongside *Nugget*, told police the skipper of "*Nugget* is a guy who works up at Furneaux. He owns the ketch "*Nugget*" which is moored quite often up around there at Furneaux."[223]

So yet again a Furneaux staff link to the MEA sightings. Yet *Nugget*'s skipper can't have seen MEA leaving unless it left after 10am New Year's Day, when he woke up. He told police, "the other boats in our raft were still there" when he looked outside.

According to another witness who spent the evening drinking with some of the people from this group of boats, they had gang connections:[224]

"A large group from the Wellington area also joined us. One of them was [Joe Bloggs] from Wellington, I heard was attached to a gang, the Nomads and another gang was mentioned. He had 3 or 4 businesses. He was about 40–45 years of age. He had his partner, a blonde, good looking, I can't remember her name.

"This group were rafted up. In the photo of the Endeavour Inlet you have shown me, one of a group, either the *Nugget*, Beau D'or Rell or *Oranui*."

So here we have an alleged crime connection as well. We will return to the significance of that shortly.

However, and here's the rub, MEA was not rafted up to *Oranui*, ever:[225]

---

223 40283 / ST / SHERRYL HANNA / RMC084 / 250398
224 40192 / ST / NICHOLAS COOPER / AS1272 / 230398
225 10197 / ST / CHRISTOPHER WILSON / GM8230 / 080198

"Just my wife and I were aboard and we stayed on board all night," *Oranui*'s skipper, Christchurch man Chris Wilson, told police. "We were moored straight off the end of the Furneaux Lodge jetty , about 20 metres off.

"The motor sailer is 35 feet long, coloured white with blue on the cabin roof and a sea coloured stripe around the top of the hull. It has a big cabin window and small portholes at the rear. It is called the '*Oranui*'.

"We arrived on the 31st December at about 4pm. Tied up to us was a mustard coloured concrete boat with brown sail covers [*Nugget*]. The owner lives on it in Wellington. He would be in his 40's. He was rough looking and there was another 40 year old guy with him who looked rough. There was another guy on board who had grey hair and looked to be in his 60's. The two 40yr olds told me on New Year's Day that they got back at about 4 or 5 am to their boat. I noticed them returning at the time and got up to look and saw one of them climbing on board the back of their yacht and telling the other to be quiet. I only saw the one of them, then went back to bed. The water taxi delivered them to the stern of their yacht, they didn't come alongside our yacht.

"I would describe them as follows;

"1. (Owner) Male Caucasian, 40years old, moustache or unshaven, scar down the side of his face, average/heavy build, 6 foot tall.

"2. Male Maori/half-caste, 40 yrs, black hair to collar, rough shaven or moustache, dirty looking, 5'8" /tall, average build, strong looking.

"3. Male Caucasian, 60 yrs, shaved grey/white hair, very fat stomach, unshaven but cleaner looking.

"I don't recall any tattoos on them.

"Tied next to them was a rental boat and I think it was called the "Del 'd Roos" or something similar. I don't know who they were but they were more roughies with tattoos up their arms. There were two jokers and a woman on board. They were even rougher than the guys next to us. They were all friends apparently, both boats. The Del 'd Roos was a fibreglass launch, 32 foot, cream colour.

"North of us was the *Toroanui* with a man and wife aboard. They are well known in the area and live on the boat. The *Toroanui* is a white ketch(2 masts) with portholes but has no blue stripe. A couple of fizz boats were tied up to him.

"South of us (left of the jetty as you look from the beach) and nearer to the area that the suspect boat was meant to be, was a group of 3 boats rafted together. One of the boats was "Monde". That was a great big, 50 foot launch. The other 2 were launches also. One I think was the *Spirit of Marlborough* and the other had Squadron written on the side of it.

"I don't recall seeing a white ketch with a blue stripe and portholes while we were there.

"The only point of note I would make is that if the water taxi driver was pissed and looked across our yacht, which looks similar to the ketch you are looking for except for our one mast, is that in the darkness the mustard coloured yacht's mast might have seemed like a second mast on our yacht and made it look like a ketch."

Wilson's wife Rebecca confirmed they were the last vessel on the raft—which meant MEA had not tied up to *Oranui*, despite what Ron 'Rippa' Farrell had told Picton police on 6 January. Police files disclose there was a ketch-rigged vessel near the *Oranui*, however, but it was the *Alliance*—the white boat with a blue stripe and round portholes which may have formed the mental template for Guy Wallace's ketch visions. Rebecca Wilson had shared New Year greetings with people on *Alliance*:

"Wilson can remember chatting to a family group on board a vessel with two masts and a blue stripe and port holes. She thought this was about midnight on New Year's Eve as she and her husband had been sleeping earlier in the evening."

All of which raises a perplexing question: police now had a clear conflict of evidence over the whereabouts of the massive sloop MEA on New Year's Eve. The skipper had given detectives a statement:

"On Monday the 29th we travelled to Picton and moored near the ferry terminal. We remained there until departing on 1 January 1998. We paid mooring fees at Picton of $10.00 per night. We spent New Year's Eve at the Federal Hotel in Picton. This was the entire group. Susan and I returned to "MEA" at about 12.30 am on 1 January.

"On 1 January 1998 we departed from Picton late morning and headed to Torea Bay. We had lunch at The Portage and returned to "MEA" at about 5.00 pm. We spent that night on the boat.

"On 2 January we returned to Picton and moored in the same area near the ferry terminal."

The skipper's wife provided some receipts to prove their whereabouts on 31 December.[226] The first was an Eftpos cash withdrawal of $50, made from the till of the Barn Cafe in Picton at 10.48am. The only other receipt from that day was for $16 for a purchase at the Western Ridge in Picton at 2.08pm. While this proved that someone was in Picton up to 2.08pm, it did not prove where they were after that and it certainly did not prove that passengers on MEA had seen in the New Year at the Federal Hotel, because no receipts were provided to corroborate that.

The MEA's owners then provided receipts from the Port of Marlborough for the yacht's mooring fees:

"Port Marlborough New Zealand Limited, receipt 4847, dated 30.12.97, for two days "MEA" to 31.12.97.

"Port Marlborough New Zealand Limited, receipt 5161, dated 03.01.98 for one day, "MEA"."

The sharp-eyed reader will notice that MEA arrived on the 29th, so needed to pay for that night's stay. The receipt recorded two

---

226 10167 / JS / MEA NZ / KY7541 / 100198

nights' berthage, so it would have also covered the night of the 30th. Did that mean MEA checked out on the 31st? If so, were they really still in Picton on New Year's Eve?

The second Port of Marlborough receipt provides confirmation of the Port's methodology. We know MEA berthed back at Picton on 2 January and overnighted there. It left for Furneaux on 3 January. The second receipt is dated 3 January for one day, but it must have been the fee for 2 January, paid up on 3 January before the boat left.

It appears then that MEA had not paid for a mooring on the nights of 31 December or New Year's Day.

It is possible, then, based on the evidence in the police files, that MEA could have been at Furneaux on New Year's Eve. But if that is the case then it appears either the skipper is wrong, or alternatively the Furneaux witnesses are wrong.

In the book *Silent Evidence*, it is reported:[227]

"Another boat discounted was the *Mea New Zealand*, which was found to have been booked in at the Picton ferry terminal until 1 January."

But based on the information in their own files, police should have known this may not have been true. They had witnesses saying MEA had been at Furneaux that night, they had a skipper denying this and claiming to have an alibi, and police failed to chase down that alibi to see if it stood up to scrutiny.

For example, in the case of every other boat at Furneaux, police tracked down and interviewed every single person on board, including children. With MEA, police collected one statement from the skipper, and nothing from the 11 other people on this vessel. No one else was asked, 'Where were you on the night of the 31st?' or 'What did you see?'.

It is policing 101: follow all leads. This was a boat that Detective

---

227 *Silent Evidence*, p108

Sergeant Wayne Stringer had told his team "this looks like our vessel". Yet when push came to shove, when police had a clear and disturbing conflict of evidence about its movements, detectives were distracted by something else.

Eighteen years after the event, the discovery of a gaping hole in the police investigation is surprising. To try and retrace the steps after so long, when memories have well and truly faded, is near impossible. Nonetheless, it was worth a try.

One of the passengers on Mea that summer now lives in Sydney. She's now a Christian. She didn't even know in 2015 that there'd been a double murder at the time and that her yacht was mentioned in dispatches.

"You're kidding!" the woman exclaimed. "Two kids were murdered in the Sounds while we were there? Why didn't I know about this?"

She then answered her own question: "I moved to Australia right after that boat trip. It's a lifetime ago. I was a different person. There were drugs, alcohol, parties, I've forgotten so much from back in those days. We were a party boat, there were about a dozen people on board maybe. I remember one family had their sons with them I think. We all sort of knew each other, we were all friends of [the skipper]."

"Did you go to Furneaux Lodge for New Year's Eve?"

"I think we did. We were partying so hard. But I used to do a lot of drugs. I can't really remember."

Another passenger tracked down denied being at Furneaux. "We were at the Federal on New Year's Eve. We were a very quiet group. We definitely didn't have partying on the boat."

Again, faced with a conflict of evidence, the next step is to follow the hypothesis, the 'what if?' scenario.

If MEA motored into Furneaux for New Year's Eve, and even if they are lying about it, how does that change what we know? If the mystery man was described as a "loner" by the bar staff, and he was, he doesn't fit the profile of someone coming in from the collection of friends on MEA.

MEA had its own inflatable and didn't need water taxis, so that's another indicator that it wasn't involved because it is unlikely Wallace would have been asked to ferry anyone back there.

Then there's the issue of conspiracy. When the crime escalates from a lone wolf to an entire boat-load of co-conspirators, there's a big leap in the amount of credibility required. In this case MEA's passengers included a mixture of men and women of varying ages.

If the crime was committed by an opportunistic passenger smuggling Ben and Olivia on board, how did he kill them and do everything else without any of the other passengers hearing? How did he move their bodies within the tight confines of a yacht? How did he dispose of their bodies without being seen and without trace?

If the passenger enlisted the help of the other passengers, are we to believe they were all psychopaths, or would they do what even normal families usually do—restrain the offender in their midst and call police?

If MEA's skipper was the "lone wolf" in the Furneaux bar, what did his wife think when he brought Olivia home and diverted the boat out into Cook Strait to dump the bodies overboard?

In fact, there were two men—both travelling with their wives—and five women on MEA on the night in question.[228] The men were aged in their mid-40s, well outside the mystery man profile.

No, even if MEA was at Furneaux, the plotline for any involvement in the murders is too outlandish to be credible. We don't know what caused Furneaux staff to have suddenly raised MEA or variations of it, but on the other hand they could equally have simply been mistaken, confusing the 3 January visit with New Year's

---

[228] 10167 / JS / MEA NZ / KY7541 / 100198

Eve and the whole thing developed into a series of Elvis-sightings.

Which brings us back to the organised crime connection. We know members of Satan's Slaves were partying at Furneaux. A witness claims one of the men who brought his partner and daughter across from Wellington was tied up with the Nomad gang.

It is a matter of public record that the gangs use commercial fishing boats and private vessels on both sides of Cook Strait to tranship drugs and black market fishing catches. People involved in these operations have sometimes turned up dead or simply vanished off the face of the earth. All that was found of one Wellington man involved with drug trafficking across the Strait was his foot, still inside a flipper, after a supposed diving "mishap".

The police were criticised for checking possible links between Watson and the September 1997 disappearance of American heiress Nancy Frey-Hershey on Great Barrier Island north of Auckland, but they had received anonymous information alleging gang involvement, as the text of a letter to Christchurch Police shows:[229]

"The disappearance of that Smart son of a bitch and that spoilt bitch are connected to the disappearance of Nancy Frey at Tryphena Harbour Rd, Great Barrier, Hauraki Gulf. When people start to find out too much or see too much it is necessary to take the action we take. Business is business and we don't like people interfering in our business operation.

"They will continue to take whatever positive action is necessary to protect their business operations. If people get in the way they simply get rid of them without leaving evidence. As you have already been informed they are well organised throughout New Zealand.

"Nancy Frey knew too much of the operations of both The Auckland Chapter and the North Shore Chapters of the Hell's Angels organisation. Drugs are being channelled through Great

---

229 20801 / LTR / NANCY FREY / AC6711 / 230298

Barrier Island for distribution through Waiheke Island. [Name Deleted], a sex worker from [Location Deleted], distributes drugs to the well organised prostitute network. The property with [Deleted] at Tryphena Harbour Road Barrier is connected to the North Shore Chapter. The gangs use the Barrier for their drug distribution bringing the drugs in by boat and then distributing by boat to Waiheke and to Manly at Whangaparaoa. They also go to the Barrier over the Christmas summer holidays.

"[Name deleted] (a [Occupation Deleted]), his daughter [Name Deleted], [Name Deleted] (also a sex worker) run the drugs through Auckland and throughout New Zealand through legitimate and well organised registered companies.

"The code of silence exists with the gangs who are involved in most of sex industry service outlets and the distribution of drugs. We cannot disclose any more information or else we will end up like Nancy Frey and many others who knew too much," ends the letter.

Consequently there has been speculation that Ben and Olivia ended up on the wrong boat at the wrong time and paid the price. It is highly unusual, however, for outsiders to be targeted in gang operations; it calls down too much heat. Nancy Frey was a Great Barrier local who could have intimately known what was happening on a larger scale. She could have seen regular shipments, and muttered something injudicious about the locals involved.

Contrast that with the Sounds murders. What could Ben and Olivia possibly have seen on a gang boat at four in the morning after a New Year's party? Is anyone seriously suggesting that on party central night "the boys" had all gathered around the table with a thousand one-kilo bags of cocaine out in the open while they all played cards? By all accounts the gang types were yahooing with the rest of the revellers. It wasn't a night for business, and many of these gang members had brought their families across.

"The only thing that stood out as being unusual," reveller Ian Baylis told police,[230] "was gang type people on very expensive boats drinking Lion Red. I think I saw about 3-4 males and a couple females. They were on a launch and a yacht with a Bayliner with them."

There's a hint in the police files that the gangs were as annoyed by the disappearance of Ben and Olivia as the police were:[231]

NEW ZEALAND POLICE JOB SHEET
OFFENCE: OPERATION TAM

07.05.98

Received the following information from a male who wishes to remain anonymous.

About two weeks ago the informant was speaking to a Christchurch gang member (name of gang not disclosed) who told him the yacht owner, WATSON, was growing marijuana and distributing to North Island gangs, namely Nomads and Highway 61.

The gang member also said Ben SMART smoked cannabis and did light "dribbling" in the drug, however Olivia HOPE was not involved.

The gangs were concerned that Police enquiries in the Sounds had severely jeopardised their drug activities in that area and to that end three gang members had allegedly travelled to Marlborough to make their own enquires into the disappearance of Ben and Olivia.

The informant said in the next two or three weeks he may be in a position to obtain further information.

---

230 11137 / ST / Ian BAYLIS / DSG765 / 260198
231 12199 / JS / ANONYMOUS / RB4089 / 110598

Another file note from early February has been censored by police. It details the aftermath of the seizure of Zappa's cannabis crop at Erie Bay, and concludes:[232]

"Note: (DELETION) was adamant he did not want his name brought up with (DELETION). Believes that (DELETION) has gang connections in North Island."

In Auckland, detectives spoke to a man who'd worked with Scott Watson near Whangarei. He told of a rumour in the wake of Watson's arrest:[233]

"The rumour was going around town that guy from a deep sea trawler had spoken to one of the locals.

"This person had said that a gang, who the locals thought was the Black Power, had brought an H28 ketch and were in the Marlborough Sounds at the same time as the pair went missing. Whilst the gang were in the Sounds they were selling LSD trips to the yachties.

"They then took the ketch up to Whangarei and sunk it somewhere off Whangarei."

Let's assume for a moment that Black Power had indeed set up a yacht to sell drugs from to boaties. Ben Smart had a known drug habit. He knew the protocol. In fact police even received a tip-off that Smart had his own gang connections:[234]

"Recently speaking with an informant who advised that [DELETION], who allegedly was a very good friend of Benjamin Smart, had, prior to depositions, arranged to purchase a shotgun from gang associates with the intention of shooting Scott Watson.

"My informant said the shotgun had been obtained and [DELETION] was going to be shown how to fire it and it was only when

---

232 10683 / JS / DELETION / RMC084 / 020298
233 14282 / JS / SEAN SAMPLE / MFC397 / 281298
234 14002 / JS / DELETION / PR8612 / 120499

some sense was spoken to the supplier of the shotgun that it was no longer made available to [DELETION]."

Again, if Ben Smart was buying narcotics, he would have known the rules and it's highly unlikely he would have come to fatal harm stumbling onto a tinny boat.

Besides, the mystery man was a small Caucasian, not a beefy Ngapuhi member of Black Power.

The source of the Black Power yacht rumour appears to have been a disgruntled Wellington man having a neighbour dispute with a Black Power associate living next door. He wrote letters to newspapers alleging the man had been at Furneaux and had then "got rid" of a yacht in early January. The man later gave a statement to police accepting he had exaggerated:[235]

"When approached by Police I cooperated and was prepared to make a statement instead of continuing to remain anonymous. I realise that it was a big leap in logic from all the facts that I had at my disposal, to saying that Jason is to be looked at as a suspect for the Furneaux Lodge investigation."

For reasons of basic logic and commonsense, then, the involvement of MEA in the murders can be discounted: this appears to have been a lone wolf opportunistic crime by someone—admittedly like many other men at Furneaux that night—hoping to score. Unlike many other men, however, the culprit may be psychopathic with a total disregard of overstepping moral boundaries. Plus, the culprit had to have control of a boat. He can't just be a guest. To complete this crime, he had to be able to direct operations himself. Any old oik can kill someone and throw them over the side, but to do it in a fashion that the bodies remain undetected to this day—that requires control of your environment.

This same evidential foundation also rules out involvement of

---

235 13976 / ST / DELETION / TFD175 / 180398

an overseas yacht. The mystery man had an ordinary New Zealand accent. He cannot have been in "control" of a foreign ketch as such. The involvement of any greater number than two men in this crime challenges credibility.

Guy Wallace, meanwhile, was changing his story as often as his clothes. On 6 February, Guy Wallace came up with yet another location for the mystery ketch:[236]

"When I was delivering Ben and Olivia to the ketch there was someone using a spotlight. I think it was from the boat Squadron.

"The ketch that Olivia and Ben got on was rafted to a boat like a Markline. I remember indicating to Andy Saunders in an early interview the Markline that the ketch was rafted to.

"Detective Sergeant Evans has shown me a photograph dated 1 January 1998.

"The boat the ketch was rafted to I can say is the boat named *Awesome*. It was rafted on *Awesome*'s port side.

"In the foreground is *Panache*. That is Anderson's Markline. I know it wasn't that one.

"The position of *Awesome* fits the position of where the ketch was."

Except, as the owners of *Awesome*—a 52 foot Salthouse launch—testified, no ketch was ever tied up to their port side.[237]

Halfway between *Awesome* and *Panache*, however, sat *Blade*, tied up to the *Mina Cornelia*.

"On three different occasions that I have spoken to Guy about the ketch," complained fellow water taxi driver Don Anderson to police,[238] "he has described three different positions to me as to where he saw the ketch in the bay.

"The first location was at the end of the jetty and out a bit and slightly to the right as you look out in the bay. The second occa-

---

236 30380 / GUY WALLACE / DE5136 / 060298
237 20824D / BRYAN MORRIS
238 10823 / ST / DONALD ANDERSON / LC8773 / 050398

sion he said it was on the end of the line on *Nugget*'s mooring, rafted up to *Nugget*. The third occasion was on the raft of *Spirit of Marlborough*. These positions changed as us guys talked about boats that were in these positions and we worked out that no such boat of that description could have been there. His story would change a bit a couple of days or so after this.

"I'm not the only person that Guy has changed his story to if you ask others directly. I don't believe everything he has said is a lie, I believe it's to give his original story some credibility, hoping that by Police continually searching they would uncover something. He's been under a lot of pressure."

It's hard to take Guy Wallace seriously, however. Not only had he woven an elaborate lie that led police down a false trail, but after telling police he was so concerned about leaving Olivia and Ben on the ketch with a strange man, he then said this to author Mike Kalaugher who—in their interview transcript—didn't even bat an eyelid at Wallace's next revelation. Wallace talked of then taking a drunk man out to the row of fishing boats and *hearing a scream from the ketch*:

> GUY WALLACE: He was standing up abusing the security guards so I drove them out to the ketch, after.. sorry, I drove them out to the fishing boats…
>
> MIKE KALAUGHER: Right.
>
> GUY WALLACE: …now on my way back… now the fishing boats are right out in the bay, they are the furthest boats anchored out there was a few of them together there. Um on the way back, I remember telling Fitzgerald this, um, further out in the bay I saw this ketch, and there was still no life on board, just dormant, and as I went passed it I heard a bit of a scream, like it was nothing blood curdling or anything like that..
>
> MIKE KALAUGHER: Yeah
>
> GUY WALLACE: …But the boat appeared to be on its own…

How is it possible that you would hear "a bit of a scream" coming from a boat in such circumstances, and you would do absolutely nothing about it? It had to be a loud enough scream for him to hear it over the noise from the Naiad outboard. Wouldn't a normal person immediately make a beeline for the vessel to see if he could hear anything else?

Although Wallace claims to have told Detective Tom Fitzgerald about the scream from the ketch, his 194 page police interview transcript does not contain the word 'scream'. Nor does he disclose this vital information, and his own inexplicable lack of human reaction, in *any* of his formal statements.

It is as if Guy Wallace's 'random access memory' (to borrow IT terminology) has truly gone random.

What can we make of Wallace's ever-changing statements then? Virtually nothing. Go back to the very first couple of descriptions of the mystery man, before his memory became contaminated, stick with those. When it comes to ketch versus sloop, the scenario that the mystery man asked for a ride to his "ketch" fits the evidence. That would easily explain why Wallace became conditioned to think of the boat instantly in terms of a ketch and in the darkness his sleep-deprived brain transposed a vision of *Alliance*. From there it was all downhill.

Add in a bunch of lawyers ready to make the most of your confusion, at $2,000 plus GST per billable hour, and you can see why Wallace felt he'd been hit by a freight train.

To give you an idea of how witnesses can be led by the nose during trials, look no further than Hayden Morresey, being questioned by Watson's lawyers.

"When you then went over next to the second boat, was it your impression at the time that that boat was a ketch?

"…Ah yes."

"It was wasn't it?

"...Yes."

"You were quite clear about that over subsequent days weren't you?"

"...Yes."

"You were quite clear about that from your own recollection of these events?"

"...Yes."

"Nobody else had made any suggestions to you, these were your recollections weren't they?"

"...Yes."

"Well, can I just ask you first of all, this second boat, the mystery boat, can you tell us does it appear to be on its own when you came up to it, as opposed to being rafted up to other boats?"

"...Yeah, by itself."

"It appeared to be on its own?"

"...Yeah."

"So it was just sitting out there on the water not connected with any other boat?"

"...No."

"And these are not the Droids you're looking for, are they?"

"...No, these are not the Droids I'm looking for."

OK, the last two lines clearly don't appear in the Court transcript, but they easily could have. The rest is a direct quote. In his original statements he'd said he couldn't remember whether it was rafted to any other boats. Suddenly, 19 months later, he's very clear it was moored on its own. Yeah, right.

The irony is, Morresey had admitted in court just before this particular sequence of cross examination that his original police statements were more reliable:

"And you spoke to the Police on the 7th and then again on the 8th?"

"...Yeah I think so."

"At that stage what had occurred on New Year's Eve was still very fresh in your mind, would you agree?"

"...Yeah, it was pretty fresh yeah."

"Perhaps a lot clearer than it is now, 18 months later."

"...Oh yeah you could say that."

Additionally, *nowhere* in his police statements had Morresey *ever* called the yacht a ketch. After his almost hypnotic cross-examination by Watson's defence lawyers however, the teenager was certain he'd always known it was a ketch.

Yet it turned out, just as we deduced from his original statements, he had never seen a second mast, and there cannot have been one because they'd approached from the front and he only saw what he mistakenly thought was the "rear" mast. If there was a front one, he would have passed it and seen it. He'd based his entire assumption that it was a ketch simply because it had some ropes up its mast:

"And was your assumption therefore that those ropes that were going up must have been going to another mast?"

"....yes."

[Judge Heron interjects] COURT: "Did you not see another mast?"

"..no I didn't look that far no."

"So the principle reason why you say that the boat that Ben and Olivia got onto was a ketch was because you could see those ropes going forward and up?"

"....that's right yeah."

"And they had to end somewhere."

"....yes exactly."

"Could you see many ropes in that fashion?"

"....um I think there was only about 2 or 3."

Clearly this is a boat with lots of ornate heavy ropework as Guy Wallace claimed. *Not*.

A little later under questioning from prosecutors, the rope issue was explored further:

"And how many ropes can you actually remember coming from three quarters of the way down this mast?"

"....at least 2 or 3."

"Apart from those ropes did you notice other ropes that weren't attached to the mast?"

"...Yes there was other ropes."

"Where did you see these ropes?

"...There was a few on the deck, pretty much everywhere."

So far, then, we have confirmed, on Morresey's testimony, a one-masted boat with ropes. It could probably describe many yachts, but it certainly described *Blade*, as you will recall:

"There was a lot of rope on board his boat, particularly down the back of the boat. These ropes were wounded up in coils but loosely lying around the deck,"[239] remembered Monique Rutte from the *Mina Cornelia*.

"I can remember were that there was rope on the deck," added Marcel Rutte.[240] "I don't know if it was an excessive amount for a yacht because I do not know much about boats. The rope was light in colour. I don't recall any of it hanging over the side, however I only saw one side of Scott's boat. That was the side parked up beside us."

"I recall the deck being quite cluttered with ropes and stuff," Deborah Corless remembered of *Blade*.[241]

Realising the smart members of the jury might also suspect it was *Blade*, defence lawyers led Morresey through this amazing demonstration of Jedi mind control—this is not the boat we're looking for:

"Can I just ask you this then when you were shown a photo or photos of a one masted yacht, did you then say that that boat was too small?"

"....yes."

---

239 20288 / ST / MONIQUE RUTTE / SHD080 / 150198
240 10653 / ST / MARCEL RUTTE / MK8254 / 060298
241 20284 / ST / DEBORAH CORLESS / MMG072 / 150198

"And by what you were referred to, was that boat was too small to be the boat that you stopped at and that Ben and Olivia got off onto?"

"…That is what I said yes."

"And you would say that about that boat in the pictures, the yacht in the pictures, 73?"

"…Ah yes, it's too small yes."

"When you were shown the photo of this sloop by the Police, did you straight away think that it was just too small?"

"…Yeah, straight away."

"Just straight away you thought well that wasn't the boat?"

"…Yes."

"And one of the reasons why it couldn't have been that boat is first, because it is too small?"

"…Yes."

"Secondly it doesn't have a stripe does it?"

"…No."

"Like the ketch that you saw?"

"…Yeah."

"It's far too low to the water isn't it?"

"…Yes definitely."

Once again you have to ask the fundamental question: how on a near moonless night, with no lights on the boat, at the very darkest point of the night, was Morresey genuinely able to discern the size of this boat?

The courtroom testimony is a game of smoke and mirrors, played with leading questions and the power of suggestion to mould the witness testimony into whatever you want it to be. By the time a case gets to trial, big agendas are at play for high stakes. In contrast, during the initial intelligence-gathering phase of a criminal investigation, police are trying to get all the information they can because they don't know at that point what will be relevant and what won't be. That's why initial witness statements are far more valuable to cold case investigations than trial testimony ever will be.

Before we leave this "mystery ketch" illusion for good, here's the straw the breaks the camel's back. You will note above the claim that Watson's sloop *Blade* was "far too low to the water, isn't it" to have been the boat Olivia and Ben were dropped off to.

Yet here's what Guy Wallace told police initially—the big "ketch" was strangely far too *low* in the water:[242]

> GUY WALLACE: Yeah but what is surprising about this particular one is that the middle of it's not that far out of the water.
> DETECTIVE FITZGERALD: Right.
> GUY WALLACE: 'Cos that's what really struck me.
> DETECTIVE FITZGERALD: When you say really far, when you say not that far.
> GUY WALLACE: What they call a wet boat.
> DETECTIVE FITZGERALD: Yeah.
> GUY WALLACE: Like if you're breaching or anything, going along on a tack and you may even have the gunnels over at times if you're trying to get a bit of speed out of it um, well the boat like that wouldn't have a displacement speed I'd be able to hold that, they'd probably just round up then again you never know.
> DETECTIVE FITZGERALD: When you say not that high you mean, it'd have to be at least, it's a ketch it's not small.
> GUY WALLACE: Oh no no, yeah you're probably looking at the middle of it about that high out of the water [indicates] 'cos when they stepped off from the Naiad it wasn't very far and I noticed I was hanging onto it from the Naiad and most boats you've gotta hold up like that [demonstrates] if you're sitting in the Naiad and I didn't, there was no strain at all.

---

242 12635 / TAPE / VIDEO INTERVIEW GUY WALLACE / TFD573 / 110198

If you can't see the writing on the wall now, go back and read these chapters again with an open mind, clear of any preconceptions. For Olivia and Ben to have climbed up onto a big ketch like the *Alliance* from the side would have been an exercise in gymnastics even on a sunny calm day. In the dark of the night it would have been a recipe for a dunking. To "hold on" to the railing of a ketch you'd need arms four foot long. Morresey and Wallace were not holding on to a ketch no matter what they truly believe today: they were hanging on to the side of a small yacht, which is why it was low enough to step onto.

"What really stood out," Wallace later repeated to private investigators for the Defence, "was how low in the middle, like the beams, the bow was quite high and the stern was quite high, but the middle seemed quite low, like banana-shaped almost and I think it would be a very, very wet boat to sail. There would be a lot of water coming on board."[243]

If you actually look at the *Alliance*, which formed the mental template for Wallace's non-existent "mystery ketch", it is nowhere near as low to the water as a standard yacht. Banana-shaped, yes, but it is not a submersible.

You can see the gears grinding in Detective Tom Fitzgerald's brain as he tries to reconcile this contradictory really low boat with everyone's usual idea of a big ketch.

> DETECTIVE FITZGERALD: But it's certainly a boat that would dominate the water, one like that.
> GUY WALLACE: Yeah.
> DETECTIVE FITZGERALD: Yeah.
> GUY WALLACE: Yeah, dominate your.
> DETECTIVE FITZGERALD: Your vision.

---

243 TRANSCRIPT Wallace interview with Carl Berryman for Defence

GUY WALLACE: Your vision.

DETECTIVE FITZGERALD: Yeah.

GUY WALLACE: As in, wow that stands out from anything else.

DETECTIVE FITZGERALD: Yeah yeah.

GUY WALLACE: Yeah definitely.

DETECTIVE FITZGERALD: For sure.

GUY WALLACE: That's why I can't figure out why they haven't tracked it down yet.

DETECTIVE FITZGERALD: Mm.

GUY WALLACE: It's just, just seems strange to me why they haven't, oh why someone hasn't said oh I've seen it.

DETECTIVE FITZGERALD: Mm.

GUY WALLACE: Like Ted, I read the paper today and he reckons he saw it and um, he may have seen it.

DETECTIVE FITZGERALD: Who said that?

GUY WALLACE: Ted Walsh.

DETECTIVE FITZGERALD: Oh yeah.

GUY WALLACE: Yeah but that's speculation again, they could've left the mooring, whose to say it wasn't another boat.

DETECTIVE FITZGERALD: Yeah.

GUY WALLACE: Whose to say the didn't jump on a dinghy, rowed ashore, gone somewhere else, I dunno—'phew'.

DETECTIVE FITZGERALD: Mm, that's the question isn't it.

GUY WALLACE: Yeah it is.

DETECTIVE FITZGERALD: That's the question. And you reckon it was Ben there that said ah.

GUY WALLACE: This guy said 'I hope that's your boat', yep have to I'd say.

DETECTIVE FITZGERALD: What about Olivia?

GUY WALLACE: If it wasn't him, no it'd have to be him 'cos he was sitting right on my left, sure it was him sitting on my left 'cos the two guys, there was the guy that I dropped off Hanns Bush Jetty and [pause] Ben, very similar, in height, everything really, build.

DETECTIVE FITZGERALD: Mm hmm.

DETECTIVE FITZGERALD: Okay so that boat [pause] like this boat worries me.

GUY WALLACE: Yeah?

DETECTIVE FITZGERALD: Yeah it worries me.

GUY WALLACE: Yeah I think it worries me. I'm right in the middle of this and [pause] I don't know what to bloody do, I'm just trying to help as much as I can type of thing.

DETECTIVE FITZGERALD: [Sigh] 'Cos it's important that we get to the truth you know?

GUY WALLACE: What do you mean?

DETECTIVE FITZGERALD: Well 'cos this boat, no one else has seen this boat.

GUY WALLACE: Well Ted saw it.

DETECTIVE FITZGERALD: No Ted didn't say he saw this boat, you said he might've seen a boat coming round the, that was blue and white.

GUY WALLACE: Yeah.

DETECTIVE FITZGERALD: No one else, you help me out. Let me give you a scenario that I've got okay.

GUY WALLACE: Yeah.

DETECTIVE FITZGERALD: There's four Naiad drivers who are working.

GUY WALLACE: Mm.

DETECTIVE FITZGERALD: Up to eight hours right? And in your own words you told me before that this boat is so dominant it stands out, anyone would see it.

GUY WALLACE: That's right.

DETECTIVE FITZGERALD: Right?

GUY WALLACE: Mm hmm.

DETECTIVE FITZGERALD: They've never seen it. They're delivering people all night.

GUY WALLACE: Yeah I know, I know what you're saying. I'm giving you my description of what I think it's like and I'm bloody sure that's how it is.
DETECTIVE FITZGERALD: They've never seen it.
GUY WALLACE: Well I'm not pricking you around.
DETECTIVE FITZGERALD: They've never seen this boat.
GUY WALLACE: Like, who was I talking to, another guy.
DETECTIVE FITZGERALD: No, no one, you haven't answered my question.
GUY WALLACE: I have answered your question!
DETECTIVE FITZGERALD: Look at it from my point of view.
GUY WALLACE: I'm looking at it from every point of view I can.
DETECTIVE FITZGERALD: Okay.
GUY WALLACE: How many times do you think it's gone over in my head.
DETECTIVE FITZGERALD: Well you look at it from my point of view, I've got four other people.
GUY WALLACE: Mm hmm.
DETECTIVE FITZGERALD: Who have worked out there in daylight.
GUY WALLACE: Mm.
DETECTIVE FITZGERALD: Right through to when you got out there.
GUY WALLACE: Yeah.
DETECTIVE FITZGERALD: And some say later, right?
GUY WALLACE: Mm hmm.
DETECTIVE FITZGERALD: And they know that harbour better than anybody.
GUY WALLACE: Right.
DETECTIVE FITZGERALD: They know every boat by name just about. People get on, take me to the *Nugget*.
GUY WALLACE: Mm hmm.
DETECTIVE FITZGERALD: Take me to the *Alliance*. They know where it is.

GUY WALLACE: Yeah.

DETECTIVE FITZGERALD: 'Cos Rachel's told me where they all are. They all know, they know it off the back of their hands, it's only a small inlet. Here's a 38 foot outstanding ketch that you've given us a brilliant description of.

GUY WALLACE: Outstanding, yep.

DETECTIVE FITZGERALD: No one's seen it. Nobody.

GUY WALLACE: Well um, I was talking to one guy. Just let me finish um, and I explained the boat that I say it was moored up next to and he said right I didn't see it there during the day 'cos I would've but um, there was something moored up to it at night and that was Tony off the *Nugget*.

DETECTIVE FITZGERALD: No.

GUY WALLACE: No?

DETECTIVE FITZGERALD: No I've spoken to Tony.

GUY WALLACE: Yeah.

DETECTIVE FITZGERALD: In depth.

GUY WALLACE: Well that's what I was talking to him the other night.

DETECTIVE FITZGERALD: And saying.

GUY WALLACE: In the bar.

DETECTIVE FITZGERALD: Nah.

GUY WALLACE: And he reckons he didn't see anything tied up against this big …

DETECTIVE FITZGERALD: Nothing.

GUY WALLACE: And this is where that was.

DETECTIVE FITZGERALD: No he remembered seeing a boat that we know is the *Alliance*.

GUY WALLACE: No the *Alliance* is *moored out by itself.* [author's emphasis]

DETECTIVE FITZGERALD: No he doesn't remember anything like this. I've spoken to him.

GUY WALLACE: Yeah so have I.

DETECTIVE FITZGERALD: I've spoken to him personally and in depth.

GUY WALLACE: Yeah.

DETECTIVE FITZGERALD: I've got a written statement off him.

GUY WALLACE: Yeah.

DETECTIVE FITZGERALD: I could show it to you.

GUY WALLACE: I'm just saying what I heard from him.

DETECTIVE FITZGERALD: Explain to me Guy why no one else has seen it.

GUY WALLACE: Oh mate I can't explain it to you! I've explained all I can to you.

DETECTIVE FITZGERALD: Well we've identified a hundred and over boats.

GUY WALLACE: Yeah.

DETECTIVE FITZGERALD: Just about, practically every single boat in that harbour that night.

GUY WALLACE: Righto.

DETECTIVE FITZGERALD: And spoken to every single person.

GUY WALLACE: Yep and no one remembers seeing it.

DETECTIVE FITZGERALD: No one, bar you, has seen this bloody thing.

GUY WALLACE: Oh!

DETECTIVE FITZGERALD: Now that's not possible. That is not possible.

GUY WALLACE: Well I don't see how it is.

DETECTIVE FITZGERALD: That's not possible.

GUY WALLACE: Not possible

If you noted the emphasis above, this next point will make sense. Wallace was trying to picture a ketch moored up to other boats. He discounted *Alliance* precisely because it was moored on its own. In his mind, he wanted *Alliance* to be tied up to *Mina Cornelia*, but to also be as low to the water as *Blade*. That would have solved his problem. Over the coming weeks and months he came to believe the "ketch" had been moored on its own. This was the *Alliance* memory gradually taking over from what little remained of the actual encounter in pitch black darkness.

So far then over the course of this book, we've established that Scott Watson fits the profile of a psychopath, that contrary to what you've heard he was prone to violence, intimidation and that he discussed having sex with a woman and killing her during the act. He did in fact try and coerce a woman to have sex at knifepoint.

We have established that Watson had a dangerous Jekyll and Hyde personality switch when drinking, and we know he'd been drinking heavily on New Year's Eve and taken drugs.

We know Watson had repeatedly boasted that he had a "double-masted ketch" out in the bay, when in fact he had a sloop. We know he was one of only two yacht owners who had sailed into Furneaux alone that day. We know that, like many men, Watson was looking to score.

We know that Watson is the spitting image of the descriptions of the mystery man, regardless of what authors and the news media have previously told you. In fact, you appear to have been subjected to deliberate misinformation about Watson's appearance on the night.

We know that none of the clothes Watson was actually photographed or seen wearing that night have been found.

We know that the mystery ketch with what looked like Ben and Olivia in the back, seen sailing towards Cook Strait on 2 January by a large group of people on a charter launch, has now been for the first time in 18 years positively identified as the ketch *Alliance*.

We know that the blonde woman in the back was most likely teenager Hollie Pickering, a passenger on *Alliance*.

We know that Guy Wallace mixed up a memory of *Alliance* and mistakenly came to believe he had dropped off Ben and Olivia to a ketch identical to *Alliance*.

We know it was too dark to actually see the detail he claims to have seen.

And we know Scott Watson lied about his movements, in ways you have never been told but which you are about to find out.

CHAPTER FIFTEEN

The Two-Trip Theory

In his book, Keith Hunter claims Scott Watson emerges from an analysis of the documentation "lie free". That contention is about to be sorely put to the test, but not before overcoming the problem of the two-trip theory.

Scott Watson's defence lawyers were outraged during closing argument in front of the jury when prosecutors suggested Watson made two trips back to *Blade* that evening not one. The argument was that he'd gone back to get a jersey and then returned to Furneaux.

The defence had made much of a trip back to *Blade* by Watson supposedly at 2am. If Watson had come back at 2am, they argued, he could not have been the mystery man on the water taxi at 4am unless he had somehow returned to shore unnoticed.

It would be fair to say that the two-trip theory remains the most problematic part of the case against Watson, not just because it raises questions about where he was, but because it also exposes other grey areas in the police case.

Let's examine what evidence exists. In his first statement to police dated 7 January, Scott Watson said:

"At about 2.00 am I took the water taxi back to my yacht. It was a Naiad, yellow. It was driven by an old guy with a hat on. I was the only passenger. I remember he wouldn't let me on until he had parked the boat. He kept telling me to wait. I don't think I spoke with him."

Police checked. The only "old guy" driving water taxis that night was John Mullen, and he wasn't wearing a hat that night, nor did he recall taking Watson out.[244]

We know Watson is either lying, or only telling half the truth, because firstly the people on *Mina Cornelia* were still on deck at 2am and did not see him return at that time, and secondly there were multiple confirmed sightings of Watson back in the Furneaux bar after that.

Security guard Michael Cronin, who had not been drinking while on duty, said the band finally packed up all their gear at 2.30am. He was supervising the garden bar and keeping a beer in the fridge for a man in a light blue denim shirt and jeans who was popping back every so often to retrieve his beer.[245] "I would recognise him again", Cronin told police,[246] and then confidently identified Watson from a photo montage saying he wasn't as clean-shaven on the night as the photo implied[247]. He said Watson wasn't causing any trouble on the occasions he saw him.

---

244 20075 / JS / NAIAD DRIVER ENQUIRY / TFD573 / 130198
245 Guy Wallace testified that he saw the "mystery man" in the garden bar at precisely this time when he came out to check on operations at the bar around 1.30am. He told the court he also went to the beer fridge and wanted to know why they were storing a punter's drink in there when that was not supposed to happen given the large number of punters and limited fridge space. He testified that he discussed the issue with Cronin. This doesn't prove the "mystery man" was Watson, although Wallace did later identify him as such, but it does prove that—just like the "mystery ketch" and the *Alliance*, always in the same place at the same time—so too were the "mystery man" and Watson.
246 11841 / ST / MICHAEL CRONIN / GT3329 / 100398
247 11761 / ST / MICHAEL CRONIN / GT3329 / 300398

The Two-Trip Theory

At one point he remembered seeing Watson talking to David Furneaux, one of Furneaux Lodge owner Rick McLeod's security coordinators. Watson had told police he'd been speaking to McLeod, although McLeod denied remembering Watson. Cronin said Watson "had obviously had a bit to drink" by then.

He told police Watson left the garden bar area about 3am, where he'd been since around 1.30am.[248] He didn't see where Watson went.

According to a raft of witnesses, Watson was still in party mode, and came into the main bar.

There is no dispute from Watson's defence that this was Scott Watson, so the descriptions are not the focus here—it is the timings and context that are important. These are the witness statements taken when memories were still fresh:

"After the band had finished," Oliver Perkins told police,[249] "a guy approached us in the bar. I hadn't seen him before. He was by himself at all times."

"I can remember about 3.00 am going over to a group of my friends were talking to a guy," Ed Sundstrum told police.[250] "The group of friends included Olli Perkins, Chris Bisman, Amanda Egden, Millie Savill. They were speaking to a guy called Scott.

"He said he was Scott from Wellington. I can't remember exactly what he was saying but he wanted the girls on to his yacht. He was getting personal and obviously wanted them to go out there for sex. He was asking for sexual favours in return for going on to the yacht. I can remember him talking about Prozac but am not sure what he said. I heard the next morning that he had offered the girls Prozac t-shirts.

"At about 4.00 am I walked back to the bay where we were staying. I walked back with the English guys."

Amanda Egden told police she returned to the Furneaux bar at

---
248 13332 / ST / MICHAEL CRONIN / MK8254 / 110998
249 10120 / ST / OLIVER PERKINS / AHD181 / 080198
250 10268 / ST / EDWARD SUNDSTRUM / MK8254 / 160198

2.30am and ended up in a conversation with Scott about 15 minutes after that. He told her he had a "double-masted ketch" and invited her on it:[251]

"I asked him where he was going on the Yacht and he said he was going to Tonga and all around the Islands. I told him that we could pull ropes on the yacht to help him sail it and to that he said 'What, no sexual favours?'

"The way I understood his comment is that he was implying that if we come aboard the yacht it would be for sex."

"I thought Scott was just some weird guy who was trying to come onto us. After we finished talking to Scott we walked back to the beach where Mr Fisher had dropped us off. That's where we slept the night. We got to the beach at about 4am we did take our time getting back. The last I saw of Scott was in the bar."

Chris Bisman was drinking outside the bar and watching his mate Ollie Perkins inside through the double doors.[252]

"After the New Year we just sat around drinking until about 3.00 am. We were still outside on a park bench by the left of the front doors of the Lodge. There were still quite a few people around even though it was 3.00 am. The bar was still packed.

"My friend Olly Perkins was inside the bar talking to a guy. Amanda Egden, Mark Tapley and Millie Savill were sitting at a table. I just went in to have a drink and stayed inside… Later, while I was still in there, I saw Olly Perkins talking with a guy over by a table to the left as you walk in the door. They were standing near a table. It was the same table that Mark, Millie and Amanda were at.

"I went over to talk to Olly because he is my friend. After a few minutes I realised that the discussion between Olly and this guy was a bit heated."

---

251 10184 / ST / AMANDA EGDEN / AHD181 / 120198
252 10055 / ST / CHRISTOPHER BISMAN / BB3624 / 120198

Perkins went outside with Bisman for some fresh air, and explained how it had come up in conversation that his sister had cancer, because Watson had called him a girl for wearing a necklace his sister had given him. Watson allegedly retorted, "she'll be dead in two years".

"I went back in," said Bisman, "and by this time this guy was sitting at the table with Mark, Amanda and Millie. I sat down beside him and I discussed with this guy about comments he had made about cancer. I said to him not to say that sort of thing about Olly's sister and he kind of agreed with me. When Olly came back in this guy actually apologised to Olly.

"By this time it was about 3.45 am or 4.00 am and Olly and I left and went outside. I had a couple more beers with Olly while the girls stayed back inside with this guy.

"I considered that he had been drinking heavily because he was kind of slurring his words. He wasn't drinking anything when I saw him and spoke to him. He could have just been fairly drunk but he also could have been spaced out from smoking dope or anything for that matter. Nothing was mentioned about dope or drugs during our conversation.

"I'm not sure how long the other girls talked to this guy for but they met up with us a short time later and we all walked back to the bay and slept on the beach."

Amanda Egden's brother Richard estimated the total length of his group's exposure to Watson was about an hour:[253]

"I'm not sure what time it was when we first saw this guy. He would have stayed with our group for an hour or so I think. The whole time we were in the top bar at the Lodge. Most of us left the bar at about 4.00 am. We walked back to the beach where we slept."

Independent corroboration of the timing of all this comes from

---

[253] 20043 / ST / RICHARD EGDEN / SID741 / 120198

Simon Bell, helping transport passengers on the launch *Equaliser*.[254]

"We came alongside the [Furneaux] wharf at 0230 hours, some of the youths we were to pick up were not there so John Murray and myself went to the bar. At the bar John and I went to find the seven that were missing. We had a couple of drinks, there would have been about 100 people in the bar at this point."

How much time does it take to walk up to the Lodge and enjoy a couple of drinks? Half an hour?

"An altercation then started between seven or eight youths hassling a single male. There was shoulder pushing and that sort of thing, the guy kept backing off, he showed no sign of retaliating or aggression, he backed into John Murray and myself. I stepped aside, let him through, then I closed the gap, as he was on his own and outnumbered.

"At the same time the Furneaux employees, two of them stepped in and spoke to the aggressors. The guy we let through pulled out his smokes and rolled a smoke. I could not believe he was so cool, calm and collected at this point.

"Soon after leaving the bar I heard someone say (one of the youths) that the guy had said something derogatory about his sister who had cancer or something like that.

"The guy, Male Caucasian, 5'6" to 5'8" in height, 70 to 80 kg, closer to 70 kg, straight dark hair, real dark, brushed around, touch ears down onto collar, 25 years to 30 years, no moustache, stubble. He was wearing a light weight denim shirt, sleeves rolled loosely to below the elbow, tidy blue jeans, faded, cross trainers, fairly scuffed. Had tattoos on forearms or back of hand that were faded, I did not see what they were.

"We grabbed the guys we could and then we headed back to the wharf. On the way we picked up other friends etc and we got on

---

254 20203/ST/SIMON BELL/PPD601/170198

the boat and headed for Punga Cove. At around 3.30 am we left to go to Punga Cove with 25 persons on board.

"We dropped 16 at Punga Cove at 0403 hours and then we arrived at Bay of Many Coves at 0430 hours," concluded Simon Bell.

What all of this means, regardless of what any commentator argues, is that Watson's movements between 1.30am and 3.30am appear to be fully accounted for, and they do not allow room for a 2am, 2.30am or even 3am water taxi ride back to *Blade*. The time between Watson leaving the garden bar at 3, going into the main bar at 3, pestering the teenagers for half an hour or so, and then making his way to a water taxi, is consistent with the timing of a 3.45am water taxi ride with Guy Wallace and only Guy Wallace. Remember, the sightings above are all *confirmed* sightings of Watson, taken not from choreographed court testimony 18 months later, but from police interviews just days after the event when memories were sharp.

No, if we are to find the gap where an earlier trip back to *Blade* could have happened, we are going to have to retrace Scott Watson's steps earlier in the night.

CHAPTER SIXTEEN

The Real Sequence Of Events

Scott Watson came ashore with Dave Mahony and the men from *Mina Cornelia* probably 9.45. We know this from a 9.58pm eftpos receipt from one of his fellow passengers onshore. He got himself noticed almost straight away, before he had even left the jetty:[255]

"The male had an 1125 ml bottle of Coruba rum in his hand," reported security guard Stewart Allen. "He was holding it by the neck when he got off the taxi. I spoke to the male the instant he stepped foot on the landing. I told him he wasn't getting past the landing with the bottle. I told him he had to drink it or leave it behind.

"The male stayed on the landing for about 30 minutes. He was there for quite awhile trying to drink the rum...He was talking to a group of people who looked quite rich, by the way they were dressed and I saw the boat they came off. They were there before the male arrived."

---

255 11476 / ST / STEWART ALLEN / AHD181 / 120298

ABOVE: The flashbulb illuminates Furneaux Jetty. **BELOW:** The Lodge Bar

This was less than an hour after Watson's "clean shaven" photo was taken on *Mina Cornelia* before they came ashore. Thankfully the security guard hadn't seen the photo and was looking instead at the real Scott Watson rather than the airbrushed version:

"He was a male Caucasian, about early to mid 30s. He looked like he drunk and smoked heavily and was quite untidy. He had several days growth on his face. He had black short hair. He had tattoos on both arms in deep green ink. He was wearing large white t-shirt that had a very open neck on it and appeared two sizes too big. He had blue jeans and possibly jandals. He was smoking 'roll your own' smokes. I saw one in his hand at one stage."

So we know Watson was stuck on the wharf between approximately 9.45pm and some time just after 10pm. It was during this time that Watson began hitting on women on the jetty.[256]

"Stephanie has blond hair and is attractive," recalled Janine Morrison. "I don't know what this male said to Stephanie but I got the impression that he was trying to pick her up. The reason that I say this is that I heard Stephanie tell him to "F*** off".

"This male stayed around our group for about ten to fifteen minutes. He seemed to move on from Stephanie to Sheree and then to Catherine. Once again I don't know exactly what he was saying other than I heard the girls telling him to "F*** off".

"I think at one stage he came up to me but I just turned my back and ignored him so he didn't say anything to me."

It was hardly the offence of the century, but it's an official Watson sighting to kick off his time at Furneaux.

There's a brief gap before the next official sighting, around 20 past 10pm:[257]

After we got into the bar, maybe 10 or 20 minutes [after 10], I

---

256 20695 / ST / JANINE MORRISON / JSD808 / 130298
257 30301 / ST / STEFAN ZAJKOWSKI / JSC422 / 050298

remember seeing Scott Watson in the bar," Stefan Zajkowski from *Mina Cornelia* told police. "Scott was by himself and I think he walked past us and disappeared."

And reappeared elsewhere in the bar to someone else. We know this next sighting turns into an official Watson one, but it appears to begin with a mystery man at the bar, trying to ingratiate himself with a girl behind him:

"At about 10.30pm all five of us went inside the bar because it was freezing outside," student Anna Kernick told police.[258] "We stood at the back of the bar by the fireplace and the pool table.

"The bar was packed. Phil, myself and Lance sat down. By this stage we were all fairly tired from the day and the drinking. I wasn't drunk. Sarah and Mary went away to get some drinks. It took them about 10 minutes."

Another friend, Amanda Percy, kept getting propositioned by a mystery man at the bar every time she'd gone up for drinks.

"During the evening," remembered Amanda Percy, "when we went to the bar we would always go in twos. When we were sitting with Annie's group, two of their friends Sarah Kernick and her friend … came back from the bar and commented on this really sleazy guy who had been at the bar.

"They wanted to throw iced water over him so Sarah and Sandra [Mary?] went back to the bar, Lance and I followed behind. I showed them the guy that I thought they were talking about. This was a person who was by himself and kept talking to me every time I went for a drink. He would say 'Hi, how's your night going, is your boyfriend here'. I got the impression he was really sleazy. He was always up at the bar every time I looked in or went past.

"He was about 6 foot tall, Caucasian, 27 years, short black hair. I can't remember what he was wearing. He had a t-shirt on. He

---

258 20294 / ST / ANNA KERNICK / RMC084 / 130198

The Real Sequence Of Events

had dark skin. He had quite muscly arms. I was surprised the barman didn't do anything about his behaviour. I remember he was clean shaven," remembered Percy, who was blonde. She had not gone back with Sarah and Mary to their seats after this and told police she therefore didn't know whether her mystery man was their mystery man.

Barman Chey Phipps had seen this kind of behaviour that night, remarking:[259]

"The only person that really stood out to me was a guy drinking at the bar in the area of Reg's corner or that side of the bar. I noticed him because he was kind of getting in the way of other customers, trying to get served, because he was leaning on the bar and not shifting out of the way.

"As different girls were coming up to the bar to get served, this guy would start chatting away to them. I can't remember any conversations but his body language was suggesting "come on baby, how about it" type of thing.

"One girl looked at him with a look of disgust and she then turned to some guy that was probably her boyfriend.

"I can't recall anything about her other than she was fairly attractive."

Imagine: you're a barman at a packed counter on New Year's Eve. There are four of you working the counter that evening, faced with a sea of drunken faces, yelling, laughing, pushing, thrusting cash in

---

[259] 20250 / ST / CHEY PHIPPS / ASD279 / 090198 Phipps, incidentally gave a different description of the mystery man from Amanda Percy, who later told police the man she had seen had recognised her and apologised to her in a Blenheim shop: 40061 / ST / AMANDA PERCY / DH6260 / 200398
"The male I refer to in my statement last night came into my parents store and said to me I look familiar. I said, "I saw you at Furneaux Lodge New Year's". The male went red and apologised to me. I just didn't like the way he talked to me and acted. I have seen him in the store before, usually on dole day. I don't know his name but will try to find it out." Significantly, Amanda Percy recognised Scott Watson as a regular customer of the store, and told police he wasn't the one at the bar she wanted to pour ice over. Percy said in 2016 that "the mystery man I saw was certainly no boat owner". She never discovered his name because she left on her OE the following month.

your face to get your attention. What if the "mystery man" at the bar was just a composite of "every man"?

There were a lot of men trying to hit on women that night, but how many had control of a boat?

"When they got back," continued Anna Kernick as she described Sarah and Mary's return, "there was this guy hanging around Mary. He was really drunk and was sleazy. Mary was leaning against the pool table and he was leaning in close and swaying back and forth.[260]

"I couldn't hear what was being said but could tell that Mary was trying to get rid of him.

"I saw him put his beer down by Mary's feet and then he asked her to pick it up and when she did he brushed his hand across her breast," said Anna Kernick.

Her sister Sarah also witnessed it, implying Scott Watson was a lounge lizard:

"A guy slid along the wall up to my friend Mary. When I say he slid, he looked like he wasn't making himself obvious. He didn't appear rotten drunk, but seemed to be swaying. He wasn't slurred in his speech.

"He asked Mary what her name was and where did she come from. Mary said 'wouldn't you like to know'. Mary appeared to be giving him a complete push off. I can't remember what else was said but he looked to lean on the pool table and knocked Mary's drink over. He then knocked her packet of cigarettes out of her hand.

"Mary bent down to pick her cigarettes up and he bent down at the same time, and he appeared to fall forward touching Mary's breast. I don't know whether he did this intentionally or not.

"When they stood up again, Mary noticed the guy had a wet sleeve. She asked him if he had pissed on it. It was about here that Mary picked up her stuff and came back to where we were standing," Sarah Kernick told police.

---

260 20294 / ST / ANNA KERNICK / RMC084 / 130198

The Real Sequence Of Events

Is this the mystery man incident bar manager Roz McNeilly witnessed out of the corner of her eye? She certainly identified Watson as the mystery man she'd seen, but her incident may have happened earlier:[261]

"I identified a person from this photo montage as the person who was in Reg's Corner at the front of the bar on New Year's Eve. I have been shown a series of 7 photographs by Detective Fitzgerald today and I know Guy Wallace served him a lot also.

"I remember thinking to myself I wonder where "Reg" is because this guy was sitting in his seat. I thought Reg must have just gone to the toilet or something but he didn't come back. I later saw Reg down the other end of the bar.

"The male I identified in the montage I remember him smoking "rollies", that is roll your own cigarettes. He was sitting there with a skinny rollie in his mouth.

"I remember someone fell over in that corner. I asked someone if he was alright and they said yes, that's when I noticed the guy had moved from that corner. I'm not sure if it was him that fell over but I presumed it was because he had gone after that incident. If it was him that fell over in that corner he would have got wet because there was a lot of beer on the floor.

"I remember this guy sitting there because there was a till right in front of him. This till was put there especially for New Year's Eve because it was so busy.

"He had a leather complexion a sea person sort of look, like he had been in the sea or worked out doors. He had brown hands like tradesman hands, definitely not an office worker. His hands were fairly skinny but not soft," said McNeilly.

Watson by all reports was unstable on his feet at this time, and falling over would explain his wet clothing. Anna Kernick says she watched Watson after the fall and the breast incident.

---

261 40330 / ST / ROZLYN McNEILLY / TFD573 / 020498

"I think it was about this time that Mary came back over from him to us. This guy just stood there staring at four young girls dancing together.

"I watched him go around the bar, he was staggering. He appeared to be by himself.

"At one stage during this guy being around he passed comments about coming down to his boat for a ride.

"I also bent down to pick up my bag and he said to me, 'Nice set you have got there love'.

"It was about this time that Lance spoke with this guy. I could hear him say to Lance that he was a boat builder and to come down to his boat. I could hear Lance telling this guy that we didn't want anything to do with him.

"I also heard him ask Lance for drugs. I heard Lance tell him he was a policeman and this guy walked away then came back and told Lance to prove it.

"This went on for a couple of minutes then he left us alone."

But how, you may be asking, do we know for sure that this person was Scott Watson?

"Lance told me after he spoke to this guy he had told Lance he was a boat builder and was staying at Furneaux on his own boat," explained Sarah Kernick to police.[262]

Lance Rairi, based in Australia, later identified Watson from a photo montage as the man who had been sexually suggestive to the girls and who had touched Mary's breast.[263] Reading his police statement however, you can see it was Watson who was the only lone yachtie at Furneaux on a homebuilt craft:[264]

"After about 45 minutes I happened to notice a man talking to two others about 3 metres away from me. He appeared to be very

---

262 20079 / ST / SARAH KERNICK / RMC084 / 130198
263   40924 / ST / LANCE RAIRI / SB8406 / 140498
264 40162 / ST / LANCE RAIRI / NG7930 / 040398

inebriated and had trouble standing. It appeared to me that he wasn't with the other two men and in fact he appeared to be annoying them.

"He was Caucasian, in his early 30s, thin to medium build, about 174 cm tall, and unshaven. He didn't have a beard, just stubble from a day or two's growth. He had dark collar length messy hair.

"He was wearing a light coloured t-shirt and dark jeans.

"I left our group for about 10 minutes while I went to the outside toilet. When I returned the man was talking to my group of friends. I spoke to Sarah and she told me that the man had said something of a sexual nature to her sister Annie. As I was talking to Sarah the man was actually talking to Annie.

"I stood next to the guy to make my presence known and then moved in between him and Annie. I started making small talk with him so that he wouldn't talk to Annie anymore.

"I said, 'Where are all your mates?'

"He replied that he was there on his own.

"I asked him if he was from around the area and he said yeah.

"I don't know how it came up in conversation but he mentioned that he'd arrived at Furneaux Lodge in a boat.

"I asked him if it was his own boat and he said yes and that he'd actually built the boat himself. I asked him if that was what he did, and he said that he was a boat builder.

"During the conversation he asked me if I had any drugs. I said no and told him that I didn't do that sort of thing. He became agitated and seemed to change his attitude. He called me ignorant and I asked him why. He said I was ignorant because I didn't use drugs. I told him that it was a personal choice and that I choose not to do that.

"At that point I came to the decision that I didn't want to talk to him anymore," said Lance Rairi. "I didn't see him again that night. We stayed in that area until about 11.30 pm."

So here we have a confirmed sighting of Scott Watson, stretching from around 10.30 until he moved away, just after 11pm.

"This would have been about 11.10pm," one of the others in the group, Philip Hale, told police.[265]

"He was a male Caucasian, about 5'7" in height, slim build, he was wiry. He had short dark wavy hair down to just past his collar. He had high cheekbones with 'slitty' sort of eyes. He had like a day or two's growth on his face. He was wearing a blue long sleeved denim shirt which had two pockets on the front. He was wearing brown cat type boots. He was wearing dark blue jeans."

Around this time, Deborah Corless, one of the *Mina Cornelia* passengers, noticed Watson "on the other side of the inside bar at the lodge. He was leaning over the bar and talking to one woman."[266]

Watson didn't have to go too far in a crowded bar to get into trouble. But he does not appear to show up again until just before midnight. Lois Knowles and her husband had been on the launch *Kaela Rose*, moored 30 or 40 metres from *Blade*:[267]

"At about 11.50 pm New Year's Eve I was in the bar area at Furneaux Lodge. My husband had gone to find a table. I was approached by a male Caucasian. He was fairly drunk. He started talking to me. I can't remember exactly what he was saying. He mentioned that he had a boat and asked if I would like to see it. I said that I wasn't interested as we had one of our own.

"He asked what boat I was on. I told him the '*Kaela Rose*'. He said he knew the boat and mentioned that he had seen a blonde with "big boobs" on board it earlier in the afternoon. I said to watch it as he may have been talking about my daughter.

"My husband arrived back at about that stage. This male didn't say much else and moved off shortly afterwards. I didn't see where he went to."

He reappeared after the midnight countdown:

---

[265] 30055 / ST / PHILIP HALE / DSC229 / 210198
[266] 20284 / ST / DEBORAH CORLESS / MMG072 / 150198
[267] 11553 / ST / LOIS KNOWLES / CSC980 / 110298

"After midnight, I think it was after midnight," Brent Newton told police, "some guy in the bar approached Ray, apparently asking him for some drugs. Ray later told me that. Ray didn't have any drugs. This guy just asked him for some.[268]

"Ray apparently told him that he didn't have any and Ray told me that this guy made the comment to him "Dog on a chain Bro". I didn't hear this guy say that but apparently he repeated it to Ray twice. I don't know what that was supposed to mean.

"At about that time this guy hassled Teresa by approaching her. The guy was pretty boozed apparently, from what Theresa told me and she can't remember what he said to her. I had my back to her at this time and didn't see what was happening.

"Theresa told me later that she felt uneasy and frightened by the guy. He was leaning right over her.

"I happened to turn around and saw this guy there. I moved over and started talking to my fiancee Teresa and this guy left at that point. There were no hassles and agro.

"I didn't get much of a look at this guy but I would describe him as: a male Caucasian, aged probably about thirties. I didn't get a very good look at him. He was slightly shorter than Ray and slightly taller than me. He would have been approx. 5' 9" I guess.

"His hair wasn't dark or noticeably blonde. I didn't even get a good look at that. He wasn't big but skinny to medium. He was wearing casuals and a blue shirt I think, I'm not even sure of that. His hair was medium length and not much over his collar. He wasn't long haired or anything like that. I didn't notice any tattoos.

"I did notice that he looked scary around the eyes. He certainly didn't have a friendly face. He just left without any problems," recalled Brent Newton.

Now let's hear from Ray Padden, the man who was first approached:

---

[268] 20045 / ST / BRENT NEWTON / BB3624 / 110198

"The atmosphere was pretty happy except for one person.

"This male person came over and started speaking to me. He said that he had built his boat and that it was in the bay. He asked me if I had any drugs. I said no. I said 'Look I don't know you, you could be a cop, anyway I don't take drugs'. He then said 'Dog on a chain bro.'

"He said this as though it was meant to relax me. I asked him what this meant and he said it is gang talk in Australia. I had had enough of him. He was in my face for a good amount of time even up to half an hour.

"The main conversation was about his yacht and the drugs, but apart from what I've said I can't be more specific. In the end I had to tell him to f*** off because he was being a pain.

"He was by himself during this time and I am unsure if he spoke to any other people in our group.

"I saw this person one more time. It was about ½ an hour since he left. I went to the toilet and on the way I saw this guy being searched by two security guys. These guys were the two that were in the bar most of the night.

"They were getting him to empty his pockets. It was a tense situation. As I came up one of the security guys fronted me up, probably thinking I was a mate of the guy they were searching. I said I'm off to the toilet.

"When I came back I'm not sure but I think they might have been still there. This happened inside the bar near the alleyway leading to the toilets and restaurant. This was the only two contacts I had with this person.

"He was a male Caucasian, he had a dark lived in colour. I would say he is in his 30s. He was wearing a blue denim shirt, with a red tag. I thought it was a Levis tag. It looked new. I think he might have been wearing jeans," remarked Ray Padden.

There is no question that this was Scott Watson, but here, just after midnight, suddenly he was wearing a shirt with a Levis tag, which doesn't appear in the *Mina Cornelia* photo, and there was no mention of a wet sleeve. Had he slipped back to his boat for a change of clothes after being asked whether he had "pissed" on his sleeve?

Ray Padden continues:

"He was about 5 foot 7, 5 foot 8. He had a small frame, but still looked athletic. I think he needed a shave. The reason it sticks out is here is this guy with a new flash shirt yet it looked like he needed a shave and a bit of a clean up.

"His hair was short dark and not very messy. I don't know if he was smoking. I think he told me his name and I can't remember it. He did have tattoos and one might have been on his hand; perhaps a flower."

Teresa Geddes, the focus of Watson's attempts at affection, also remembers "his hair was quite tidy and collar length at the back."[269]

Yet only an hour earlier, with a wet sleeve, Lance Rairi had described Watson's hair as dishevelled:

"He had dark collar length messy hair. He was wearing a light coloured t-shirt and dark jeans."

Is it possible that in his booze-fuelled haze even Scott Watson had realised he needed a change of shirt and a quick brush of his hair if he was to have any chance of female company that night? Is it possible that between 11.15pm and midnight he slipped back to *Blade*, a 90 second trip, and cadged a lift back in from someone in the huge tide of revellers flowing into shore in time for the New Year's countdown? His boat didn't have a name, he was just another face in the crowd, just another marine hitchhiker on a night of general goodwill—a passing tender may not have realised to this day that they picked up Watson.

Of course, this is mere speculation, but it's unusual that Watson

---

269 20046 / ST / TERESA GEDDES / CHC045 / 110198

went from dishevelled to shevelled in the space of an hour on a night when people normally look worse for wear as time goes on.

It's also hard to get past that flash new shirt, when three hours earlier as he caught the inflatable to shore, Brigette Radford on *Cornelia* said Watson was wearing "a soft blue shirt, not denim but it looked like it. The shirt looked as if it had been through the wash a few times."[270]

Radford was the only one on the boat to pay close attention to the state of Watson's shirt.

Ray Padden's encounter with Watson in the "new flash shirt" with red Levis tag, was over by around 12.30. But Scott Watson wasn't done with trouble. In this next encounter he begins stalking an 18 year old girl, eventually grabbing her—signs of an increasingly unstable state of mind.

Harry Featherstone and his wife had brought their children's 18 year old nanny Kristal and her friend Delina to the New Year's party.

"I guess it was close to 1.00am then," Featherstone told police.[271] "While there a guy approached our group. I don't know where he came from but it was in the direction of the middle of the first chalet and the laundry of Furneaux Lodge.

"He came from a direction of bush. He was by himself. The guy approached the two girls. Louise was standing near them then.

"He walked straight up to them and he said something to the girls like, 'Do you want to come and see my yacht?'"

Note the possessive. This was a predator who owned a boat. There were only just over a hundred boat owners at Furneaux that night. Most had brought large groups with them, making them unlikely suspects. The police claim only two lone yachties were there, and one of those was Watson while the other was portly, middle-aged and fully bearded.

---

270 10667 / ST / BRIGETTE RADFORD / JSC422 / 050298
271 30336 / ST / HENRY FEATHERSTONE / JSC422 / 070298

Featherstone continues:

"He said something else to them that I can't remember. I immediately picked him as sleazy. I stepped in and said, 'Leave my daughters alone'. He turned to me and said, 'Who are you?'

"I said, 'I'm their father' and that I'd started early.

"He was quite confident and you could tell he backed himself. He then asked me, 'What do you do?' to which I replied, 'I'm a farmer'. He then turned around and walked away.

"He was about 5'8" tall, medium but muscular. I'd say he was around 35 to 40 years old. He had dark coloured hair, not long but just over his ears in length. It was not untidy looking. He was clean shaven and I didn't notice if he was carrying anything. In fact he wasn't holding anything, not even a glass like most people. He was wearing clothing of some description but I can't even tell you what.

"He was quite close to me when he spoke to me and I never noticed his clothing.

"When this guy left us he walked straight towards the beer garden. I had no doubts what this guy wanted that night. He was trying to pick up a girl. He was very direct in his manner. I thought he was quite sleazy," said Featherstone.

Delina Mihaere, one of the girls, kept an eye on Watson:

"Harry told him to go away and he walked over to a tree not far away. He stood there and looked at Kristal." [272]

Kristal Baillie got a good look at Watson because one of the big outside lights was shining on his face. [273]

"I would describe this person as male, Caucasian, quite tanned, his face was quite burnt. He was short, about my height which is 5'4" or 5". He was reasonably solid build but not really big. He had brownish hair with a slight bit of curl. It was tight curls and his

---

272 10672 / ST / DELINA MIHAERE / MK8254 / 070298
273 30335 / ST / KRISTAL BAILLIE / MK8254 / 080298

hair was short above his ears at the side. I cannot remember if he was clean shaven or not.

"He was wearing jeans. I'm not sure if they were blue or black. He had a light blue denim shirt and some kind of white top on underneath. I don't know what type of top it was but I can remember seeing some white. I think his sleeves were rolled up.

"He was dressed tidy. I do not recall if he had any tattoos," said Baillie.

"After this guy had left we stayed talking to Harry and Louise. They then left a short time later. Me and Delina went back down to the garden bar. We ended up dancing on the stage.

"The same guy who had hassled us earlier came up to Delina and asked her something about the band. I didn't notice it was him until I looked over. When I realised it was the same guy I said to Delina, 'Let's go'.

"We jumped off the stage and started to walk away. As I did walk away this guy went to grab my arm. I was holding Delina's jersey as I was following her.

"Delina saw this guy trying to grab me so she took my other hand and pulled me away. I managed to shake off this guy. We left the garden bar and I did not see this guy again," said Baillie.

Delina Mihaere told police the man made a solid attempt to hold onto Kristal:

"He had already grabbed her around the stomach and tried to do it again."

"When the guy was talking to Delina," added Baillie, "he didn't sound drunk but I could tell he was. I do not think he had an accent. I was trying to avoid him so I did not take a lot of notice.

"He made me feel uneasy and uncomfortable because of what he had said earlier," said Baillie.

As she later told the court, using more polite language than originally used, the man who grabbed her had earlier on their first meeting wanted to "sleep" with him:

"He started talking to me and making disgusting comments about the way I looked and what he thought of me."

"Can you recall now what it was he said to you?"

"...not exactly what he said, no, but it was to do with that I was nice looking and that he would quite like to, yeah," murmured Baillie.

"Well I am sorry to push you on this," explained the crown prosecutor, "but it is important—could you do your best to tell us what it was he said?

"...roughly that he probably wouldn't have minded sleeping with me that night and for me to go off with him."

"He used the word 'sleeping with you', that type of phrase, or did he use some other phrase?"

"...no it was yeah, just dirty comments, um, making suggestions to me that, like, sleep with me and you know—I can't remember specifically what it was that he said, but it was yeah, that..."

"How long had you been in his presence before he suggested that to you?"

"...not even a minute, it was pretty straight off."

"And when that was said was there any reaction from anyone else around you, or did you respond to that?

"...I responded to it."

"What did you say to him?"

"...I told him to get lost."

"Are those the words you used?"

"...no."

"You see it is important that we try and capture accurately what happened, you understand why don't you?"

" ...yes."

"And so if the words are a bit colourful, you just tell us anyway do you understand?"

" ...yes."

"So you tell us what you said as you remember."

"...I told him to f*** off and leave me alone and stop dreaming."

Having been told "no", Scott Watson had nonetheless waited for an opportunity, stalking the girls in the garden bar, and this time drunk enough to grab one.

"We got up and walked off and as we were walking through the crowd we have to weave in thru the crowd, so my arm was dragging behind me and as we walked up –

"So you were walking with one shoulder ahead of you to get thru some narrow gaps or something?"

"...yes to get through the people, and as I was walking off he grabbed my arm and tried to pull me back and Delina saw this and when she saw this she just tugged me through the crowd and I eventually lost his grip on my arm," Baillie testified at trial.

It is odd that—despite having access to the original witness statements—authors working on this case have failed to accurately nail down the timeline, choosing to use the much more unreliable court testimony.

The garden bar is where we know Scott Watson hung out between 1am and 3am, when he went into the Lodge bar and clashed with Ollie Perkins.

Baillie would later positively identify Watson in two different photo montages.[274]

"Further to my statement made on 8 February 1998, I am quite sure if I am shown a photograph of the person who grabbed me after midnight at the New Year's celebrations, I will be able to identify him. It has been a long time but I will try.

"Constable Faraimo has shown me a montage of photographs— labelled Montage B— showing 8 photographs of male Caucasians aged between 30-40 years old. At the time I thought this guy was in his 30's.

"I am 90% sure that photograph number 3 is the guy that grabbed

---

274 40490 / ST / KRISTAL BAILLIE / MFF568 / 300398

me at the New Year's celebrations at Furneaux Lodge. I am certain that it is not the others in the montage. It has been sometime since the incident but again I am 90% sure that the person in photograph 3 is the same guy."

This, then, takes us full circle. We can trace Scott Watson's movements right up to around 11.15pm, shirt beer-soaked, hair all over the place, and he reappears again just in time for the midnight countdown. He reappears apparently wearing a "new flash shirt", hair "brushed".[275]

Did he cut back to *Blade* to freshen up? Watson's defence insisted (as reported in *Ben & Olivia*) that Watson did get a water taxi ride to his boat—not with Guy Wallace at 4am but two hours earlier with water taxi driver Don Anderson. The only problem is, as we have now seen based on the first accurate timeline ever published on this case, such a journey was not possible unless Watson also returned back to Furneaux. He had to have returned because we can prove he was onshore up to the point of the fateful water taxi trip.

It therefore doesn't really matter whether he made two trips, because we know he was in the right place at the right time for the only trip that did matter.

For the sake of completeness, however, let's explore the possible window of opportunity.

---

275 20203 / ST / SIMON BELL / PPD601 / 170198

CHAPTER SEVENTEEN

Which Water Taxi?

There can be little question that Watson should have been waiting for a water taxi at the same time when Hayden Morresey, Sarah Dyer and Guy Wallace turned up.

But if that's the case, how on earth do we explain this testimony from water taxi driver Don Anderson? Anderson had initially disavowed any knowledge of the mystery man, but he was asked to think again:[276]

"I remember several days after Ben and Olivia went missing I was contacted by a Police officer [who]... asked me if I could remember taking a person/s to a boat called *'Blade'*.... I said I couldn't remember, that I would think about it and get back to him. Later that day the same officer rang me back and I told him that I could remember taking a person out to a boat called *'Blade'*. I told him that I could recall taking a male person out to a yacht that this male

---

[276] 10670 / ST / DONALD ANDERSON / MW7124 / 060298

person referred to as *Blade*. I'm just guessing but I thought that I did this trip at about 2.30 to 3.00 am on New Year's day."

Don Anderson was "just guessing" about the time. For the reasons already outlined, we know Watson was in the garden bar at that time, and in a clash with Ollie Perkins after that. However, timings aside, Anderson continues:

"The boat I took this person to is the one identified as *Blade* in the Police photograph dated 31/12/97 6-7 pm. The person I took to *Blade* would have been medium to slight build. He was wearing a denim shirt, a lighter colour than his jeans I think. He was wearing blue denim jeans. The shirt was long sleeved and had a collar. I can vaguely recall that he was wearing a T-shirt under the shirt. The clothes looked clean but the guy looked scruffy. He looked like he had 3 or 4 days of growth on his face and unkempt "curlyish" dark hair. It looked like he needed a haircut."

In another statement Anderson put it this way:[277]

I remember pulling up to the floating wharf and this guy was standing by himself on the wharf. There were no other people waiting for a ride but there may have been others on the wharf. I can't recall. As I got closer to the wharf I could see this guy and thought he looks like a rough bugger, a fisherman sort of character.

"He had several days growth, not just two days growth. It was like quite a few days growth on his face like you got to the point where you thought about keeping it for a beard. He had a dark olive complexion not Maori but someone who had been in the sun or a hardened complexion.

"His hair was dark, more black than brown and his stubble was dark too. His hair was very unkempt like he hadn't done anything to it for a very long time, it wasn't really long. His hair was like the guy in the identikit picture that was in the paper, not quite as long as the

---

277 10823 / ST / DONALD ANDERSON / LC8773 / 050398

one with the longer hair in the sketches. His hair was almost getting curly, like wind blown. He didn't have a fringe, like his hair was off his face. He could have been receding but I couldn't say for definite.

"I would say his age was between 26 yrs to mid 30s.

"He had a blue denim shirt, light denim and I thought a white tee shirt underneath. He had normal blue colour Levis jeans on but I don't know about his footwear, I think it was more likely boots."

You could argue his mind was simply filling in the blanks with the by this stage widely reported description of the mystery man, the boat *Blade* and Scott Watson; however his next comment is unique:

"I remember that he asked me politely for a ride out to his boat, which didn't really fit his appearance. He was by himself and I said that we would wait until we got some more people. He said that's not a problem and then I decided to give him a ride anyway. There weren't many people on the wharf at this stage, and there weren't any waiting for a ride."

This aspect of Anderson's evidence opens up a number of possibilities. If it was Watson (and there's no guarantee it was), then the immediate question is what time could this be?

Although we've explored timelines, all Watson needed was a window of ten to fifteen minutes. He could even have decided to go back to his boat for something before actually leaving the jetty. Anywhere between 10pm and midnight is viable, because most people at the Lodge were hanging around for the midnight countdown and would not have been leaving before that. If Anderson was noting a lack of people wanting to go out to their boats, the hour just before midnight fits best—most of the boaties were already ashore, no one was leaving yet, except this mystery man.

On the other hand, between midnight and 3am there was a steady stream of people wanting rides out.

There are several clues to timing. Firstly, Anderson says he put on a ski jacket as the evening started to cool, but "I don't think I had the jacket on when I went to the *Blade*."[278] In other words the trip was earlier rather than later.

The biggest clue, however, is physical. Look at this description of Anderson pulling up to *Blade*:[279]

"The back of his yacht was facing in towards the jetty. The boat was rafted to two others. I pulled up on my portside which meant the front of my Naiad was pointing in towards the jetty. The male got off the Naiad and on the side of the yacht. He climbed over the wire rail running around the boat."

When Anderson dropped Watson to *Blade*, the yacht's bow was pointing out to sea and the stern was facing the Furneaux jetty. This indicates the yachts had swung to face the incoming high tide. The only time that could have happened was between 10pm and midnight, as a police file note discloses:[280]

"In relation to the vessels on their mooring over the evening Mahony said that as depicted in the photo the boats were initially facing towards Punga Cove. By 11.00 pm he said that they had at least swung 90° and were facing towards the head of the inlet. The 180° swing had been completed by the morning and they were facing towards Furneaux Lodge itself."

High tide was 10.49pm on New Year's Eve. Low tide was 4.07am on New Year's morning. When Guy Wallace dropped off the mystery man just before 4am the yacht's bow was facing towards Furneaux as the tide raced out of the inlet.[281]

"And you have told us that the bow of the vessels that you were passing were *all* orientated so that they were facing back to the shore or back generally in the direction of the jetty?

"…that's correct."

---

278 10823 / ST / DONALD ANDERSON / LC8773 / 050398
279 40980 / ST / DONALD ANDERSON / TFD573 / 040598
280 13043 / JS / DAVID MAHONY / BM6952 / 180698
281 Guy Wallace Evidence in Chief at trial

Which Water Taxi?

When Don Anderson says he dropped Scott Watson to *Blade*, the yacht's bow was facing out to sea. Don Anderson's trip to *Blade* cannot have taken place at 2am and it certainly could not have taken place as late as 4am. The evidence that *Blade*'s bow was facing the sea at 11pm, leaving "the back of his yacht...facing in towards the jetty" is incontrovertible physical proof that if Scott Watson did slip back, he probably did so between 11.15 and midnight to spruce up before the countdown.

The two-trip theory thus stacks up; it was possible, but much earlier than the jury was told, and the water taxi driver who'd made in excess of 100 trips to different boats simply got his timing wrong when trying to pinpoint this one trip.

We could spend the next 30 pages nailing down every piece of other circumstantial evidence or trying to squeeze in every definite (as opposed to purely photo ID'd) sighting, but at the end of the day they are irrelevant: the tidal movements show Anderson's trip to *Blade* must have happened around high tide before midnight. Those tide readings are decisive. There are only three questions remaining—why didn't anyone hear Scott Watson return to *Blade* the first time, where was the mystery man at this time, and was it possible for Watson to get back from *Blade* without being noticed?

We'll deal with these questions in reverse order.

Paula Woolman was employed as security on the jetty that night. She noticed a man on his own waiting on the wharf sometime before midnight and when she next turned around he'd been whisked off toward the Pines (in the general direction of *Blade* or other boats moored out that way, in other words) in a water taxi also carrying another passenger:

"I have been asked about the male that I saw down at the end of the jetty prior to midnight. I cant think of anything else about him other that what I have already said. I guess it would have been between 9pm and 11pm, I cant be any more accurate than that.

"The man was a Caucasian, late 20s, solid build ie overweight (had a bit of a gut on him), 5'-6" to 5'-7" in height, I got within about 3 metres of him and he was shorter than myself (5 8"), short thick wavy hair, I cant remember whether he had any facial hair. He was wearing blue jeans, white tee-shirt with a picture (not words) in the centre, he also had a blue denim shirt over top. I remember vividly that he had a noticeable gap between his front teeth.

"I would recognise him again if I saw him in person. I had a very good look at him when he was on the jetty and I can still remember his face.

"He didn't look drunk to me, I say that because he wasn't swaying or staggering around. I could see him clearly because the lighting was good on the lower jetty. I don't recall what type of lighting was there but I know it lit up the area well.

"The man in the denim shirt looked creepy to me. I think it was the way he was standing there staring at people (no one in particular). I remember I said to someone (I have no idea who) "I don't like the look of him". I work in a mall as security staff and you find that you get a certain feel about people, I had a bad feeling about this person for no other reason than the way he stood there staring at people.

"I did not notice him carrying anything in his hands, nor did I see him carrying any small bags or luggage.

"I first noticed him when he was standing on the jetty as I described above, I don't know how he got there. I have marked on the jetty sketch where I saw him.

"Sometime later (possibly around 5-30mins) I saw him on a Naiad with a female. He was sitting on the side of the boat with his arm outstretched on the pontoon. The girl was just in front of him off to the left sitting on a seat. I didn't see them get onto the boat. I remember her leaning towards the driver talking to him as they took off. I got the impression that she didn't know the man but I could be wrong. I really can't pin-point why I got that impression.

"The boat took off in the direction of the Pines although I lost sight of it very quickly. I have marked on the sketch where the taxi left from. [Watson's *Blade* was anchored on the way to the Pines]

"I would describe the girl as Caucasian, 18 years, shoulder length dark blonde/brown straight hair wearing a white singlet type top. I did not see her face well enough to describe it.

"I have absolutely no idea who was driving the water taxi. I don't remember anything about him.

"A short time later (less than 20 minutes) he returned back to the jetty. I didn't see him arrive back. I just noticed that amongst the people coming and going, he appeared again at the end of the jetty, I'm not sure where exactly.

"He was by himself but I really can't remember anything else

LEFT: "I remember vividly that he had a noticeable gap between his front teeth"

about what he was doing or how long he stood there for."[282]

The take home point is that somehow this person, who appears to in fact be Scott Watson on that pre-midnight trip with Don Anderson, arrived back at the jetty without security seeing how.

"You know you turn your back on someone and that is it," explained another security manager, Neil Watts, to police.[283]

Water taxi driver Robert Mullen said revellers seemed to have no shortage of rides if the water taxis weren't around:[284]

"The only incident we really discussed was a guy we took back to his boat several times and we couldn't work out how he was getting back to shore. I had dropped the guy off at least two or three times and so had Anderson."

So one of the big objections to the two-trip theory crumbles. "How could he have got back?" Easily, it turns out, probably by hitching a ride like everyone else.

Which gets us to the next question—does the two-trip theory rule out Scott Watson as the mystery man? The answer is no.

Bar manager Roz McNeilly didn't notice the mystery man until after midnight, which fits this construction of a quick trip to *Blade* and back after 11.15:[285]

"I think that the first time I noticed the guy I have described was after midnight. I certainly served him more than 5 times—it was like he was constantly getting drinks. There was a girl that was near to him that he seemed to be buying drinks for also. She was sort of standing behind him."

She told police he was in the Lodge bar for an hour to 90 minutes, which dovetails nicely with Michael Cronin seeing him arrive in the garden bar around 1.30.

---

282 11782 / ST / PAULA WOOLMAN / DRD506 / 240398
283 11584 / ST / NEIL WATTS / DL7209 / 270298
284 11780 / ST / ROBERT MULLEN / AHD181 / 200398
285 40587 / ST / ROZLYN McNEILLY / BM6952 / 200398

Barman Chey Phipps says he didn't notice the mystery man at the bar until at least 11.40pm, and says he spent about two hours there.[286] Again, this is consistent with the Watson timeline.

Guy Wallace, tired, busy and consistently dodgy on timing throughout his evidence, is the outlier, thinking it might have been much earlier:[287]

"This person to the best of my knowledge turned up just before or just as it started getting busy. I guess about 7.30-8.30 pm."

It was a "guess".[288] It started to get really busy after ten pm when all the boats were unloading passengers ashore for the New Year's Eve countdown. Wallace could well have seen Watson who was in the Lodge bar solidly between 10.15 and 11.15, and from about 11.45pm through to 1.30am.

"I saw this male consistently off and on throughout the night. I called last drinks at 2.25 am and was told by Rick McLeod to keep the bar open. I can't remember whether this male was in the bar then."

Watson was out in the garden bar at 2.25am, but he wandered back into the Lodge at 3am to clash with Perkins.

"I next recall seeing this male was on the way down to the jetty with Hayden (Morresey) and his girlfriend. I can't recall whether he walked down behind us and I noticed him by the "Hoby Cat", a yacht which is by the boatshed by the bush line. I think he came over from the Hoby Cat. He may have been over having a leak or something. It is possible that he asked for a light. I recall that someone asked for a light when we were by the boatshed.

"When I first saw him I thought that's the guy that had been at the bar. I might have even said to him 'What are you doing down here' or something similar.

---

286 20250 / ST / CHEY PHIPPS / ASD279 / 090198
287 40365 / ST / GUY WALLACE / SM7883 / 030498
288 10081 / ST / GUY WALLACE / TFD573 / 090198 / W In one of his first statements to police, Watson said, "I first noticed the male who I described in my first statement at about 9.00 pm."

"The only other thing I can recall as I have thought a lot about that night is that I think that this person introduced himself to me earlier in the night, probably as he got his first drinks. I can't recall his name, but I am reasonably sure that he said he was from Picton. I thought it was strange at the time because he said he was from the same town as me and I didn't recognise him. I thought I had mentioned that to someone—possibly Roz.

"As for who served this male, I have said Roz and I, but also Chey (Phipps) would have served him also. The main bar staff that served this male was Roz and I."

So the mystery man, just like Watson, told Wallace he was from Picton. Who knew? As we've seen previously, both were smoking "rollies". Maybe the mystery man even happened to mention when he first started chatting to the suggestible Guy Wallace that he was on a "double-masted ketch" and planning to go to "Tonga". There was, after all, a guy in that bar saying such things. It would explain why Wallace came up with this in his police interview on 11 January 1998:[289]

> GUY WALLACE: "I reckon myself it's on the way to Tonga."
> DETECTIVE FITZGERALD: Do ya?
> GUY WALLACE: Yeah.
> DETECTIVE FITZGERALD: Yeah well you're dreaming.

Nothing of the mystery man's movements is inconsistent with the known movements of Scott Watson, or a pre-midnight trip to *Blade* for a new shirt. Like the mystery ketch shadowing *Alliance* wherever it sailed, Scott Watson and the mystery man were both described in near identical terms, with the same kind of behaviour—although Watson's was worse. Both men were in the same room, at the same bar, for hours. Yet they were never seen together. Eyewitnesses asked

---

289 12635 / TAPE / VIDEO INTERVIEW GUY WALLACE / TFD573 / 110198

to report anything suspicious in the very first days of the inquiry filed incident reports repeatedly and independently tracking back to a man we can prove was Scott Watson, long before Watson was a twinkle in a cop's eye. Yet if you take the current tortured memories of the Furneaux bar staff at face value, they never noticed badly behaved Watson, only his quieter doppelganger.

It's a murder mystery with not only a shadow ketch but a shadow man. What are the odds?

Actually, it's more akin to the old Hindu proverb about the six blind men who stumbled upon an elephant—each touching a different part. One, holding a leg, insisted it was a tree. Another mistook the tail for a rope and another the trunk for a snake. Was Scott Watson the mystery elephant in the room that night, perceived slightly differently by each witness but there nonetheless?

The final remaining question is why no one heard Watson return to *Blade* the first time?

Mina Cornelia skipper Dave Mahony was the only person left on the raft of boats including *Blade* and *Bianco* after everyone else had gone to shore. But Mahony had not returned to his boat immediately after dropping off Watson and the others at 10pm. "I didn't wear a watch" that night, he told police.[290]

Instead, Mahony's inflatable was commandeered by two people who thought it was a water taxi. Rather than argue the point, Mahony took them to their vessels and then spent a further 20 minutes or so on a "tiki tour" around all the boats. He did not see the mystery ketch in his travels.

He was back on *Cornelia* some time between 10.30 and 11pm— remembering he did not wear a watch.

"I got back on my boat and stayed there all night. I was inside for most of the night and I remember it was quite a cool night.

---

290 10669 / ST / DAVID MAHONY / DE5136 / 080298

While I was on board our boat I just read, slept, drank coffee and that's about it really."[291]

Dave Mahony told the court at trial that he also had the radio on. If Don Anderson is insistent that he dropped someone off to *Blade*, we can only presume that—between the radio and the noise of the rock band playing a couple of hundred metres away on shore—Mahony either didn't hear it or that it possibly happened before Mahony got back to *Cornelia*.

Or, as Keith Hunter has tried to argue, maybe Scott Watson returned to *Blade* on a different water taxi altogether. Will that scenario hold water, or sink like a stone? Let's find out.

---

[291] 20084 / ST / DAVID MAHONY / RHD118 / 120198

CHAPTER EIGHTEEN

Keith Hunter's Taxi Theory Sinks

In *Trial by Trickery*, journalist Keith Hunter is skeptical of a Don Anderson water taxi ride but highly favours another option—middle-aged John Mullen. Mullen was never asked at the trial whether he had taken Watson or someone like him back to his yacht, and Hunter says the answer would have surprised the court.

Hunter makes much of the fact that he was the first to ask John Mullen the hard question about a trip to *Blade* as described by Scott Watson.

"He did describe just such a trip to me when I asked him about it in a videotaped interview for my film in February 2003. This is not because I asked the question more perceptively. It was simply because I *asked* the question. Mullen did not describe such a trip in court because prosecutor Raftery did *not* ask him the question."[292]

---

292 *Trial By Trickery*, p232

Apparently Hunter had not properly understood the police files. Two things became apparent. Firstly, that private investigators hired by the Watsons interviewed Mullen in early 1998 and concluded he was not the taxi driver who had uplifted Watson from the wharf.

"I do not recall taking only one passenger on my Water Taxi out to a yacht. The procedure we adopted was to fill the taxi with as many people it could take, in a safe manner.[293] I doubt if I would have left the wharf with only one passenger, although it could have occurred but I can't remember doing it."

Secondly, after Watson had described his water taxi ride, police appeared to have indeed asked the question of all the taxi drivers, "Can you remember taking a male of this description out to a yacht called *Blade*?", and here's the answer they got:[294]

"John Patrick Moera MULLEN (as per statement does not remember anyone of that description). Scott WATSON stated he was taken to his yacht by an older man wearing a hat. John MULLEN was the only older person driving the Naiads that night. John MULLEN states he was not wearing a hat that night, and very seldom wears a hat."

No, the one normally wearing a hat was John's 21 year old son Robert:[295]

"I wear a cowboy hat all the time but that night I wasn't wearing it because I was wearing a Furneaux Lodge Cap as it was the only form of identification I had to wear."

But Hunter's straw-clutching doesn't get the matter any further, because Robert Mullen said he had not taken anyone out to *Blade* either:[296]

"Robert John MULLEN cannot remember taking anyone fitting

---

293 Statement of John Mullen to Defence 25 Feb 1998
294 20075 / JS / NAIAD DRIVER ENQUIRY / TFD573 / 130198
295 11780 / ST / ROBERT MULLEN / AHD181 / 200398
296 20075 / JS / NAIAD DRIVER ENQUIRY / TFD573 / 130198

the description of the unknown male to a yacht (as in his statement). He believes it would be unusual to take anyone out to their yacht by themselves at that time of the morning (around 2.00 am) because they were so busy, the Naiads were always loaded up with people."

Hunter quibbles with the John Mullen denial of 13 January 1998, trying to explain it away by saying he was asked about the description of the unknown man, "not of Watson". This appears to be Hunter's version of "the big lie". Let's remind ourselves firstly of the Guy Wallace description of the mystery man:[297]

"The guy that got on board with Olivia and Ben was a male, Caucasian, aged about 32 years. He was about 5'8" tall, wiry build. I think he may have had tattoos on his arms but I can't be sure. His hair was a brownie colour, wavy and medium length. He had about two days growth on his face. He was bourboned up, like his eyes weren't focussing.

"He was wearing a Levi shirt with short sleeves, 100 per cent cotton. It had a collar with a button-up front. I saw the Levi brand on it. It was a short sleeved shirt and the colour was between khaki and very pale green. He was wearing blue jeans and I think sandshoes."

Secondly, let's look at a few confirmed descriptions of Scott Watson that night:

Lawrence McKay, a passenger on *Mina Cornelia*, met Scott when Watson tied up *Blade* alongside *Mina Cornelia* on the afternoon of New Year's Eve.

"Scott looked about 5.10 tall, 75 kgs, Caucasian, slim build, unshaven, a couple days' growth, scruffy appearance.[298] I noticed he had tattoos on him. He had brown straggly hair. It wasn't long, but it wasn't short either, possibly to his collar."

"Scott had light coloured sneakers on and blue jeans," confirmed

---

297 10017 / ST / GUY WALLACE / ASD279 / 050198
298 20286 / ST / LAWRENCE MCKAY / MBD353 / 150198

Cornelia skipper Dave Mahony when he dropped Watson into Furneaux."[299]

"Philip Hale described Watson as:[300]

"...a male Caucasian, about 5'7" in height, slim build, he was wiry. He had short dark wavy hair down to just past his collar. He had high cheekbones with 'slitty' sort of eyes. He had like a day or two's growth on his face. He was wearing a blue long sleeved denim shirt which had two pockets on the front."

Keith Hunter keeps claiming that Scott Watson in no way resembled the mystery man. He has repeated this often enough that even he may now believe it. Certainly a large chunk of the public have been persuaded by him. Unfortunately it just isn't true.

It follows that Keith Hunter's videotape interview with John Mullen for *Murder On The Blade*, conducted five years after the events in question and flying in the face of what Mullen remembered at the time, is arguably worthless—a triumph of TV flash over journalistic substance, especially given the reservations the Watson family's own private investigators had.

Turning to the heart of the alleged Mullen trip, we see Keith Hunter has again failed to do his homework in the police witness statements.

The police argued Watson was Guy Wallace's mystery passenger. Not so, says Hunter.

Watson's lawyers claimed Watson returned to *Blade* alone with Don Anderson. Not so, says Hunter.

"My conviction," says Hunter, "is that the only trip Watson took to his boat that night was with the water taxi driver who matched his description of the man who took him, John Mullen.[301]

---

299 20084 / ST / DAVID MAHONY / RHD118 / 120198
300 30055 / ST / PHILIP HALE / DSC229 / 210198
301 *Trial By Trickery*, p212

"He went back both alone, and later than 3.30am," Hunter says.[302]

Again, a simple read of the witness statements blows Keith Hunter's theory out of the water, and with it any credible alternative explanation of how Scott Watson did actually get back to *Blade* after 3.30am. In running a John Mullen trip up the flagpole, Keith Hunter actually sinks his entire case.

Was John Mullen driving water taxis after 3.30am?

No.

"I worked until about 3.15 am when I got taken back to my boat, *Southern Comfort*, by Don [Anderson]," John Mullen told police.[303]

It's a little bit hard to get a 3.30am ride out to *Blade* with The Man Who Wasn't There. John Mullen, in fact, had already gone. Don Anderson recalled dropping Mullen to his boat between 2am or 2.30,[304] and Rachael Veitch who was coordinating boats and taxis put it around 2.30 as well. He was certainly long gone by 4am when Dave Mahony was woken by Watson.

Deprived of Mullen as an alibi, and with the Anderson trip timed around 11.30pm because of the tidal evidence, and security guard Paula Woolman witnessing it, we are left with Guy Wallace as the likely driver for the final trip back to *Blade*.

Imagine that. Both Scott Watson and his shadow doppelganger are on the same wharf at the same time, waiting for a taxi. The latest in a string of such incredible coincidences. And just one taxi driver remembers taking a man of that description.

---

302 ibid, p209
303 10404 / JS / JOHN MULLEN / MR8667 / 200198
304 10070 / ST / DONALD ANDERSON / RRC196 / 050198 / W

ABOVE: *Blade* in foreground. **BELOW:** *Blade* rafted to *Cornelia*

CHAPTER NINETEEN

The Deception Widens

In Scott Watson's first statement to police, he was definite on when and how he got back to *Blade*:[305]

"At about 2.00 am I took the water taxi back to my yacht. It was a Naiad, yellow. It was driven by an old guy with a hat on. I was the only passenger. I remember he wouldn't let me on until he had parked the boat. He kept telling me to wait. I don't think I spoke with him."

Watson had claimed to have arrived back at *Blade* about 2am, but he can't have—the people on *Mina Cornelia* tied up next door were still awake:

"We stayed up until about 2.00 am socialising and then went to bed,"[306] recalled skipper Dave Mahony.

"When we got back to our boat we all stayed up until about 2am

---

305 10083 / ST / SCOTT WATSON / DSC229 / 080198 / W
306 10084 / ST / DAVID MAHONY / RRC196 / 070198 / W

when we slipped off to bed," remembered passenger Ernestus Rutte Jnr. "I was last to bed because I slept on the floor. I didn't hear anything happen on Scott Watson's then. His yacht appeared to be empty."

Debbie Corless told the trial she couldn't sleep initially, and stayed awake until 2.45am. Scott Watson did not return inside that time, and as we know he could not have—he was still up at the Lodge bar.

Instead, an hour after the "old guy" taxi driver John Mullen had gone off duty, Watson woke up passengers on *Mina Cornelia* and the *Bianco*:

"At around 4.00 am," said Mahony, "although I'm not exact on the time—that's what one of my passengers told me—Scott stuck his head into the cabin. He was drunk and wanted someone to get up and socialise with him. We all ignored him and I heard him go across to the Raven [the *Bianco*] and try to get them up as well.

"Between 3.00 and 4.00 am it was dark and a male person came on to our boat," stated Andrew Crawshaw from the *Bianco* to police.[307] "He put his head through the hatch, squatted down and talked to us. The whole conversation made me feel uneasy."

We'll get to the substance of what Watson did on these other boats in a moment, but first—realising his story was not stacking up, Watson became more vague about the timing and detail of his return when he was called in for a second police interview:[308]

"I was pretty written off. I was wasted. It was New Years.

"I can remember being in the beer tent talking to Rick McLeod.[309] Then I went home. I can remember getting on my boat. I remember the guy saying to me not to get into the taxi from the wharf. I don't know what he was up to. I think he was making it safe for me to get off the wharf onto the Naiad.

---

307 10414 / JS / ANDREW CRAWSHAW / SCC539 / 090198
308 20029 / ST / SCOTT WATSON / JMD684 / 120198
309 McLeod denied this at the Depositions hearing: "I do not know the accused and cannot remember speaking to him or seeing him during the night at Furneaux." 10129D / RICHARD McLEOD

"I think he had a hat on, a cap on. I think he was old. I had seen him earlier on that afternoon whizzing around dropping people off, picking them up. I'm not sure whether I got a lift in with him or not. I had no trouble getting off the Naiad onto my boat.

"I think it was about 2.00 am. I have got a feeling it was about then. I'm not exactly sure."

"I went out alone to my boat. There was only myself and the Naiad driver. I got onto my boat first then I think I jumped straight onto Cornelius, and woke them up. I don't know who I spoke to. It was a guy that was laying there in his bunk. I couldn't see his face. I said to him to get out of bed. I wondered why they had all gone to sleep.

"The boat would have been full of people but it was dark so I couldn't see. I don't know. I was standing up by the cockpit, and leaned my head in the door," said Watson.

Here's what *Cornelia* passenger Ernestus Rutte Jnr told police:[310]

"I was woken up by Scott coming on our boat, I heard someone stumbling around on our boat. We couldn't see him, it was really dark. He said something along the lines of 'you pikers, you shouldn't be in bed, you should get out of bed and party.' I replied 'f*** off'. He replied 'oh you pikers', I then heard him moving down the side of the boat. I thought at the time that he was checking the rafting lines that secured the boats together. After about 5 minutes it went quiet. I recognised it as being Scott's voice. The next day I spoke to Dave and he said the same thing. He didn't respond at the time in the hope that Scott would go away."

According to Watson, he got the hint: "So I went back to my boat, had something to eat cos' I was hungry. Then I went to bed."

Because of the way police statements are drawn up, a little bit of reading between the lines can sometimes reveal a lot. The inter-

---

310 10327 / ST / ERNESTUS RUTTE / MHF680 / 150198

viewing officer has noted Watson claiming he went to bed, but you can bet on the fact the officer then asked, 'did you go to any other boats?'. The question is not recorded in the statement, but Watson's answer is:

"I went onto the boat next door. It wasn't Warwick's boat. It was a little Raven boat. I had met them when they first tied alongside. I didn't say anything to them. They were asleep. So I went and had something to eat and went to bed."

Keith Hunter staked his reputation as a credible investigative journalist with this bold statement in *Trial by Trickery*:

"[Watson] was cheaply labelled a liar...The documentation does not support the label. He emerges from an inspection of it lie-free."[311]

Let's test that theory. Watson says he went to the *Bianco* "next door...I didn't say anything to them. They were asleep."

Funnily enough, Andrew Crawshaw and Deanna Cunliffe don't remember it that way at all:

"We went to sleep at about 1.30 am," Cunliffe told police.[312] "While staying in the Sounds I can recall that it started to get light at about 5.00 am.

"We both fell asleep. A couple of hours later I woke up. It was still dark. I cannot recall exactly what woke me up. It may have been some talking. Andrew and I were sleeping on a bed that doubled as the table in the cabin. The head of the bed was about a metre from the doorway to the cabin. When we had gone to bed we left the cabin door open.

"I woke up and looked towards the door. I looked there because I heard someone say, 'What are youse doing in here?' It sounded really uneducated and either drunk or drugged.

"He then said, 'Are youse sleeping in here?' At first I thought it

---

311 *Trial by Trickery*, p9
312 10340/ST/DEANNA CUNLIFFE/MCD438/150198

was our friends from next door and was not too perturbed. He said words to the effect of, 'Come out and party'. Andrew said something like, 'Look, we're not interested, we're asleep, go away'.

"The conversation took a turn for the worse because he kept pushing us to get up and party. He was very drunk and it was at that point that Andrew got angry and shouted at him to 'f*** off'.

"At this point I got really worried because I then knew it was someone that we did not know and that there was or may have going to be trouble. I remember thinking that it may have been the guy from the other boat. It was then I took my eyes off him. I was frightened.

"He thought for what appeared a moment and then said, 'Give her to me mate, I'll look after her'. He then said something to the effect of, 'I'll show her a good time'.

"The way he said it I took it to mean that Andrew could stay there and he would look after me. They were sexually driven comments and I was really scared. I felt that what he said he meant. By this time I thought that it was the guy from the other boat and after what I had heard earlier about him being strange it all seemed to fit in.

"Andrew by this time was really angry and told him to 'f*** off' again. The guy didn't say anything more and just left. I didn't see him leave.

"I didn't hear anything else after that. There was no noise at all. The Sounds were very still and quiet and I would have heard another boat leaving or arriving," stated Cunliffe.

It's pretty obvious that Scott Watson lied about not saying anything to the couple, making Keith Hunter's assurances about Watson's honesty utterly worthless.

Andrew Crawshaw told police:

"He had a drink in one hand and a cigarette in the other and he was leaning in through the hatch... he must have seen Deanna because he said, 'Give her to me, I'll look after her'. I said 'look mate, just go away' and he did.

"At the time there were no lights on in our boat but the night was quite clear, there was moon so it was reasonably light outside.

"I could tell that person in the hatchway was unshaven, he was of a wiry build, his hair was short and dark. You could also tell from his demeanour he was quite drunk, and that he wasn't well educated just from the way spoke. I can't describe his clothing. The cigarette he was smoking was quite sweet smelling like a roll your own. I could not smell the alcohol.

"At the time when he asked me to give Deanna to him his voice had very lurid sexual overtones. At this stage I felt there were going to be serious problems and I got ready to get out of bed and confront the guy.

"This comment unnerved me that much that I mentioned it to a number of people the next morning in particular the crew on the [*Cornelia*] and various friends when I returned to Auckland."

Now, you'll remember that Watson claimed he said nothing to this couple but instead returned to his boat, cooked some bacon and eggs and went to bed. If that's true, one would have expected the highly intoxicated and "wasted" Watson to sleep like a baby. Even *he* made that observation in a statement:

"I don't think I had a sleep or anything like that because if I had I would have still been there the next day."

Yet despite recognising what normally happens when you fall asleep drunk, he then claimed to have gone to bed after waking up the people on the other boats. Miraculously he must have micronapped, because here's where another alleged lie emerges:

"After waking up, checked the oil in the motor, and left. It was about half past 6, 7 o'clock when I left. It was dawn anyway. It was daylight. I am guessing it was that time. It was early, but it was a nice day.

"The neighbours weren't up and about. I didn't see anyone else. I untied my boat and left."

It sounds plausible but for two things. Firstly, how does someone blind drunk fall asleep near dawn then wake at sparrowfart motivated to greet the new day? Secondly, at the time he claims to have left, the neighbours were already up, and he had already gone.

"I woke up around 6 am," Ernestus Rutte Snr told detectives. "Dave [Mahony] was also awake. We both had a cup of tea outside... Scott's boat had gone."[313]

"The next morning when we got up the boat was gone," said Rutte's son Ernestus Jnr. "This was a real surprise. I remember thinking that he was pretty drunk last night, he hadn't sounded much better when he stumbled on board in the early hours of the morning."[314]

The sun was already up by 6am. It began to get light gradually from 3.47am onwards. Around 6am, Punga Cove water taxi operator Marko Doblanovic had dropped a female friend back to Furneaux. He noticed a small yacht leaving Furneaux in the direction of Cook Strait. It was the only boat on the move.[315]

"I remember it was ahead of me and on the left hand side of the bay going out. It was under power not sail. I can't recall what type of boat it was or the colours except to say it was light coloured. I can say it wasn't a big yacht.

"When I first saw it, it had passed all the yachts that were moored. I don't recall seeing any people on the yacht. I was heading for Punga and it was going out to the strait."

Scott Watson's *Blade* had been moored to the left of Furneaux. For a trip to Erie Bay his yacht would have veered right, cutting across Furneaux. This yacht wasn't going to Erie Bay. And it wasn't a ketch.

Doblanovic wasn't the only one to see a boat leave. Back onshore at Furneaux, teenager Jeremy Brown had decided to pull an all-nighter to welcome the dawn:[316]

---

313 20422 / ST / ERNESTUS RUTTE / TV8075 / 260198
314 20675 / ST / ERNESTUS RUTTE / JSC422 / 040298
315 10869 / ST / MARKO DOBLANOVIC / TFD175 / 180298
316 20218 / ST / JEREMY BROWN / SID741 / 140198

"I saw a yacht which was heading away from the Furneaux area. This boat was definitely white with a stripe along the side. I don't know what colour the stripe was. I couldn't see anyone on board.

"I saw a light, I'm not sure how many, at the top of the mast or masts. I don't know what colour the light was. I would say the boat was about 40 foot long, I could see the outline quite well. It had safety rails on it as well."

Wayne Robertson was awakened on the launch *Wild Honey* around 5.30am.[317]

"Twenty minutes later at 5.50 am I heard a fizz boat and I got out of bed. I had a look and saw a white with yellow topped boat head directly towards Punga. It was driven by a young male Caucasian. He was going pretty fast. I remember after he cleared the boats he put his head on his arms like he was hungover. He was the only occupant of the boat."

Robertson's testimony puts Doblanovic's Furneaux to Punga dash at 5.50am. In the wider detail of his statement, Doblanovich had laid out the timings of each part of his journey, and working backwards that indicates he'd arrived at the Furneaux jetty around 5.20am. He hadn't seen a yacht leaving on his way into Furneaux, which suggests the mystery yacht must have departed some time between 5.20am and 5.30am, or alternatively that it was too dark for him to notice during the trip in.

"I got up at about 5.30 am and I noticed then that Scott's boat wasn't there," *Unicorn* skipper Warwick Eastgate told police.[318]

This is final proof, if needed, that Watson had lied in his police statements about going to sleep after getting back to his boat. No one drunk, who has been awake nearly 24 hours, falls asleep and then wakes in the space of an hour, noiselessly unties his boat and

---

317 10226 / ST / WAYNE ROBERTSON / DSC229 / 160198
318 20085 / ST / WARWICK EASTGATE / ASD279 / 120198

slips away before sunrise. That's not how New Year's hangovers work. Something sobered up Scott Watson pretty quick. Something motivated him to leave the area immediately.

Now here's something else he lied about.

CHAPTER TWENTY

Cracking The Case

For the past 18 years, debate has raged about Scott Watson suddenly deciding to paint his boat a different colour. We reported the 'official' version from the trial in *Ben & Olivia*, that Watson had arrived at 'Zappa' Keating's place in Erie Bay on 1 January, and then:[319]

"The next day Watson came ashore, and then rowed back out to his yacht to get some milk as the family had run out of milk for breakfast. He got back to the house and the children realised that Scott had left a trail of blood on the kitchen floor. He had cut his foot on the beach while going out to his yacht.

"Watson inquired if the man still had some paint he'd seen several months ago, that he could use. On previous meetings they had discussed repainting *Blade* and the man had suggested white and blue with the cabin blue. The man gave Watson the paint and he went and shifted his boat into a more sheltered area in Erie Bay nearer

---

[319] *Ben & Olivia*, p147

the point. He then changed the colour of the cabin from a reddy brown to blue. That night Watson was invited for tea and they sat around watching a television movie again. The following morning the Erie Bay family got up and noticed that Watson had left with no indication that he was going to."

As explained, that's the official version and it was all we had to go on at trial. There's no question that Watson had clearly signalled his intention—a week earlier in fact—to repaint his boat. There were independent hostile witnesses who remembered the conversations. That's why in the previous book there was cynicism about the police using the repaint as proof of criminal intent.

"If *Blade*'s owner was the killer, he must have kicked himself repeatedly after painting his yacht to change it from the colour it had been on the night—only to discover the police were looking for a boat the same colour as his new paint job."

If only it were that simple. The police files disclose something we didn't know, something much more suspicious: there's evidence Scott Watson painted his boat alright, but not moored at Erie Bay. Instead, the evidence suggests he painted it on 1 January, at sea.

Who does that? And who does that after nearly 24 hours on the turps and no sleep? More to the point, it appears to show Watson did not tell police what he had been up to:

"After waking up, checked the oil in the motor, and left. It was about half past 6, 7 o'clock when I left. It was dawn anyway. It was daylight. I am guessing it was that time. It was early, but it was a nice day. The neighbours weren't up and about. I didn't see anyone else.

"I untied my boat and left. I headed down to Tory channel to Erie Bay. I had a hangover. I wasn't sick. I'd had a feed and heaps of water before I went to bed.

"I suppose I got to Erie Bay about half past 9-10 o'clock on New Year's day. I went and saw my mate. I moored up on the only wharf in Erie Bay.

ABOVE: Erie Bay, with the Cassels jetty at left. **BELOW:** Close up.

BEFORE 1 JAN 1998

AFTER 1 JAN 1998

"I went to see "Zappa" the caretaker. It's me bosses house, or a guy I work for sometimes. His name is Alister Cassels. He wasn't there, and I ran into "Zappa" I don't know his real name.

"I was there for 3 days moored up at the wharf. I didn't go anywhere. While I was there I dug up the water supply for the caretaker's house and Alister's house.

"I had told him (Zappa) that I would see him there New Year's Day.

"I stayed on my yacht for the 3 days in the bay and at his house."

That's Scott Watson's claim, now let's see how true it is.

We know Watson did not leave in "daylight". Dawn was 5.54 that morning. His boat was gone before 5.20am, possibly earlier.

There was no "waking up" because there's a very strong inference available that he never went to sleep.

One thing entirely missing from both of Watson's police statements is any reference to painting his boat. He talks above about digging up the water supply for the Erie Bay house, but chooses to omit the fact he had painted his boat. Why?

Watson talks of being "moored up on the only wharf in Erie Bay...I was there for three days moored up at the wharf."

Really? Here's how Keating remembered it:[320]

"I looked up and saw that Scott had arrived in his yacht. *He had it anchored in the bay.* I didn't see it sail in. He came out of the blue, I can't even tell you what time he came in. I would put the time about between 10 am and midday."

It's a little thing, but for some reason Watson didn't tell the truth about coming to the wharf.

"We looked out of the kitchen window and saw that Scott had sailed into the bay," said Keating's 13 year old daughter.[321] "I saw

---

[320] 20066 / ST / *KEATING / TFD175 / 140198
[321] 20064 / ST / *KEATING DAUGHTER / TFD175 / 140198

him in his dinghy and he was coming into the shore. He was by himself and walked up to the house."

Keating's 10 year old son confirmed it:[322]

"Scott came this year around New Year's Day. I think it was lunchtime...Scott came ashore. I didn't see how he got ashore. Scott was wearing a blue woollen jersey. He had black jeans on too."

Anchored out in the bay, there was no chance of Keating or his children running down to the wharf and jumping on a moored *Blade*. Anchored out in the bay, Scott Watson maintained total control of his yacht and who had access to it.

Here's the really interesting thing however. Look at how the children, staring out the window at *Blade*, described the boat on its arrival:

"He came on his boat. It was a different colour than last year. It was blue on the top," the son told a detective.

Interviewed separately by a different detective, the 13 year old daughter told police:

"He was wearing a black or dark blue wool jersey & blue jeans. I would say his face was prickly. He needed a shave.

"I remember that his yacht was sort of navy blue & white in colour when he arrived."

Out of the mouths of babes. These witness statements are utterly contradicting the official painting story. How is it that Watson could possibly have painted his boat in the time it took to sail 15km from Furneaux Lodge to Erie Bay?

The answer is, Scott Watson did not sail *Blade* directly to Erie Bay.

Geraldine van Wijngaarden, her husband Alex, their children and some friends motored into Erie Bay on New Year's Day, close to the jetty, around 1pm:[323]

---

322 20082 / ST / *KEATING SON / RHD118 / 140198
323 20854 / ST / GERALDINE VAN WIJNGAARDEN / SCC539 / 020398

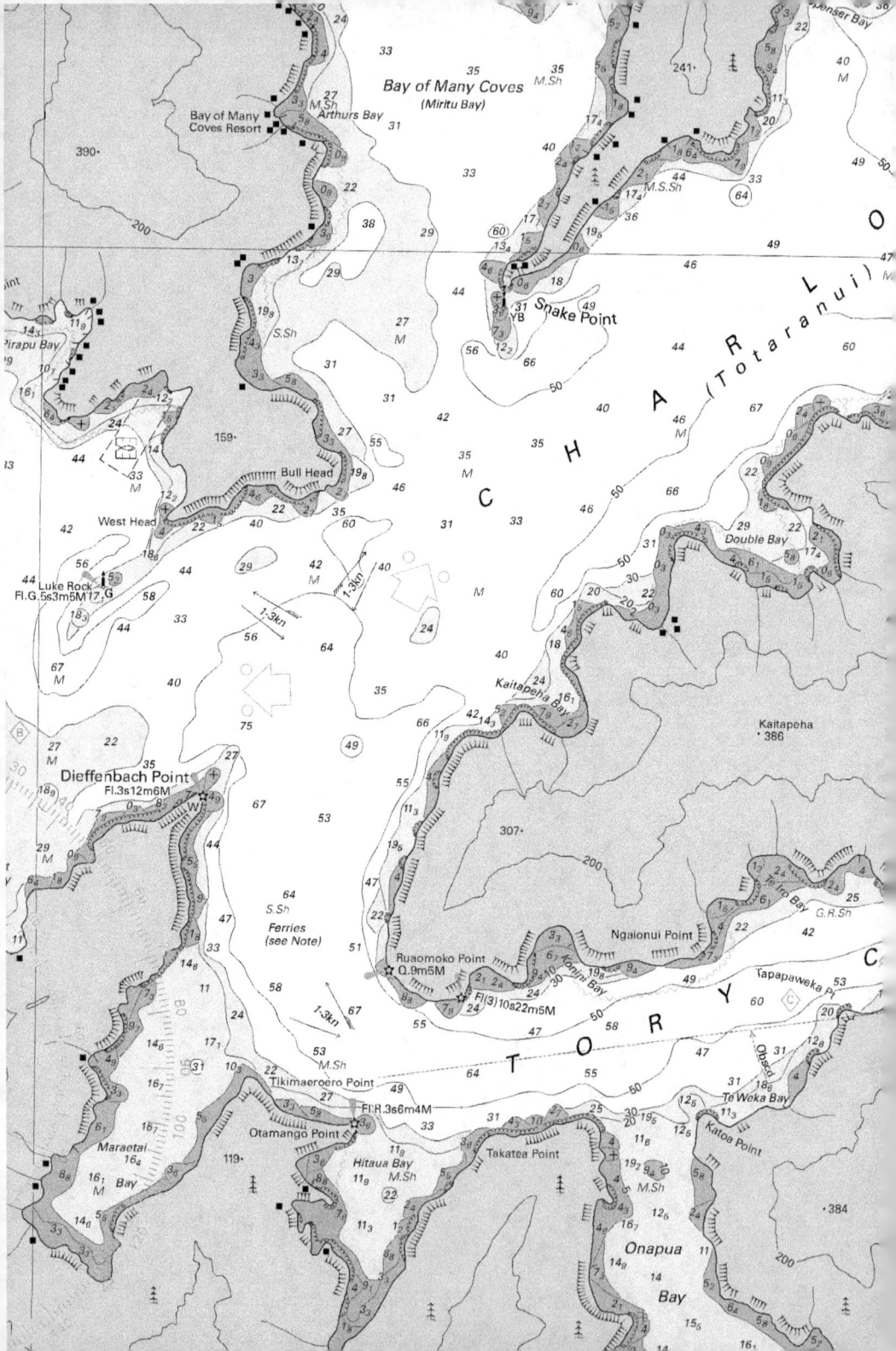

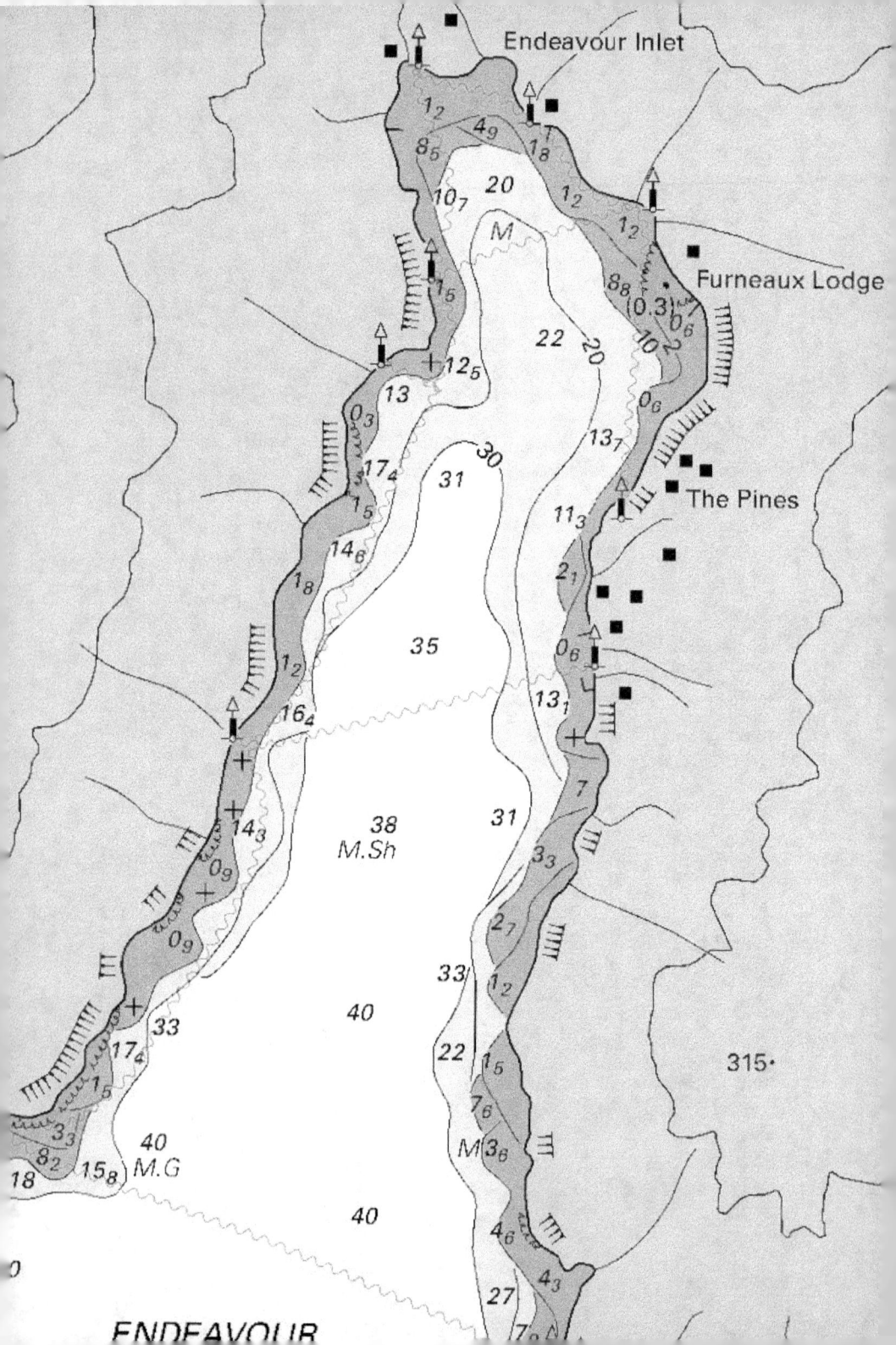

"When we come into the bay, we always go in via the western side of the bay and come into the area near Mr Cassells' mooring. We don't ever cut across the bay straight for the mooring because it's shallow in parts.

"When we first arrived we got lunch, then I relaxed for the rest of the afternoon, inside and out. It's the type of bay that you'd notice boats coming in and out. There were definitely no other boats in the bay where we were on the 01.01.98 when we arrived. And there were no boats that arrived while we were there.

"The children biscuited around the bay and swam in the afternoon, jumping off the new platform at the back of our yacht."

And no sign of *Blade*.

"I'd say we were in Erie Bay for a good three to three and a half hours that day," she told police.

Her daughter, 14 year old Karyn, confirmed the absence of *Blade*:[324]

"There were no other boats moored in Erie Bay when we were there on the 1 January 1998.

"On the 1st when we were in Erie Bay I remember seeing the caretaker. I don't know his name. He was on the jetty and it was in the afternoon."

Alex van Wijngaarden—also the Picton Harbourmaster, knew Scott Watson's yacht well, and never saw it that day.

"There were no other vessels in the bay anywhere near the vicinity of Cassels' place. I am familiar with the yacht owned by the accused Scott Wason and I am quite certain that it was not in Erie Bay on 1 January 1998 while I was there with my family.

"I left Erie Bay shortly after 5.00 pm on 1 January 1998. I know this as I passed the passenger vessel *Seabourn Legend* as it sailed out of Queen Charlotte Sound and into Tory Channel, in the vicinity of Ruamoko Point light at about 6.00 pm."

---

324 10805 / ST / KARYN VAN WIJNGAARDEN / SCC539 / 280298

This absence of *Blade* in Erie Bay until at least 5pm, and probably even later, is important, because a conspiracy theory has grown up around this aspect of the case. The caretaker, Keating, was arrested when police found a large cannabis plantation on his property. He then changed his timing on the arrival of *Blade* to 5pm, and he got his kids to change their statements as well. Pay close attention to the evolution showing Keating was in this up to his neck:

KEATING on 14 January: [Backstory, Scott arrived between 10am and midday, 1 January] "He came and had a cup of tea and a biscuit. At about 1 pm we both headed up the back to check our water supply. I just cleaned some gravel and we returned.

"I told him that me and the children were going up to the top of the hill for a walk. He said that he would go back to his yacht for a sleep and he left.

"Scott must of had his dinghy because I never took him in or at.

"He went out to his yacht and I didn't see him again to speak to. He stayed on his yacht until the next day when he sailed off.

"He didn't come ashore again.

"When he left on New Year's day I offered him an invitation to join us for a bar-b-que. He didn't say if he would come back or not.

"That afternoon of the 1st January we all saw Scott on his yacht. I'm not to sure what he was up to, he could of been painting but I can't swear to it. I saw him around the side of the yacht. At about 4 pm-4.30 pm the bar-b-que was cooked. My daughter and I went out to the end of the tennis court and yelled at Scott to join us. He was on the yacht but didn't come out. We didn't even see him. We didn't see him or try to contact him for the rest of the day. The next morning I got up at about 6 am. The yacht that Scott was on was still at the same place in the inlet.

"At about 9 am Scott left on power heading toward Picton. Scott didn't say goodbye he just left. He never told me the day before his arrangements for travel.

"On the 1st of January 1998 Scott was wearing blue jeans and a dark coloured jersey. I think he had a cut foot and might of been in bare feet.

"He had a bit of shadow of growth on his face. He wasn't clean shaven."

OK, that was statement one, a massive fabrication because we now know Watson wasn't there on 1 January. All this talk of cups of tea, invitations to barbecues—didn't happen. The essence of statement one is that Watson visited briefly then went back to his yacht to sleep, never came back to the house and sailed away on the morning of 2 January without notice.

Two days later, realising Watson has mentioned painting the boat, the story changes:

KEATING on 16 January:[325] "I didn't speak to Scott until I saw him on New Year's day. I looked up and saw that Scott's boat was anchored right off the tennis court and in close to the shore. This is where he normally anchors.

"Scott came ashore in his dinghy. I didn't come down to see him.

"Scott came into the kitchen and sat down. I asked him how Furneaux was for New Year. He said that it was OK. He said that he had a bottle of rum. He mentioned having a drink with a couple of jokers on some boat. He didn't say if they came on to his boat, or if he went to theirs.

"He did mention something about a scuffle but he didn't elaborate on it. I don't know if punches were thrown.

"I asked if there was any spare women & he said there was lots of couples—he didn't say anything about himself finding a woman.

"The water pressure was down so Scott & I walked up 50 yards to fit it. It only took 10 minutes. We cleared a bit of shingle away & went down to the house again.

---

325 20141 / ST / KEATING / TFD715 / 160198

"I told him shortly after that the kids & I had planned to go up the hill. He didn't want to go for a walk & said he would go back to his boat.

"He said to me have you still got that paint in the bucket. We both walked to the boat shed and found the paint. It was in a white 10 litre bucket. I can't remember if he said if he was going to paint it that day. I can't recall but he may of said it. The boat was still anchored off the tennis court. I didn't give Scott any paint brush only the paint.

"We were away for an hour or so.

"When I came back to our house the boat was now anchored 50 yards north of where he was. He was now on the far side of the bay. I can't say what way the yacht was pointing because it swings around. I didn't notice what he was doing on it but I presume he was painting because I gave him the paint. He was in & out of his cabin in his yacht.

"I didn't actually see him with a brush in his hand. I can't be sure if I noticed boat with a different colour—but I think I commented later that night that by being blue it makes the cabin look lower.

"At about 4-4.30 I called him for a bar-b-que but he didn't answer.

"I now remember that Scott came up later at night. I recall it because he ate a pie and a couple of sausages.

"I don't recall what we talked about. I think that Scott and the kids watched a film on TV. It was around mid evening. I think it might of been *Geronimo*. We didn't have anything to drink—he was just his normal self.

"The movie ended & he went to his yacht. I said something like I'll see you tomorrow if you're still here.

"In the morning his boat was still in the same position but he left at 9 am.

"He has phoned me once since I spoke to you on Wednesday. He phoned after midday and wouldn't say where he was. He said his lawyer had him tucked away.

"He apologised for saying about the paint. I told him not to worry because it was true. He didn't ask what the police had asked me or anything like that."

Suddenly, there's a fabricated story about offering some paint, and this time Watson has returned to the house for dinner and a movie. Keating was lying like a flatfish. He was trying to give Watson an alibi after the fact.

But wait, there's more:

KEATING on 23 January:[326]

Q: Are you happy with the two statements that you have already made to police? Other words are they correct?
A: No, I've been thinking and talking with the kids and I think I have got my dates and times wrong.
Q: When did Scott arrive? Was it still New Year's day?
A: Yes.
Q: What time was it?
A: It was in the afternoon I think. Like I said previously I didn't see him sail in. I looked up and he was moored off the end of the tennis court. This is where he usually moors; he always anchors and doesn't use the fixed mooring.
Q: How do you know it was in the afternoon and can you be more specific with the time?
A: We had a barbeque for lunch and he hadn't arrived. The races were on, it was Auckland cup day. I also did some lawns. I would now put the time at around 3.00pm.
Q: When did he come ashore?
A: The kids were playing badminton and I was inside. I think he came ashore right away.
Q: What happened when he got inside?

---

[326] 20392 / ST / KEATING / TFD175 / 230198

A: I gave him a cup of tea and we had a chat about New Year. He stayed and ate some bread. We all watched that movie Geronimo—afterwards he went out to the boat.

Q: What time would that have been?

A: 10.30-10.45.

Q: What did you talk about for seven hours?

A: Just general stuff. He never said anything out of the ordinary. We talked about the movie. I can't remember anything specific except I asked him about the word Geronimo when they jump out of a plane.

Q: Did he have his dinghy?

A: Yes—that old wooden thing.

Q: What happened the next day?

A: Kids slept in and Scott came ashore at about 8.00-8.30am. When he came ashore he was there for breakfast. I said that we didn't have any milk. He said he had some Long Life milk on his boat and that he would go and get it. I reminded him about a book that he had told me about the previous day. He said he would go and get the book as well.

Q: Where was his yacht at this point?

A: Still off the end of the tennis court.

Q: What happened over breakfast?

A: Nothing, he had some toast and a cup of tea. Afterwards he came and gave me a hand with the water supply behind the house.

Q: Had he cut his foot at this stage?

A: Yes he cut his foot at the time he went for the milk and the book.

Q: How long did he stay at your place on 2 January 1998?

A: Twenty minutes to do the water. He then asked about the paint that was in the bucket. I would say it was after nine o'clock in the morning. We walked down to the boat shed and I gave him the paint. I didn't give him a brush or sandpaper. He went out on his dinghy to his boat.

Q: When did he move his boat?
A: That morning I heard the chain being pulled up and moved over to the other side. I heard him move across the bay but I didn't see him, actually see it. He anchored on the right hand side as I look out.
Q: Did you see what he was doing?
A: No he was out there all day. I presumed he was painting.
Q: Do you remember if he had any sails on the boom?
A: I can't say definitely but he probably did.
Q: Did you call him for tea?
A: Yes, I yelled out but got no reply from him. He might have been having a snooze.
Q: Did you notice the paint colour of the boat?
A: It was blue when I yelled out for him to come for tea.
Q: Did he come to your house that night?
A: Yes about 5.30 for pie and sausages. He then stayed and watched a movie called Fortress.
Q: Did the kids watch it with you?
A: Yes.
Q: When did Scott leave?
A: The next morning I saw the yacht there and then he left. He never came ashore on 3 January—he just left.
Q: Why is this statement so different than the first two?
A: My kids and I have talked about it all the time. They have jogged my memory. The reason I'm so vague is that I can't remember what we talked about but I remember certain things.
Q: Is this all you can remember?
A: Yes.
Q: In the first statement did you leave anything out on purpose?
A: No not at all—that is what I believed. I haven't got any reason to leave anything out.
Q: Is this your memory of events or your kids?

A: From what my kids have told me it has helped me remember. To me it is just a normal day, so I didn't take any notice of events.

Supporters of Watson have long argued the timing changed because of police pressure. But the truth is Watson was not there, he was elsewhere. All three Keating statements are vast fabrications. Suddenly not only has the arrival time changed to late afternoon on 1 January, but Watson is now present for the whole of 2 January and departing on 3 January.

It's clear that Keating's children were persuaded to sign false statements:

"A Policewoman spoke to me on 14 January about Scott Watson coming to my dad's place at Erie Bay on New Year's Day this year. Some of the things are not correct because I forgot Scott stayed for two days," said Keating's 10 year old boy.[327]

That wasn't all they forgot. Suddenly, among other things, the boat had miraculously returned to brown when it arrived:

"On New Year's Day Scott came to our place again in his boat. I think it was about lunchtime because I saw him walking into the house. I didn't know Scott was coming. His boat was brown on top.

"Scott had some dinner with us and then watched a movie. I went to bed about 10.00 o'clock and Scott was still there. He stayed on his boat that night.

"Dad and Scott didn't speak about painting Scott's boat the next day. I didn't hear them say anything that night about painting the boat.

"Scott came up for breakfast the next day at about 8.00 o'clock in the morning.

"After breakfast, dad and Scott went up to check the water because dad told us they were going up to check the water. Dad and Scott were only away about ten minutes or so.

---

327 10378 / ST / KEATING SON / LC8773 / 230198

"Dad came back and said he gave Scott some paint out of the shed. I didn't look down at the boat then but looked down later around lunchtime and saw the boat was blue. I couldn't see Scott on the boat then.

"Scott had a sleep on his boat and he came up to our place for tea later that night. We yelled out to him to come up for tea but we couldn't get him. He came up later though, about half to an hour later.

"Dad said his boat looked lower because it was painted blue.

"I don't know what Scott was wearing when he got to Erie Bay on New Year's Day. The next day he had a blue woollen jersey on and black jeans. It was the second day he was there that Scott cut himself."

What did Watson have over Keating that was forcing him to make ten year old children lie to police? The poor child was forced to lie again in a further police statement in March:[328]

"I have already made two statements to the Police. I have had my statements read back to me and they are correct. When I said that Scott came to Erie Bay on New Year's Day I didn't give a time.

"I think that the time was about 3 pm. I know that we had eaten lunch before Scott arrived. When we are at Erie Bay we have our dinner early. By early I mean 4-5 pm each day. I know that Scott got there before we ate dinner.

"When Scott arrived he sailed his yacht over to the far side of the bay. I have drawn on a sketch the position that he put the yacht in.

"The rest of my statement is correct.

"Dad has never told me what to say to the Police and if anything it is the other way around. We talked about Scott coming to Erie Bay at New Year and helped dad remember things that he had forgotten.

"I am sure that Scott was the only boat is Erie Bay on the afternoon of New Year's Day."

---

328 20999 / ST / KEATING SON / TFD175 / 100398

Keating knew he could face possible perjury charges for giving this load of baloney to the cops. By blaming his changing story on his children—who were too young to be criminally prosecuted—Keating was trying to weasel out of his predicament. In doing so, he made his son and daughter morally culpable as accessories after the fact to a double murder.

His daughter, too, was forced to give false testimony:[329]

"Further to my original statement, myself, my brother and dad have thought about things that happened on New Year's Day. Scott Watson arrived after lunch. We had a barbecue lunch at about 12 'ish. We ate our lunch inside at the kitchen table. Right in front of the table there's a window where you can see the whole bay.

"About half an hour after lunch we were all sitting at the table when we saw Scott coming in. I don't remember which way he was coming in from. I think he was motoring.

"He put his yacht on the right-hand side of the bay.

"I am positive his yacht was the brownish colour."

Except, of course, we now know with absolute certainty that Watson's boat was blue before it ever got to Erie Bay.

We know Keating lied about Watson's arrival time of between 10am and midday. We know Watson lied about an arrival time of 9.30am to 10am. We know Watson's yacht had already been painted blue when it did arrive.

Why? How? And why did Keating lie? Keating is dead now so we will never know his reasons. Watson, on the other hand, still has some explaining to do. Where did he go in those missing hours immediately after Ben and Olivia went missing?

Terrence Stevens was sailing his wife and children in their yacht from Tawa Bay, in Endeavour Inlet, south to the Bay of Many Coves and the shop at Gem Resort. They left at 9.30am, four or

---

[329] 10373 / ST / KEATING DAUGHTER / SCC539 / 230198

five hours after *Blade* had silently slipped its mooring at Furneaux. *Blade* could have covered some 30 kilometres over that time. Yet, as they came out of Endeavour Inlet, Terrence Stevens came across a small yacht heading south.[330]

"I noticed a boat directly ahead of me. I could see the stern and it looked like an old fashioned boat, approximately 26-27 ft long, in that region. It had browny red cabin sides, white lee cloth around the stern, whiteish coloured hull travelling south at a slightly slower speed than us. We believe that we were travelling at about 6 knots—so I would say it was doing about 5.5 knots. My yacht does not have a functioning Log therefore my assessment of speed is based on time & distance recordings I had made in the past. My yacht was travelling at full motoring speed which previous time on distance recordings earlier in the trip indicated that it was 6 knots.

"The day was fine and the water was flat, not dead calm but flat. It was North Westerly.

"We picked it up somewhere between Edgecombe Point and Kurakura Point. I believe we were to its starboard side, so it was on our left. I cannot recall overtaking it, but was surprised sometime after to see the boat that had been ahead of us, behind us. I may have gone down below to get something for the kids or something. When we overtook it I must have been doing something else.

"All of my family steers the boat, and we were taking turns that morning. I particularly encourage the children to steer the boat.

"I would have seen this boat shortly after 10am. I know this because we were roughly half way between Tawa Bay & Gem Resort and I know that we arrived at Gem Resort at about 10.30 am that morning.

"The boat seemed for its length quite beamy. Beamier than the impression I had gained from the photographs of the seized sloop

---

330 40302 / ST / TERRENCE STEVENS / SCC539 / 170398

in the newspaper. It was a single masted yacht that was definitely motoring. It didn't have its sail up and I can't remember whether it was towing a dinghy.

"From memory we got to within 50 metres of the yacht and then my next memory is the yacht being behind us.

"I definitely thought that someone was steering the boat. I remember seeing a person or persons and I wasn't suspicious about the boat at the time. However I can't remember how many there were or what they looked like. I can give this more thought though.

"I have always remembered this boat because we were following it for some time, and it was matching our speed and was then within short space of time it was behind us, and matching our speed, almost like it slowed down to put distance between. Given the closeness of our speeds and direction I would have thought that we would have stayed alongside it for a long time and that didn't seem to be the case.

"After we had passed him he kept pace. I would have thought that if we overtook him quickly that he would have lagged behind, but he didn't. For some minutes, at least ten, he maintained a relative position dead astern, behind us.

"My last recollection of the boat was when I last saw it about 100 metres behind us when it was near Spencer Bay. It was still heading South West... We approached Snake Point, at about 10.15 am."

Terrence's eight year old son Matthew was actually steering the family yacht on this occasion, and he got to see it up close:[331]

"Dad and Mum & me and Jonathan saw a wee boat just before Snake Point. I was steering the boat and looking towards it because it was ahead of us. We were going at almost full speed because we were charging the battery up and you can only charge it up on full speed.

"We got about 10 metres away from it. It took us about 5 minutes

---

331 40371 / ST / MATTHEW STEVENS / SCC539 / 190398

Cracking The Case

ELEMENTARY

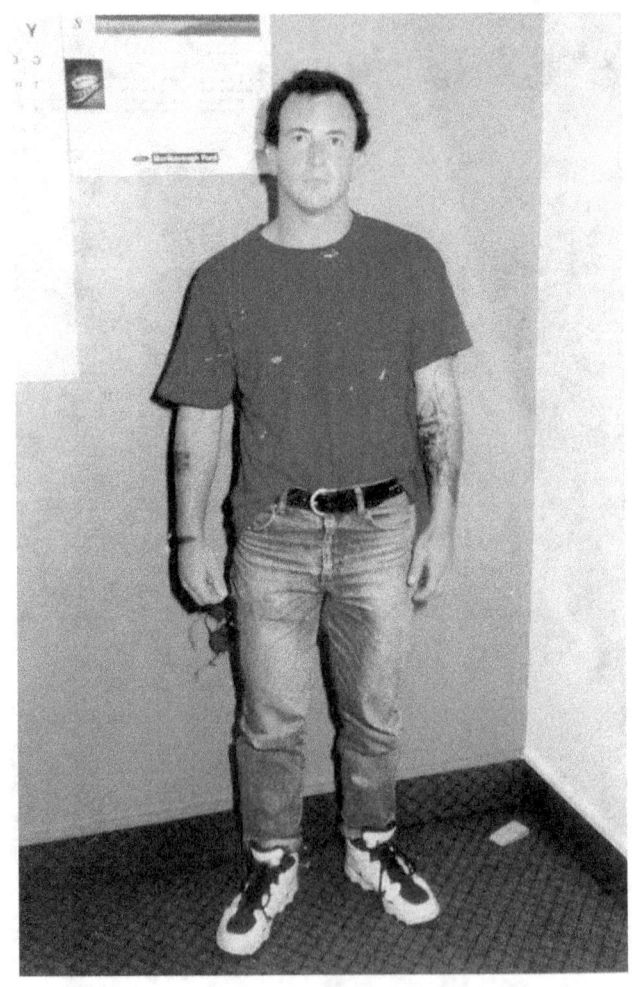

to catch up with it because it was going quite slow and we caught up quite quickly.

"It looked like the wee boat was heading to Picton or Waikawa, I never saw it come into Gem Resort. The best view that I had of the boat was from the side.

"When we were coming up beside it I could see some of the floor and the seats at the stern of the boat. It had black stripes going down towards the back of the boat on the brown wood. This was on the seats & the floor. I could see it was a keeler boat. It looked the right size for a keeler.

"The hatch was open and was made of wood and it had a little metal ring to open and close it. I saw the hatch was closed but the washboards weren't there. I couldn't see into the cabin. It was black.

"The boat had cloth around the back. It went halfway from the back into the middle. You couldn't see through it. The cloth was white. It was about 2 feet tall. It was about 1 metre long side on.

"I'm not sure what shape the windows were or how many there were but I saw cream coloured curtains that were shut.

"It had just 1 sail. It was on the boom. It was quite little. It wasn't covering much of boom. It was tied up with green and white ropes. I couldn't see any other sails on the boat.

"There were ropes down the sides and on the top of the cabin. They were coloured. 1 was black. The ones on top were figure of 8's. The ones on the sides weren't tidy. I think the side ones were jib sheets.

"It had safety lines down the side—one on the top and one on the bottom. They were white. The mast was white. It had one spreader."

So far so good, but what eight year old Matthew Stevens said next casts a whole new dimension on the case—there were two men on board *Blade*:

"There were about 2 people on it. They were both men. Both had black hair. One was steering. The other was on the starboard side. They were sitting down. One had a glass or something in his hand—the one who wasn't steering. The man steering had a green t-shirt and the other guy had a black sweater. It might have been a woolly jersey.

"I think one was Maori. He had a round face. The guy steering had white skin and a skinny face. I saw most of his face but I didn't see all of it. I don't think they were talking. I couldn't see what colour their pants or shoes or socks were.

"The guy steering had quite short hair and the guy on the starboard side had longer hair that came down to the middle of his neck. It was long on top like Mum's but I couldn't see if it was curly or straight. I could only see the back of his head. The guy steering had short sleeves and the other guy's sleeves came all the way down like a sweatshirt. I'm pretty sure it wasn't a t-shirt.

"I have been shown a page with men's faces on it. I picked out the guy steering the boat. I think he had the same hairstyle and same head. It had a curl on the top on the right and had a few curls at the back and the rest was straight.

"It was number three on the page. "

Sonya Currie, the police officer who took Matthew's statement, filed her own report on this crucial interview:[332]

"After he described the yacht they had passed I showed him the picture of the sloop when it was the brownish/red colour and then when it was blue. Matthew positively identified this yacht as being the one he saw just short of Snake Point.

"I found Matthew to be a very knowledgeable child with an incredible memory for detail. When I obtained a statement from him, his mother was within earshot in the next room entertaining her younger son. She came and sat in on our interview about halfway through.

---

[332] 12020 / JS / MATTHEW STEVEN / SCC539 / 190398

"She described Matthew as an honest child.

"Matthew has obviously spent a good deal of time with his father on yachts and is very familiar with equipment and procedures used when yachting.

"He also knew boat lengths and compared the size of the yacht he saw with the size of his parent's yacht.

"After having obtained the descriptions of the males on board the yacht I showed Matthew Photo Montage B, a collection of 8 males' faces.

"Without hesitation, Matthew pointed to the male marked Photo 3, Scott Watson as the male he had seen steering the yacht him and his father overtook just short of Snake Point."

The description of the boat is almost certainly *Blade*, with its distinctive white lee cloth around the back and the reddish brown cabin (as of 10am on New Year's Day). But how and where had Watson suddenly picked up a passenger? How had two men ended up on *Blade*? Where were the sails? And why were the curtains on all the cabin windows shut?

The Eastgates had run into Watson at the Furneaux bar and remarked on a man he was talking to:

"Vicki and I were at a leaner in the middle of the room," remembered Warwick Eastgate, "and we were talking to a Maori guy who was at the same leaner as us. He was talking to other friends as well.[333]

"Scott came over to us and chatted for about 10 mins. It could have been up to ½ an hour. Scott had had a fair bit to drink but didn't appear to be out of control in any way. He was just his normal self.

"When we were at the table with a Maori guy in the bar at Furneaux, the Maori guy asked if we were with Scott when Scott was away at the toilet or something. I got the impression he didn't

---
[333] 20085 / ST / WARWICK EASTGATE / ASD279 / 120198

think much of Scott and thought Scott a bit of a trouble maker. The Maori guy wasn't a local. I don't know where he was from or his name," Warwick told police.[334]

"This guy was tall, solid, with a beard, not a lot of hair on the top," said Vicki Eastgate. "He may have a ponytail as well. He had a roughish look about him but seemed like a nice guy."[335]

"I don't know his name. He told us that Scott had tried to pick a fight with a gang member earlier on."

It is drawing too long a bow to say that somehow this man is the one who ended up with Watson, but it is virtually the only lead in the entire police file. Detectives did find someone who looked similar, but the man denied being at Furneaux and was "hesitant" about speaking to police:[336]

"Appeared hesitant about speaking to self.

"Description: Male, Maori. Heavily tattooed, arms and neck/throat area. Goatee beard, hair in ponytail. Solid build."

Then there was Bryan Badger's evidence:[337] "I've also seen a Maori guy on the boat of Scott's," he told police. "I don't even know what the Maori guy looked like but I've never seen him before. I don't know who Scott gets round with. I would say he used to get round by himself."

Terrence Stevens and his son Matthew were not called to give evidence at trial, because the sighting possibly did not suit the Crown reconstruction that was trying to put *Blade* at the entrance to Tory Channel in Cook Strait at 4.30pm, to fit the "body-dumping" scenario.

That scenario was based on an alleged sighting of *Blade* by passengers on the Cook Strait ferry, but it was a sighting from a distance, not from as close as ten metres.

---

334 20435 / JS / WARWICK EASTGATE / LC8773 / 190198
335 20038 / ST / VICKI EASTGATE / RHD188 / 120198
336 10720 / JS / WITNESS ENQ / RMC084 / 270198
337 10513 / ST / BRYAN BADGER / LC8773 / 270198

Thus, the evidence line towards establishing *Blade*'s real movements took a different turn.

However, the Stevens family were not the only ones to see *Blade* that New Year's morning.

At the same time, the launches *Wild Honey* and *Cheers* passed two yachts in the exact same spot—quite possibly the first yacht was the Stevens' one coming up on *Blade* but still behind it. Wayne Robertson on *Wild Honey* describes what he saw:

"It was approximately 10.00 am and we were near the head of Endeavour Inlet.[338]

"As we passed Bull Head heading to Snake Point, we passed a fibreglass 30 foot sloop with a flat, low cabin. It was one I had seen earlier in the Furneaux Inlet. The cabin and sides were cream. It was motoring and had sail up. There was no wind there though as they were in the lee of the hill. It was being powered by a British Seagull motor.

"Just in front of it, about 75—100 metres away, was a yacht similar to the description of the seized yacht that I have seen in the paper. It was under motor.

"There were two people on board. One was steering it. I think it might have been tiller steering. There was another person on the port side. He had a paint brush in his hand, holding on to the side stays. Tony in "*Cheers*" went behind the two yachts and I went the other side. The yacht had to turn to avoid the wakes.

"It was then that I noticed the *two* colours. The colour he was painting was a bluey grey colour similar to the one in the paper. The original colour on the starboard side was pinky looking, like an undercoat had been put over red.

"It looked as though the port side was nearly completed and the starboard side hadn't been done at all. When he turned it caused

---

[338] 10226 / ST / WAYNE ROBERTSON / DSC229 / 160198

the person painting to lose his balance and swing out slightly."

This element of Wayne Robertson's sighting is crucial. Robertson could see *Blade*'s port side—it was being painted blue over red, in real time, on the ocean. This is how we know the vessel was *Blade*—not just the description matched but the unusual yacht was actually seen in the very process of being repainted. The starboard side, which was the side seen by the Stevens family, was still reddish brown, painting had not started on the starboard side. So the man Matthew Stevens described as holding something in his hand was actually holding a paintbrush. Who was Scott Watson's accomplice and why have we never heard of him before?

Wayne Robertson's evidence continues:

"The person who was painting I would describe as male, race unknown. He was wearing very dark clothing. I only got an impression of him and couldn't describe him at all. I don't think he was very big. He was young, in his 20's. Black hair.

"The guy steering had grey curly hair, possibly in his 30's. I remember him looking at us. He was wearing lighter clothing, possibly grey.

"I remember passing comment to someone about, "He's keen" and, "He better grab his paint tin" because he was about to get hit with *"Cheers"'* wake and our wake. The yacht was a sloop, about 30 foot. It was hard chine. I can't remember if it had a lee cloth.

"I think the guy steering might have been standing. I can't remember if it had sails on deck. It was motoring. It did not have sails up. I can't recall anything else about these persons on the yacht.

"Very shortly afterwards the ship "New Zealand Explorer" came past us in the opposite direction. It would have passed the yachts.

"We then passed the yachts, rounded Snake Point into Bay of Many Coves."

This is where the police pursuit of Scott Watson lost a crucial lead. The obsession with placing *Blade* in Cook Strait later in the day meant this vital evidence was sidelined. Wayne Robertson did not give this evidence in Court, and we never knew about it when we wrote *Ben & Olivia*.

There is utterly no question this was *Blade*. There is utterly no question that *Blade* was being repainted while the boat was motoring down Queen Charlotte Sound at maximum speed at 10am on New Year's morning. There is utterly no question that Scott Watson had an accomplice on the boat. There is utterly no question that Keating's kids had let slip the truth: *Blade* was already blue and white when it allegedly slipped into Erie Bay late on 1 January. There is utterly no question that Keating lied about Watson repainting his boat on January 2nd at Erie Bay.

Wayne Robertson's sighting was backed up by Robert Aitken, a passenger on *Wild Honey*:[339]

"We travelled back towards the Bay of Many Coves on the west side of Endeavour Inlet.

"When we were off Kurakura Point I noticed a vessel similar to that in photograph two of the before and after shots. It was towing a dingy. I have no description of the dingy.

"The yacht itself I cannot recall a colour and it was under motor. There was a male standing in the back deck of the boat. I could not see his legs because of the canvas windbreak on the back of the boat.

"The male at the rear had short hair, that's all I can tell you about him. One of his arms was behind him like he was steering the yacht. There were three other yachts in the area all going the same way, as in going back to Picton / Waikawa area.

"When I passed this yacht on its starboard side so I was in the middle between the yacht and the Point. This would have been about 11 am. I had my mind on the Point, the depth gauge and this yacht so I wasn't paying a lot of attention to the yacht."

---

339 11178 / ST / ROBERT AITKEN / KM5725 / 260198

In case readers are in any doubt that this was Watson and he had an accomplice on board, read the evidence of water taxi driver Sam Edwards who knew Watson and his boat well:[340]

"On the 1st January at about 10.00am, I saw his boat again somewhere between Edgecombe Point and Snake Point. I'm pretty sure it was off Kurakura Point and he was heading south. I was heading to Ship Cove in *Felix* and when I passed him, I would have been about 50-150 metres away when I saw his boat. His boat was still reddy/brown in colour then. Scott was sitting in the cockpit and waved to me and I waved back. It was definitely Scott on board.

"I'm pretty sure that I saw a second person in the cockpit."

Edwards' sighting of the old paint scheme is dependent on which side of the yacht he saw. The sighting of someone else on *Blade* is consistent with everything we now know.

Scott Watson's yacht was normally moored at Shakespeare Bay, near Waikawa, is that where he was steaming for at 10am on New Year's Day? If Watson did kill Ben and Olivia, was he planning to rendezvous with someone who could help get rid of the bodies, and/or was he dropping off the mystery man on board?

Coincidentally, also heading into Picton later that afternoon were charter boat operators Ted and Eyvonne Walsh, who were picking up clients from the Cook Strait ferry at 1.15pm.

"We headed out and went to Waikawa," Eyvonne Walsh told police, "we went to get petrol.[341]

I'm not exactly sure but as we came into Waikawa near the 5 knots side on your left I heard someone say 'Someone's painting a boat'. I made the comment 'who would want to paint a boat on a nice day like this?'.

"I probably would have glanced towards whoever was painting but I

---

340 20150 / ST / SAMUEL EDWARDS / ASD279 / 160198
341 20235 / ST / EYVONNE WALSH / JSC422 / 300198

didn't take any notice. I was getting ropes ready to come into the jetty I think. I remember Ted said the guy had more paint on his hands than what he had on the boat. I can't be accurate where this boat that was being painted was but I feel it was outside Waikawa Marina."

Ted Walsh was also clear on seeing someone painting they yacht in unusual circumstances, but not so clear on precisely where:

"In my last statement I mentioned about a boat being painted. I admit that I am having trouble saying for sure where I saw this happening but I do have the nagging thought that I remember thinking what a strange place for someone to be painting a yacht. I believe it definitely was the 1st January 1998 because Eyvonne said 'who the hell would paint their boat on New Year's Day?'. The only movements I did on New Year's Day was to come into Picton to meet the 1.15 pm ferry and then travel to Waikawa Marina for fuel before going back to Furneaux. That was the only time I went out of Endeavour Inlet on New Year's Day."[342]

In another stunning twist, Ted Walsh told Watson's own private investigators that he'd seen a boat similar to *Blade* being repainted:

> BERRYMAN: You have seen his yacht in the media—had you seen that yacht in the Sounds prior to that?
> WALSH: No, not really. Not that I recall. It's a pretty basic sort of a yacht. We saw someone painting a boat similar to that on New Year's Day when we went to town, but we've had conflicting argument really, I suppose is more than confliction, of where it was. So I'll leave that out really.
> BERRYMAN: Where do you think you saw a boat?
> WALSH: I reckon it must have been Waikawa, because we were going fairly slow.
> BERRYMAN: Waikawa Bay?

---

342 30620 / ST / EDWARD WALSH / JFD014 / 050298

WALSH: Yeah, as we were going to shore, we went in to get some fuel and that's where I think it was, although I remember thinking that it was…, better keep going slow, someone will be pissed off if I disturb his paint.

BERRYMAN: We'll move on from that.

A search of the police file reveals another fascinating report, one that only makes sense because of these new revelations about the at-sea repaint. John Forrest was operating a water taxi service on a trip to Ship Cove, at the entrance of Queen Charlotte Sound from Cook Strait:[343]

"On the morning of the 1st Jan 1998 at about 8.50 am I was coming into Ship Cove with Dr Kelly Johnson and some other people, and going across Resolution Inlet, one of the passengers made a comment about a yacht. The passenger said something like 'What a horrible paint scheme, somebody must have had some left over paint'. The reference was apparently to a strangely coloured yacht in the bay."

Now that we know—an hour later—that the boat had been completely painted on one side, it raises the real possibility that a half-daubed *Blade* was at the entrance to Cook Strait at 8.50am on New Year's Day, four hours after slinking out of Furneaux. The sighting is consistent with *Blade* then heading south and reaching Snake Point by 10am on an incoming tide.

It's consistent, in fact, with *Blade* reaching Waikawa by just after 11am.

There is more overwhelming evidence that Watson's boat was painted on the move on New Year's morning, not at Erie Bay on 2 January.

Holidaymakers Bridget and Michael Edmonds were cruising the Tory Channel in their fizz boat, heading back to their vehicle at the Waikawa Bay mooring, as they came to enter Queen Charlotte

---

343 10690 / ST / JOHN FORREST / SD5025 / 050298

Sound by hanging a left at Dieffenbach Point, they came up to and overtook a yacht heading the same way, out of Tory Channel into Queen Charlotte Sound:[344]

"We packed up and left at approx 3.45-3.50 pm. I remember the time because I didn't want to get back home to Blenheim too late and I remember asking my husband the time. We travelled back to Waikawa in our Crestacraft Fizz boat. There was myself, my husband Michael and our 2 children. It was quite windy and the water was quite choppy.

"We travelled up through the Tory Channel heading back towards Dieffenbach Point.

"Just short of Dieffenbach Point, on the same side I saw a yacht. It sat low in the water and you could only see the cabin part in the water. It was blue—the cabin part. There were 3 square portholes on the side of the cabin and a bigger one to the back. It had one mast and it was going very slowly towards the point, probably only 50 metres from shore. I would say it was a wooden yacht.

"It was definitely bigger than our boat, I would say it was about 26' long. It didn't have its sails up and there were no other sails apart from the one attached to the mast.

"I didn't see a dinghy—there was no dinghy out the back. It was moving very slowly and definitely not anchored. I didn't see anyone on board. Maybe that's why I looked too, because there was no one on board that I could see.

"I commented to my husband that it was sitting low in the water, and he commented to me that it was quite close to shore, especially coming up to the point—because there are a lot of rocks close in and it's shallow there as well.

"I looked at this yacht for about a minute. It would have taken us about 4 minutes to travel from Te Iro Bay to where we saw this yacht—which would have made the time probably approximately 3.55 pm.

---

344 20321 / ST / BRIDGET EDMONDS / SCC539 / 180198

"When we passed the yacht we took a wide turn, going down the left hand side of Queen Charlotte Sounds towards Waikawa Bay.

"I have never seen the yacht, that I saw at Dieffenbach Point before. I didn't see it again after that and I don't know where it went.

"As we came up to Karaka Point we saw the Lynx heading out towards Tory Channel for Wellington.

"The day that the Police said they'd be looking for a ketch and when they released the picture, that's when I said to my husband that it wasn't the one I'd seen at Dieffenbach Point.

"Then when they said they'd seized the yacht, I saw a picture of it in the *Marlborough Express* paper and recognised it as being the one I'd seen at Dieffenbach Point—and it was definitely blue.

"I'm certain that the one in the paper (*Blade*) is the one that I saw—it's just a pity I didn't see anyone on board.

"I have been shown a photograph of a yacht coloured red and then blue, and it's definitely the same one that I saw," confirmed Bridget Edmonds.

We now know Watson was seen with a mystery man on his boat at 10am at Snake Point, heading at full throttle towards Waikawa. He could have gone anywhere, but we know he did not go to nearby Erie Bay until sometime after the Wijngaardens cleared the bay around 5.20pm. But if Keating was lying about Watson's arrival at Erie Bay—and he was—how do we even know Watson went to Erie Bay at all on 1 January?

The evidence suggests he didn't, or, if he did visit, it was not for long, it was not for the night, not for dinner and it was not for a repaint. The Dieffenbach Point sighting at 3.50pm was maybe half an hour south of Erie—and *Blade* was already heading towards Picton. It means that if *Blade* snuck into Erie it had done so only briefly and left again before the Wijngaardens left.

Water taxi driver Sam Edwards thought he saw Watson's boat at Erie Bay sometime after 3.30pm, "could have been as late as 7.00pm.

I don't remember seeing anyone on it and just remember seeing it out of the corner of my eye."[345]

He may have seen Jeremy Bradley's small yacht, white with a maroon stripe, which had broken down at the entrance to Erie Bay around 4.30pm.[346]

Sam's girlfriend at the time, Lisa Campbell, thought the Erie Bay sighting might have been 2 January:[347]

"I also remember seeing Scott's boat in Erie Bay I cannot remember if it was the 1st or 2nd of January and what time of the day it was. I am sure that it was Scott's boat. It is definitely the same style of boat that is shown in the photo of the boat the Police have seized. I think it was blue when I saw it."

Kimberley Still was staying at a bach in Erie Bay and says there was definitely no *Blade* at dawn:[348]

"I ...got up at about 7.00am on the 2nd of January. That morning we went over to Moioio Island. I am unsure of the time we went there but it was the first thing we did that morning. I remember looking over to the area marked on the map as *Keating/Cassels and there were no boats there that morning."

Jennifer and Peter Sutton owned a bach in Erie Bay. They arrived about 10pm on 1 January after flying in via Auckland from Los Angeles. Coming in on the water taxi Felix they saw no boats in Erie Bay on the evening of New Year's Day. Jetlagged, they woke up mid morning on 2 January to go and set a fishing net. While they were doing this, *Blade* turned up.[349]

"It was probably late morning when I saw a boat come into the harbour. It was similar looking to the yacht that you have shown me

---

345 20150 / ST / SAMUEL EDWARDS / ASD279 / 160198
346 10659 / ST / JEREMY BRADLEY / AS1272 /
347 40345 / ST / LISA CAMPBELL / MK8254 / 010498
348 40093 / ST / KIMBERLY STILL / ASD279 / 170398
349 30991 / ST / JENNIFER SUTTON / DCC611 / 060398

in the photograph. It was a hard chine yacht, which is the same as the yacht in the picture. The yacht was definitely not red but other than that I do not know what colour it was. I cannot be sure how much of this has been suggested by the news and media. I'd like to say it was definitely that yacht in the picture but I cannot say for sure.

"The yacht I saw had the nose of the yacht facing towards the direction of the Cassels which is on the south eastern side of Erie Bay. I would have been about 200 metres from the yacht.

"I did not see anyone on board the yacht. The yacht had one mast and it would have been about 24 ft in length. The yacht was definitely coming into Erie Bay when I saw it on the 2nd of January 1998.

"It would have been about late morning or close to twelve o'clock. The reason I am sure about those times is because I know that it wasn't late afternoon and we hadn't had lunch yet. I did not see where it ended up. My impression is that it was going to the Cassels in Erie Bay," Jenny Sutton told police.

But it didn't stay there long. By 1pm, *Blade* was seen leaving Erie Bay by a group of fishermen, utterly contradicting the false stories of Keating and his children:[350]

"Between 12.30 pm—1.00 pm I saw what I call a sloop, single mast, it was coming out of Erie Bay into the Tory Channel and heading towards Queen Charlotte which is the next Sound," said Myles Coburn.

"I would describe this boat as a sloop, single mast, old wooden colours blue and white spring to mind but that might be because I've seen it on TV and papers. The boat was under motor not sail. I didn't see anyone on board at any time. The boat turned left from Erie Bay into Tory Channel.

"I have been shown photographs of two boats (marked photograph 1). The top photo looks more like it to me as the boat I saw,

---

350 11921/ST/MYLES COBURN/GT3329/030498

I don't recall it towing a dinghy. The colour of the boat was blue and white like the boat in photo no. 2 on the same page. The boat passed us about 200 metres away but I didn't see anyone on board. The boat was probably doing about 5 or 6 knots, nothing flash.

"I noticed this boat because there were so many boats and yachts around that were new and this one was an older style boat. It was mainly wood on the deck which I noticed as being older."

Friend Fergus Sproull added:[351] "I don't recall if it was towing a dinghy or not. The rear of the boat appeared to be closed in along the back railings. I noticed that it had self steering gear mounted on the back of the boat.

"The boat was motoring close to the coast and may have been about 50 yards or so off shore. The boat was heading in the direction of Picton."

Unluckily for Watson, Sproull knew the boat and had once spoken to Watson directly. It was definitely *Blade*. "It looked familiar to me and if it had been the same colour as it was when I saw it two years ago, I probably would have recognised it."

It should be patently obvious now, even to Keith Hunter, that Scott Watson lied through his teeth in his police interviews and—knowing what he was being accused of—the Keating family have given false evidence in a murder investigation. Watson wasn't at Erie Bay for three days. He was barely there three hours.

That would mean police have failed to account for Watson's movements not for a mere few hours, but in fact for 30 hours. The construction of a false movement trail for 1 January means Operation Tam analysts actually missed a full day of potential leads—including finding Watson's accomplice—thanks to the false testimony of Watson and caretaker Keating and his children. Watson could well have been at Tory Channel at 4.30pm, because he was *never* at Erie

---

351 20815/ST/FERGUS SPROULL/RHD188/280198

Bay on 1 January, certainly not at any time that can be corroborated—the Keating evidence, all of it, was corrupt.

And if he was never at Erie Bay on 1 January, Keith Hunter's *Murder on the Blade* documentary was a waste of airtime and public funding, *because there was no mad dash from Cook Strait to Erie Bay that evening.* The whole debate about how fast *Blade* was turns out to be totally irrelevant. Watson had the whole of New Year's Day and night to get his problem sorted, and turned up at Erie Bay late morning on 2 January, and only stayed for a couple of hours before speeding back to Picton.

Keating and his kids were not lying about the 10am-midday arrival, *they were lying about the day he arrived. Nothing* about the testimony of Keating and his two children can be trusted. The alibi they created for Watson is false. The books, documentaries, newspaper and magazine articles built on that alibi are false.

That leaves one inevitable, inescapable, *elementary* conclusion: the killer of Ben and Olivia was Watson.

It's not hard to figure out why the children lied—their father put them up to it. But why was Keating lying? And what kept drawing Watson to Picton like a magnet? Where was his dinghy? What were police missing...

CHAPTER TWENTY ONE

The Final Piece Of The Jigsaw

The new evidence you've just read has rocked the Scott Watson case to it's very core, but what if we could follow this stunning new evidence trail wherever it leads? What if we can get closer to the truth of what happened to Ben Smart and Olivia Hope than we've ever been?

The police had it within their grasp, but one gets the feeling they felt the bird in the hand was easier to prosecute than the bird still in the bush somewhere. The police files given to the Watson family disclose this document:[352]

"I was working at the Barn one evening when Paul Maker said to me that the identikit that Police had put out looked like his neighbour. He said it was the spitting image or words to that effect. He didn't tell me his neighbour's name. Since then I have worked out he was referring to Scott Watson.

---

352 40044 / ST / ROSALIND BENSON / TFD175 / 040398

"When Police took Watson's boat out of the water the topic came up again. This time he said that he had it on good authority that Scott had sailed from Furneaux in the early hours of New Year's day and gone straight to Grizzy's Place in Onapua Bay. He never mentioned that Scott went to Zappa's after Grizzy's place.

"Paul didn't say who Grizzy was. I know that Paul knows Grizzy because he has asked my partner Dick to go past his place while looking for Paul's son sometime ago.

"Paul told me on one occasion that Scott tends to play up when he has been drinking and that he goes for young girls when he was drunk.

"I don't know Grizzy but my partner has marked on a map where he thinks Grizzy lives in Onapua Bay."

It makes sense. Scott Watson had to have someone close he could turn to after the murders, not just close as a friend but close in terms of distance. Watson didn't have a cellphone in January 1998—such toys were for yuppies and the likes of Watson couldn't afford the bill. He would not have used VHF radio, capable of being overheard. But he went somewhere, he picked up someone.

You could write that conversation off as idle chatter, except that the man who allegedly blurted this out to a cafe waitress about Watson's movements was indeed a key Watson confidante:[353]

NEW ZEALAND POLICE JOB SHEET
OFFENCE: OPERATION "TAM"

14.01.98

1606 hrs At Picton Police Station with Detective DALTON who is interviewing a possible witness.

---

353 10430 / JS / SCOTT WATSON / MW7124 / 140198

Scott WATSON arrives with a person by the name of Paul MAKER. Advise WATSON that I have two cameras that I wish to return to him.

MAKER advises me that he will sign receipt for cameras.

Both cameras returned. WATSON asks what the photographs turned out like. Advised films not processed yet and that he will be provided with negatives.

M C Weir
Detective Sergeant
30 January 1998

When police drew blood from Scott Watson, one man was there:[354]

"I arrived at Picton Station following a request from Operation "Tam" staff to receive a voluntary blood sample on their behalf as I had not been involved in the investigation. The donor, a Scott WATSON, was waiting for me in the foyer of the Station with an associate, Paul MAKER.

"While awaiting the arrival of the doctor I prepared the various forms and explained to Mr WATSON in terms he understood the various matters required by the legislation.

"Doctor LINTERN completed the procedure and left the Station along with Mr WATSON at 5.25 pm. The other person, Paul MAKER, was present during the taking of the blood sample."

When the Watson home was searched, the man was there:[355]

"WATSON then requests identification from everyone at the warrant. She is given this by Detective Senior Sergeant STRINGER. Carry out search while Sandra WATSON is kept in the lounge. During search she is visited by Paul MAKER and her father, Chris WATSON. At conclusion of search an attempt is made to interview her."

---

354 10363 / JS / SCOTT WATSON / JH7157 / 140198
355 12310 / JS / SANDRA-JO WATSON / PB6735 / 250698

Police attempted to find a "Grizz" in Onapua Bay, but the trail went cold.

Some believe Watson could have roped Keating in after he killed Ben and Olivia. Indeed, as we've seen, he did. But it was impossible for Keating to have been on Watson's boat painting it on the high seas, yet on the jetty greeting Picton harbourmaster Alex Wijngaarden later that afternoon.

Keating clearly had knowledge of the crime, but he cannot have been the accomplice seen on the boat. So why would Keating lie to save Watson? The police files disclose rumours:[356]

"Boyti told me about a conversation that Ike had had with "Zappa". I don't know "Zappa". I have never met him or spoke to him. The conversation had been relayed from Ike to Boyti. As far as I know, it was made after the time that the Police had been out to Erie Bay.

"Zappa had said words to the effect that he was looking at porridge and water for the next 8-10 years. This had been relayed to Boyti via Ike and he said it in a manner that it was in relation to Scott Watson's yacht and the goings on with that.

"Boyti also told me that "Zappa" had helped Scott Watson to paint his yacht after New Year. Boyti and Ike are good friends. I can guarantee that they won't approach the Police about this themselves.

"Boyti told me about the conversation on about Tuesday 27th of January. I haven't' got a clue when Ike had spoken to Zappa. I am sure that they spoke over the phone.

"I don't know anything about Watson threatening Zappa's children. I don't know how my wife Tui came up with this. It has not been mentioned to me."

Boyti was contacted by detectives and claimed Twose had it all wrong, that the conversation related to the drug crop police had

---

356 10681 / ST / GARY TWOSE / RMC084 / 300198

discovered on Keating's property and the charges he could face. Those charges, however, pale into insignificance compared to perjury and accessory after the fact to murder.

If Watson did have some kind of hold over Zappa, it would explain Keating's part in the conspiracy.

And conspiracy it was. Scott Watson may have been the psychopathic lone wolf killer, but he had enough influence to call in favours after the event—the Keatings and his mystery man accomplice.

We know *Blade* could have reached the entrance to Queen Charlotte Sound after leaving Furneaux Lodge, but the idea of dropping bodies overboard in broad daylight with other boaties beginning to appear seems foolish, which is why the 4.30pm sighting at Tory Channel never seemed convincing. If you wanted to carry out burial at sea then the dark of the night would be a far better option, and the police files show Watson had plenty of experience sailing the Sounds at night.

Instead, it's entirely likely an adrenalin-drenched, rapidly sobering Watson realised a quick disposal of the bodies was going to be impossible, so instead made a dash for his home mooring at Shakespeare Bay near Waikawa. Time to regroup, time to think, time to repaint on the way.

We know a strangely painted boat was seen at Ship Cove at 8.50am. We know a half painted *Blade* with Watson and his accomplice was seen further south at Snake Point heading for Waikawa by three sets of witnesses, including one who knew Scott well, at 10am. We know a yacht "similar" to *Blade* was seen being painted near Waikawa in the early afternoon. We know Watson had another man on board. But we don't know what happened in between—on their arrival at Waikawa.

Well, maybe now we do.

While police focused their entire case on body dumping in Cook Strait, and even hired submersible robots and sonar equipment to find the missing pair, if Rob Pope had re-checked his files he might have saved himself the heartache.

The obvious place to get rid of the bodies was Cook Strait. Scott Watson, however, chose the least obvious place—Shakespeare Bay at Picton, as 37 year old builder James Eric Keenan told police:[357]

"I am speaking to Detective Merrett of the Christchurch CIB about something my nephew, his friend and I saw on New Year's Day 1998 whilst at my nephew's address in Shakespeare Bay.

"My nephew's name is Anthony Keenan and he is 24 years of age. He lives at 943 Queen Charlotte Drive in Shakespeare Bay. From his balcony you have a good view of goings on in the bay from about 400 metres away. Tony's house is halfway up the hill and the view is looking on to the bay.

"At 10.55 am on 1.1.98 I left my home address in Blenheim driving my wife's Holden Barina coloured grey and headed to my nephew's address in Shakespeare Bay.

"Anthony and I were going to go to the Arapawa Maori Rowing Club to measure up the club with a view to renovating the club. The rowing club is situated in Waikawa Bay. The reason I know it was 10.55 am is because I remember I was running almost an hour late because I had previously arranged to meet Anthony at his home at 10 am. I also remember checking my watch as I arrived I checked my watch and it read 11.15 am or thereabouts.

"Anthony and I were both sitting down watching out into the bay and Anthony was trying to get dressed and ready and keep making conversation with me. Anthony's bedroom can be accessed from the balcony and he was popping in and out whilst he was talking to me.

"About 5 minutes later after I arrived one of Anthony's friends arrived by the name of James Chapman. James works for Tranz Rail in Picton and I think he had been at work because he was in

---

357 12232 / ST / JAMES KEENAN / PMC692 / 080598

overalls. He came out on to the balcony and he sat down beside me.

"At about 11.30 am whilst I was seated on the balcony I saw a yacht that had just arrived in Shakespeare Bay. As I walked on to the balcony I saw it coming into the area where the boats are.

"I don't recall if the yacht was on a mooring or not. I saw the yacht also had a dinghy with it on the right-hand stern side of the boat. The stern of the boat was pointed towards the beach.

"There was a male on board the yacht and one male was in the dinghy.

"I don't believe the dinghy was taken off the boat. I remember watching the yacht and not thinking too much about it and I turned away to talk to Tony or James and when I looked up I saw the dinghy.

"My impression was that the dinghy had met the yacht as opposed to the dinghy coming off it.

"When the yacht arrived I remember seeing a male on the boat and I saw a male in the dinghy. In other words I saw the male in the yacht and the male in the dinghy at the same time. I don't know which male was on the boats when they met ie who piloted each vessel but I can recall where they were when I saw them.

"The male on the yacht when I saw him I would describe as a male, Caucasian, thin build, 40-50 years who had grey hair and I think he had grey facial hair which I thought was almost a beard. He was wearing a hat of some description but I can't recall exactly what it was. I think he was wearing a light-coloured top of some description but I recall anything else about his clothing.

"The yacht he was in I would describe as being a small light-coloured yacht which had a different coloured cabin. I would guess it was about 15 feet possibly up to 20 feet. All I can say is that there was a marked difference between the colour of the hull and the cabin itself but I could not be confident of the colour of it. It also had small portholes and their surrounds were a different colour. I can't comment on shape. The yacht had some sort of sliding top on the entrance to the cabin and my impression was that was a different colour to the cabin.[358] The yacht had a mast.

"Where the guy was standing it was very compact at the rear of the boat ie there wasn't a lot of room. I am not a boat person so my estimates of size etc may be slightly inaccurate but in terms of its colour and the sliding top etc I am confident. The colour of the cabin I have in my head is like a brown colour sort of like a wood colour.

"The male in the dinghy I would describe as a male Caucasian, 20-30 years, not much bigger than the other guy in the yacht in terms of build, dark hair. Because of the distance it is difficult to estimate height but I definitely don't believe he was a tall man ie 6 foot plus. That applies to the guy on the yacht also.

"He had dark clothing on but other than that I can't recall what it was.

"The older guy on the yacht I saw go into the cabin and he backed out of the cabin and he appeared to be dragging something out. He appeared to be having great difficulty with it. When he went in he was only away for a few seconds before he emerged from the cabin.

"The item he pulled from out of the cabin looked like a big bag or sack coloured off white or similar. In terms of its dimensions I would say it was of similar size to him.

"He lifted the item up by inter-linking his arms and dragged it up to the side of the boat where the guy in the dinghy was. He laid the sack or bag over the railing so that half of it was over the railing and half was still in the boat.

"I remember thinking what the hell is that guy doing and thinking it looked very odd.

"The guy in the dinghy was just standing there and he wasn't doing anything. He made no attempt to put the item in his dinghy at that stage.

"The guy on the yacht went back into the cabin and he was away

---

358 *Blade* had a sliding wooden panel.

a similar time before he emerged with another sack or bag which appeared to be very similar to the other one. He again appeared to have difficulty with it and he placed it half over the rails again.

"At that point I mentioned to Anthony and James that it looked like they were getting rid of bodies as they were watching this also. They both agreed with me. We had a laugh about it because we thought we were a bit silly thinking about that.

"I watched the older guy in the yacht pick the sacks or bags or whatever they were up from the bottom and slid it over the boat whilst the guy in the dinghy received them and put them in it.

"It appeared that the dinghy was struggling with the weight of the guy and the things that were in it.

"Both of the males appeared to muck around doing something on the respective vessels. I started talking to the boys about it and when I had another look the yacht had gone as had the dinghy.

"I looked and I saw a male rowing off towards the other side of Shakespeare Bay where all the dinghies were tied up but I could not see the yacht.[359]

"I could not say if the male in the dinghy was the same male who had been standing up receiving the items I have described.

"When I saw the yacht initially arrive it was under motor. It left also under motor and it did not raise a sail whilst I saw it.

"The day was warm and sunny and there was no wind to speak of. The sea was flat like glass.

"The dinghy I saw I would describe as being a dark colour and I don't believe it was plywood. I can't be accurate and I don't believe it was plywood. I can't be accurate as to what it was made of and I could not accurately state its dimensions.

"Anthony and I left his house at about 11.55 am. I know that because I consciously remember looking at my watch. I was late so

---

[359] Which explains why Watson's dinghy and oars disappeared

I remember I was trying to catch up. We also had to pick up the key for the rowing club.

"Anthony and I both left in my wife's Holden Barina. As we headed around Shakespeare Bay and began to head up the hill I noticed a reddy/orange small stationwagon possibly a Nissan parked on a grass verge on the side of the road at a place called Reda's Inlet Shakespeare Bay.

"I had not seen this vehicle when I went to Anthony's address earlier in the morning. At that time there was no-one in the vehicle.

"We carried on around to Ben's and picked up the key and did our work. I dropped Anthony back to his house at about 1-1.30 pm.

"I then headed back to Blenheim and I spoke to my wife Shelley Keenan about what I had seen. We had a discussion and I thought possibly I hadn't seen what I thought I had and that there may well have been an innocent explanation for what had occurred.

"When I first heard reports of Ben Smart and Olivia Hope missing I thought perhaps what I had seen may have been relevant. But even then I thought they were only missing and that this type of thing doesn't happen in Picton so I didn't really think much about it.

"As things progressed and the Police said they were looking in Endeavour Inlet, Tory Channel and Cook Strait. I began to think it was of less importance.

"I really thought I should contact the Police when I watched a Crimescene Programme which stated that the Police were looking for sightings of a yacht between 11-3 pm on 1.1.98 and I commented to my wife I should go and tell the Police. I have been worried about this because I have waited so long but I would rather tell you about it and let you guys determine if any of this is relevant or not.

"I have been shown two photographs of a vessel coloured orange and blue respectively. The vessel coloured orange I believe is remarkably similar to the one I saw on 1.1.98 but I would not go as far as to say I am 100% it was the vessel.

"It is the colour that stands out to me the most. The cloth or whatever it is at the back of the boat was not up when I saw it."

What are the odds of yet another incredible coincidence in this investigation? A boat that looks like homebuilt *Blade* arriving in the bay that *Blade* usually moors, at almost the exact time *Blade* would have arrived motoring at full tilt from Snake Point. Two men, two human-sized bundles being offloaded. And the yacht then disappearing while the dinghy rowed to the far side of the bay.

It is pertinent that *Blade* was sighted without its dinghy on several occasions after this. Again, what are the odds?

James Thomas William Chapman remembered it well:[360]

"Jimmy saw a yacht in Shakespeare Bay and he said words to the effect of 'what are they doing?'. At that point I looked down and saw a yacht and a dinghy in Shakespeare Bay with a person on each.

"From the balcony we have an excellent view of Shakespeare Bay which is about 350 metres or so away. The 1st of January was a lovely sunny day. The yacht's bow was pointing out of the bay and the dinghy was on the yacht's port side.

"I would describe the yacht as a small one of some 24-28 feet in length, with a rusty coloured cabin.[361] I don't believe it had a sail up at all. I can't really remember much else about it but the colour of it stood out. It also had a raised cabin on it.

"The dinghy that was beside it was a grey colour about 10-12 feet in length and it had some sort of red colouring around the top of the bulwark i.e. on top of the rim of the boat.

"The guy in the yacht I would describe as a male European, in his thirties, slim build, had some facial hair. I remember he had a jersey on and some sort of jacket but I can't recall colours. I can't remember much else about him.

"The guy in the dinghy was also a male European, also in his thir-

---

[360] 12280 / ST / JAMES CHAPMAN / PMC692 / 270598
[361] The painting of *Blade* may not have been completed at this point, given that the Walshes saw more painting later.

ties, slightly bigger build than the guy in the yacht. He was about 5 ft 8-9" tall and was similar in height to the other guy.

"I gained the impression that the dinghy had met the yacht as opposed to coming off the boat when it arrived. My impression was that the guy on the yacht was always there and the other guy was coming to get something from him.

"I saw the guy on the yacht picking up a large object off the deck and placing it over some rails and the person was placing it in the dinghy. It looked like the object was heavy and they were having a lot of difficulty loading it.

"I saw this happen twice. On both occasions the objects appeared to be similar in size. I would describe the objects as being similar in size to an adult person wrapped in a white material of some sort.

"The parcels were wider at one end and tapered off at the other. When this was happening Jimmy said 'look they are getting rid of bodies' and we had a bit of a laugh about it. The reason for that was because we thought that couldn't be right.

"There were a few boats moored, but the bay was really quiet. I do remember seeing a little fizzboat or similar fishing off what I believe is called Dolphin Point. It may not have seen it going into the bay but it may well have seen it at some point.

"After that I came inside and I didn't really see much else. The one other thing I recall is that the guy on the yacht was turning around a lot and it looked like he was looking around to see if any cars were around or something.

"I thought it looked really suspicious.

"I have been shown two photographs of a sloop coloured orange and blue respectively. The orange coloured sloop is very similar to the vessel. I saw but I can't be 100% on that at all because of the distance. The colour stands out as does the raised cabin and the curved hull.

"On the way into Anthony's house I do not recall seeing any vehicles parked on the grass verge where the track to the dinghies goes. I left Anthony's place at about 11.50 am to go back to work as I had a ferry coming in at 12.30 pm.

"On my way back I recall seeing two vehicles on the grass verge where the track goes to the dinghies. They were parked in front of one another. The one in front was a silver/grey four door vehicle similar to a Mazda 626 or 929. I do not know a registration at all. The car behind was a 4 door vehicle coloured white similar to a square shaped Toyota Corolla close to an 87, 88 model. The grey car would have been an 85 or 86 model.

"I arrived back at work at about midday."

The final witness, Anthony Linton Keenan, adds more detail:[362]

"Jimmy said to me 'Look at that guy, it looks like he is trying to get rid of some bodies' or words to that effect. I turned around and looked out into the bay and saw one guy in a dinghy and one guy on a yacht.

"The guy on the yacht was passing one off-coloured white cloth that had something wrapped in it to the guy in the dinghy. I gained the impression that the item was similar in size to the person on the yacht and he was having difficulty manoeuvring it into the dinghy.

"This item when I saw it was half on the boat and half over a railing or similar. I commented to Jimmy that he was right and it did look like they were trying to get rid of some bodies.

"At that point I went back into my room to get something and when I came back out and I sat down I saw the same guy on the yacht with a second item that was longer than he was but similar to the first item.

"The guy on the yacht was interlocking his arms to drag the item along to the edge of the boat. The back of the boat was quite compact. He lent this thing over the railing and gave it to the guy in the dinghy and he placed it in there.

"At that point they appeared to have some sort of conversation and I popped into my room and when I came back out a minute or

---

362 40935 / ST / ANTHONY KEENAN / PMC692 / 080598

so later and the dinghy was gone and the boat/yacht was going past the front of the reclamation. I believe it was leaving under motor as I did not see a sail get raised or one up at all.

"The man on the yacht I would describe as a male Caucasian, average build, 20-30 years, with thick dark hair. I don't recall what he was wearing at all.

"I would describe the dinghy as being quite low in the water because of the load on it. I do remember seeing a yellow/orange fender/bender on it to prevent damage to the boat that tows it. I can't recall anything else about the dinghy as to what it was made of etc.

"My impression was that the dinghy came from the shore as opposed to being taken off the boat. That's not to say it wasn't or that someone was dropped off on the point to pick it up and row it out.

"My clear impression was that the dinghy came from shore to meet the yacht.

"The guy on the dinghy I would describe as being a male, Caucasian, 35-45 years of age and he was markedly older than the other guy. He was of medium build but I could not estimate height. I cannot recall clothing at all I'm sorry.

"I have been shown a series of two photographs of a vessel coloured orange and blue respectively.

"The vessel coloured orange is very similar to the one I saw on 1.1.98 although clearly I cannot be 100% on that. The similarities between the boat I saw and the orange boat is the colour and the cabin configuration in that it is raised up above the rest of the deck.

"I did think what they were doing was quite suspicious but I didn't really think too much of it until Jimmy mentioned it to me after he watched Crimescene. When Jimmy brought it up about whether we should tell the Police, I told him that he should tell the Police as soon as he could.

"We all definitely saw something but as far its relevance we thought you should definitely know about it even given the time delay.

"I didn't even really think about it at all particularly given that the Police were looking for a ketch."

And there, the trail ends. The last known probable sightings of Ben Smart and Olivia Hope. What happened next? Scott Watson knows, and one or two accomplices still out there who helped dispose of the bodies.

Would they have brought them all the way to Picton and off *Blade*, only to take them back out to Cook Strait again? Unlikely. The logistics of lifting two dead weights back up onto a boat from a dinghy seem difficult in the extreme and Chaplinesque in execution. So here's a possible scenario.

The bodies, wrapped in sails and looking just like rolled up sails are unloaded at the shore into a vehicle and driven to a destination far away. They are buried on land by an accomplice, probably at night. The arrangement is to rendezvous again at Picton so Watson can uplift the sails, and then there is nothing linking him to the burial should the site ever be discovered. That's why *Blade* was seen steaming towards Waikawa on the evening of 1 January—for a night rendezvous.

Watson returns to *Blade*, taking the sails and any contaminated items or clothing out to Cook Strait, probably at night, and disposes of them in a weighted bag in the deepest area he can find. In the unlikely event they ever surface, the sea will have erased any forensic link to the victims, and the gear may not even be traceable to *Blade*.

The boat is wiped down as thoroughly as possible. Regardless of how well Sandy and Scott had cleaned before Christmas, Watson made doubly sure that any surface Ben and Olivia could have conceivably touched, is wiped down regardless. He then spends the next few days trying to lay the footprint of an alibi, calling into Keating's place for the remainder of the paint he needed on January 2, before inviting Sandy on the boat so that a new set of fingerprints, hairs and the detritus of daily usage can be overlaid on the cleaned surfaces.

It was the anatomy of an almost perfect crime, but for one thing: Scott Watson had not planned to kill anyone that night, so he had not prepared in advance. He drew attention to himself, because that's what he did when he drank. People remembered the unkempt, unshaven fisherman type with the all over the place collar-length haircut from mum, tattoos on his arms, 5'8 with the blue denim shirt and dark jeans.

When, in his drunken, drugged stupor, Watson decided to strangle the sleeping Ben and move his boat away so he could attack the still sleeping Olivia out of earshot, Watson was following his Jekyll and Hyde programming. He could not, however, avoid the impression he left behind.

Given what we now know, the police were lucky to get a conviction out of the jury. The evidence line the police followed was wrong, and that's what allowed authors and critics to attack the soundness of the conviction. Careers have been built on arguing the pro's and con's of an evidence line that turned out to be false and irrelevant.

Emotional appeals to scratched hatch covers were purely theatre without substance, as was the tired old trick of wheeling out jailhouse "secret witnesses" that Watson allegedly confided to. By the time the case got to trial, witnesses had forgotten much of the detail contained in their original witness statements and their timings were all over the place. The confusion sown over the mystery man and the mystery ketch was a masterclass from the Defence in how to engender reasonable doubt. In the circumstances, the guilty verdict was a miracle.

So, to recap, what have we learnt in this book?

That Scott Watson was, and remains through genetics, a psychopath prone to violence and sexual assault—regardless of what others say about him.

That Watson's description was an exact match for the mystery man.

That Watson did in fact make another trip to *Blade* before midnight and was seen doing so and returning.

That the so called "mystery ketch" heading into Cook Strait on 2 January 1998 was in fact the *Alliance*.

That the mystery blonde on the back was teenager Hollie Pickering.

That Guy Wallace did not in fact drop Ben and Olivia off on a 'very low' ketch, but to an ordinarily low sloop named *Blade*.

That Watson slunk out of Furneaux around 5am with his guests onboard.

That after murdering them he picked up an accomplice to help him get rid of the evidence.

That both men were seen on *Blade* repainting it on the high seas.

That Watson's alibi at Erie Bay was false.

That Watson and his accomplice sailed instead to Picton and took the bodies onshore.

Did Scott Watson commit these murders? You be the judge.

This book now opens up the possibility that Ben and Olivia could still be found. I pray their families get that result.

***

Postscript: As this book was going to press, former Det. S.Sgt Wayne Stringer told me Watson had not just 'confessed' to Zappa about the murders but actually boasted about it, in the same breath making barely veiled lewd threats about Zappa's 13 year old daughter. Zappa told Stringer this directly, years later.

To obtain a text searchable copy of this book, get it on Amazon Kindle from this link:
http://www.amazon.com/gp/product/B01ASUG3WK

Or visit the Ian Wishart page on Amazon.

Or visit www.ianwishart.com for more format options. If you think other people need to read this book, please spread the word by leaving a review on Amazon or Goodreads.

www.ingramcontent.com/pod-product-compliance
Lightning Source LLC
Chambersburg PA
CBHW071953220426
43662CB00009B/1111